ELEMENTS OF A POST-LIBERAL
THEORY OF EDUCATION

ELEMENTS
OF A
POST-LIBERAL
THEORY
OF
EDUCATION

C. A. BOWERS

TEACHERS COLLEGE, COLUMBIA UNIVERSITY
NEW YORK AND LONDON

Published by Teachers College Press, 1234 Amsterdam Avenue,
New York, NY 10027

Copyright © 1987 by Teachers College, Columbia University

Library of Congress Cataloging-in-Publication Data

Bowers, C. A.
  Elements of a post-liberal theory of education.

  Bibliography: p.
  Includes index.
  1. Education—Philosophy. 2. Education—United
States—Evaluation. 3. Educational sociology—
United States. I. Title.
LA217.B68 1987   370'.1   86-30135

ISBN 0-8077-2849-7
ISBN 0-8077-2848-9 (pbk.)

Manufactured in the United States of America

92 91 90 89 88 87   1 2 3 4 5 6

Contents

Preface

THE use of the word "post" in a title, like post-modernism or as in the title of this book, suggests something about the complex relationship that exists between language and how we understand experience. If language were simply the conduit for communicating ideas, I would not have to use the word "post," as it is really used here to signify that the term liberalism, with its gestalt of culturally specific assumptions and emancipatory ideals, is inadequate for understanding the world we live in today. When a paradigm, like liberalism, begins to lose its explanatory power, we should simply be able to introduce a new word that communicates the new set of presuppositions about the political and educational possibilities of human experience. But we cannot introduce new words, as physicists seem to do, without losing our ability to communicate with a wider audience. Thus we remain in the grip of the conceptual conventions embedded in the terminology of our language. Although terms like "interdependency" or "ecologism"—to coin a word that contains the necessary political designation of being an "ism"— more accurately highlight the kind of awareness appropriate to this era, they are, as political metaphors, totally inadequate for introducing the way of thinking necessary for a new and widely shared political guidance system. Like other words that reproduce older ways of understanding now recognized as faulty (e.g., matter, data, autonomous individual, and so forth), the word liberalism thus must be viewed as our point of departure rather than as designating a fixed and fully accepted conceptual framework.

In addition to suggesting that we will be operating, so to speak, beyond the boundaries of traditionally defined territory (while still keeping in touch with valued reference points), the phrase "post-liberalism" is also meant to alert the reader to the inappropriateness of connecting this analysis of educational theories with the tradition of educational philosophy that was characterized by the work of R. S.

Peters and Israel Sheffler. I deliberately avoided using the word philosophy in the title of the book in order to distance my approach from the kind of culturally decontextualized and largely depoliticized analysis that has dominated educational philosophy in this country since the demise of Dewey's influence. Two of the educational theories that I deal with as archetypal interpretations of educational liberalism—the neoromanticism of Carl Rogers and the behaviorism of B. F. Skinner—would not be viewed by philosophers of education operating within this tradition as worthy of attention, nor is it likely they would take seriously the ideas of Paulo Freire and John Dewey, the two other major interpreters of educational liberalism that are central to my analysis. The more academic tradition of educational philosophy, with its concern with language analysis, has not captured the public imagination or provided educational reformers ways of viewing the relationship between education and the problems of society. In contrast, Rogers, Skinner, Freire, and Dewey have provided both educational theorists and reformers powerful if not always correct ways of viewing the relationship between education and social reform. Thus it is their more widespread influence rather than their legitimacy within professional circles that makes their ideas the central focus of this study.

The peculiar relationship between language and experience can also be seen in how my approach to the question of empowerment differs from so-called "radical" educational theorists who are concerned with fostering resistance, freedom, and self-determination. My arguments with them are not over the general picture of a more just society, but over the unexamined presuppositions upon which they build their metaphorical constructions. By ignoring the metaphorical nature of language, specifically the connection between iconic (e.g., individualism, autonomy, freedom) and root metaphor (e.g., paradigm or conceptual gestalt) from which these image metaphors are derived, they fail to recognize that the assumptions of the Enlightenment, formulated in response to a different set of problematic social conditions, may no longer provide the basis of empowerment. Again language, including the language of emancipation, keeps us in the grip of the past, even as we attempt to use language to clarify aspects of our collective experience that were not foreseen by the Enlightenment thinkers.

Like the "radical" educational theorists, I will make recommendations on how the reform of curriculum and pedagogy can contribute to empowerment, but I will base these recommendations on a fundamentally different and more contemporary root metaphor, one that involves a different way of understanding the nature of the individual, the rational process, and our embeddedness in the cultural and biotic community. Thus to think about the nature of a post-liberal approach to educational empowerment is to update our language by taking account of developments in contemporary social theory and by addressing the problematic aspects of modernization—including the ecological crisis— that were beyond the level of awareness of the thinkers who laid the conceptual foundations of modern liberalism. The pecularities of the binding-facilitating process that characterize the language-experience relationship will persist, for, as Nietzsche observed, an essential charac- teristic of our thought process is that we fit the new into the old schema. That is, we will continue to understand the new in terms of the familiar, which is continually reconstituted in the epistemic and metaphorical patterns of our language. But a post-liberal way of thinking about the prospects of empowerment will involve treating the "old schema" as essentially problematic.

Dewey's view of intelligence as social in nature applies to the writing of this book. In addition to the thinkers whose works have stimulated me to think against the grain of a number of conceptual orthodoxies— their names fill the reference section of this book—I am also indebted to a number of graduate students who have listened patiently as I have formulated and reformulated the main themes of the argument for a post-liberal theory of education. Their critical stance, as well as their recommendations of works that I might read in order to strengthen or abandon part of the argument, helped to shape the final outcome. But recognizing the social nature of writing a book does not eliminate the need for me to assume the final responsibility for the use (and misuse) of ideas. I also wish to acknowledge the contribution made by Phyllis Wells in typing numerous drafts of the manuscript. Her competence and cheerful attitude made my task much lighter. Finally, I want to thank Audrey Kingstrom, the acquisitions editor for Teachers College Press, for helping to get the manuscript through the critical prepublication stages. Taking seriously a manuscript that does not fit the conventional categories of educational thought took a good deal of professional courage, and it is reassuring to find this quality in a person who performs such a critical gatekeeper role.

ELEMENTS OF A POST-LIBERAL
THEORY OF EDUCATION

1

Language and the Reformulation of Educational Liberalism

SINCE the time of John Dewey it has been the liberal educational theorists, rather than the conservatives, who have written in the "language of possibility," to use the phrase of Stanley Aronowitz and Henry Giroux. The language of the liberal educational theorists has provided both a moral vision of social regeneration through education as well as the conceptual compass headings that served as a guide to new educational practices. Both theorists and classroom teachers could choose from a rich and highly metaphorical vocabulary that included such terms as emancipation, equality, freedom, self-realization, critical consciousness, efficiency, and predictive control. But as the diversity of the vocabulary suggests, educational liberalism was not contained within a single stream of thought and classroom practice. Different interpretations of educational liberalism emerged, each using a different set of metaphors to provide a distinct conceptual orientation. Neoromantics, Deweyians, libertarians, and neo-Marxists, along with the behaviorists and technocratic followers of Frederick Taylor, were all able to find within the language of liberalism a basis for promoting their own interpretation of reform while managing, at the same time, to reject the equally liberal principles of other educational theorists.

The criticism directed toward alternative interpretations of educational liberalism was often sharp and insightful. An example is the criticism directed by neoromantic and neo-Marxist educational theorists toward the educational practices of the behaviorist and technocratically oriented reformers. But the most fundamental issues were seldom raised because of the failure to recognize that the competing approaches to educational reform were rooted, at the deepest level, in a shared set of liberal assumptions about the nature of reality. In effect, the debates were within the conceptual boundaries dictated by the conceptual categories and assumptions embedded in the language of liberalism. For the behaviorist-technocratic reformer, the liberal language of possibility meant a more rational ordering of classroom activities and a closer relationship between the classroom and the needs of the workplace; for the neoromantic it meant progress in freeing the child's potential for growth from the distorting influences of a driven and overly materialistic adult world; and for the neo-Marxist educational theorists (and now Critical Theorists) the language of possibility meant achieving greater freedom and equality through the educational practice of consciousness raising. The conceptual boundaries of the liberal paradigm were indeed wide, allowing for distinct visions and journeys in educational practice. Yet the shared points of departure are clearly visible to anyone who looks beyond the programmatic differences. These include the assumption that change is inherently progressive, that the individual is the basic social unit within which we locate the source of freedom and rationality, that the nature of the individual is to be understood as either inherently good or amenable to being shaped by the environment, and that rationality is the real basis of authority for regulating the affairs of daily life.

This "language of possibility," which will hereafter be referred to as the discourse of liberalism, was part of a rich political lineage that goes back to John Stuart Mill, Jeremy Bentham, Thomas Hobbes, and John Locke. Its roots can also be traced back to the Enlightenment concern with establishing the foundations of rationality. In spite of this connection with the most dominant and progressive traditions in Western thought, the language of liberalism (perhaps it would be more correct to say the languages of liberalism) is conceptually limiting. A major consequence is that criticism and programmatic efforts based on the conceptual foundations of liberalism are increasingly seen as inadequate for addressing the crisis of authority and social purpose that have now become a central part of the public debate. There is even a growing sense of awareness that the basic assumptions upon which liberalism rests may be causally related to the deepening of the ecological crisis, the loss of meaningful community life, and the nihilism that now permeates the moral and conceptual foundations of society. In the next chapter we shall examine briefly the discrepancy between the liberal vision and generally acknowledged social problems; this will enable us to put in clearer focus the ability of liberal educational theorists to address the problems we now face. Now our more immediate tasks are to identify the major arguments developed in subsequent chapters and to situate these arguments within the emerging understanding of the power of language to organize our thought and experience.

The basic argument is that the conceptual foundations of liberal educational theory, in its variant forms, have become atrophied and that basing criticism and recommendations for educational reform on these foundations simply will further our collective problems. A further aspect of this argument is that any serious attempt to renew the conceptual foundations of educational liberalism by taking account of recent intellectual developments, particularly those influenced by the recent linguistic turn in social theory, is likely to lead to such a basic transformation that it might make more sense to think of it as a post-liberal theory of education.

The suggestion that we are entering a period of cultural development that cannot be understood in terms of the old political categories should not be taken to mean that it would be desirable to abandon the genuinely progressive achievements of political and educational liberalism. Nor should the full elaboration of the argument, as it will appear in subsequent chapters, be viewed as an attempt to make a judgment about the ideas of the many educational theorists who situate themselves in either the liberal or radical tradition. To put it another way, by focusing on the conceptual foundations shared by the four distinct interpretations of educational liberalism we have witnessed since the emergence of progressive education, I am not suggesting that all the streams of liberalism today can be fit neatly into one of the four variants of liberal thought. There are many distinct voices in the area of educational theory and some are clearly giving expression to educational concerns that go beyond the conceptual possibilities of the four archetypal forms of liberation.

For example, theorists such as Thomas F. Green, Henry Giroux, and Maxine Greene include in their analyses elements of thought that reflect the current reconceptualization of the guiding liberal paradigm. Establishing where current educational theorists fit in terms of ideological subcategories is not, however, nearly as important as examining how the distinct liberal discourses influence the conceptual boundaries, create areas of silence, and give a particular orientation both to social analysis and proposals for reform in classroom practices. The four liberal discourses—neoromantic, technocratic-behaviorist, Deweyan progressivism, and Freireian liberationism—not only represent the basic conceptual archetypes for past reform efforts, but seemingly remain today for many educational theorists as the only legitimate ideological framework for thinking about the connection between education and the problems of society. Educational theorists, such as Giroux, may uphold values that are essentially conservative in nature (Aronowitz and Giroux 1985, p. 203), but it would be difficult for them to acknowledge the true ideological origins of the borrowed ideas. It is easier, particularly in an era in which the basic political vocabulary is being debased through general ignorance of the intellectual traditions represented by such terms as liberal and conservative, to quietly mix in with one's own conceptual baggage the ideas and values borrowed from an ideology that is still held to be a pariah. This is what happens when the technicist and behavioristic reformers use humanistic values that cannot really be justified in terms of their interpretation of the liberal paradigm. It also happens when educational theorists argue for the emancipation of the individual and at the same time uphold the value of a revitalized community and an understanding of tradition.

That educational theorists should adhere strictly to the traditional conceptual boundaries of our main ideological genres is not the point being argued here. In fact I shall later argue that the boundary lines are artificial and restrictive. The point has more to do with the intellectual integrity of the arguments used to advance proposals for educational reform. In his superbly lucid essay "Standing By Words," Wendell Berry goes to the heart of the matter by suggesting that the increasingly unreliable use of language "parallels the increasing disintegration, over the same period, of persons and communities" (Berry 1983, p. 24). Accountability in the use of language, as he sees it, should involve meeting both internal and external criteria. The internal criterion requires that the writer (or speaker) must not only believe in what is being communicated, but must be willing to act on it. The external criterion for insuring against the degeneracy of language requires an accurate representation of the complexity of the external world (note that we are not referring to an objective world). The key is to find the balance. And this brings us to the deeper problem connected with the atrophied state of the liberal paradigm, which still provides what is seen by many as the only legitimate language for thinking about educational reform. Internal accountability in writing about a more enlightened set of educational practices, where theorists are prepared to make theory on the basis of their own experience, can only be achieved as the external criterion is successfully met. The key question then becomes one of determining whether the language used to think and communicate is adequate for representing the complexity of the world we live in. The liberal paradigm that has given rise to distinct language frameworks for thinking about educational reform, these frameworks themselves, and the set of assumptions underlying both are too restrictive and too embedded with what can now be viewed as mythical elements for clear thinking about either the reforms that need to be made or the theorists' own relationship to them.

A more accountable use of language will not by itself resolve the fundamental problems our society faces, but it is essential to a clearer understanding of our relationships with each other as a society and with the environment. It is also essential to putting our guiding values in order. When used in an unreflective manner, language can subjugate the mind, and it can do this by creating the illusion that we are on the right track when it is actually causing us to mistake abstractions for the actual patterns within which our lives are embedded. In order to understand the connection between the atrophied state of the conceptual foundations underlying the four distinct liberal discourses, it will be necessary to put in focus how a lack of sensitivity to the controlling power of language can lead to educational theories that are better attuned to conceptual abstractions (including the remnants of cultural myths) than to the actual world we live in—with its mix of empowering and outmoded traditions. Getting beyond the conduit image of language, that view given to us by Locke which holds that language serves as a neutral transmitter of the individual's thought, will help us to account for the role that language plays in shaping our thought about the purpose of education. It will also provide a way of addressing a basic weakness in educational practice based on the liberal paradigm—namely, how students are taught to think of themselves as autonomous and rationally self-directing.

There are two levels of argument that can be made for taking seriously the connection between language and the atrophied condition that characterizes the conceptual underpinnings of liberal theories of education. At one level is the argument, as Michael Shapiro put it in *Language and Political Understanding*, that what "people say is . . . usually a matter of giving voice to discursive practices that represent a selection from a fixed set of practices permissible in the language" (1981, p. 130). This is really a restatement of Benjamin Lee Whorf's insight that the epistemological code inherent in a language organizes the sense of meaning in terms of preestablished categories and rules of association acquired as the person becomes a member of the language community. This view of language, in addition to challenging the autonomous standing of rationality, suggests that the conceptual basis for defining and negotiating the patterns that regulate social life are, to a large extent, linguistically determined. The language of educational theory, in terms of this view, is limited to a culturally embedded scenario that influences not only what will be talked about as politically problematic but which areas of existential and social life will not be recognized as in the domain of political discourse. It also suggests that the hidden epistemic codes regulate understanding and thus our ultimate goals for education.

The debate over the issue of linguistic determinism is likely to go on indefinitely. But we need not wait for the final outcome to recognize that the conceptual categories we acquire when becoming members of a language community exert a significant influence on both our patterns of thought and experience. As will be discussed later in more detail, the "invisible band" of language appears to be at work in organizing the most basic conceptual coordinates used by nearly all liberal educational theorists—neo-Marxists, neoromantics, progressivists, and technocrats. In spite of surface and even substantive differences that separate these liberal educational theorists, they share a dichotomous pattern of thought that neatly separates enlightened from unenlightened, progress from tradition, the individual from the sociocultural, and critical rationality from myth and false consciousness. Similarly, the pattern of thinking that establishes a temporal orientation appears to have led these diverse liberal educational theorists to adopt an escalator view of history, where more exposure to emancipatory forms of education automatically represents a progressively upward and forward movement. It also enables them to view resistance, and even social revolution, as inherently progressive and, within a certain group of liberal educators, to view all technological innovation as a sign of progress. Their seemingly shared view of how to locate authority, as well as to identify the pedagogical and social processes that contribute to it, also appears to be more an expression of a shared conceptual formula than the result of individual thought. The separation of liberal educational theories from personal questions of power, as well as the tendency of the theorists to align themselves with truth, emancipation, and social justice, must also be considered as a reflection of the mythologies embedded in a shared language.

Regardless of whether we accept the strong case that language provides the conceptual categories that organize thought into predetermined patterns and set the boundaries on discourse, or the weak case that facility in using the language is essential to the political efficacy of the individual, language must be viewed as exerting a profound influence on the nature of educational and political discourse. I personally find persuasive Shapiro's argument that "language contains the field of possibilities from which the speakers select" (p. 129), but I am willing to base the subsequent analysis of the discourse of liberal educational theorists on the weaker position that avoids the extremes of linguistic determinism. This position does not entirely dethrone the sovereignty of rational thought, but it clearly points to the possibility that the ideological map used to locate the terrain of educational discourse, and thus the substance and direction of recent educational debates, reflects the vocabulary and attendant theoretical frameworks available to the educational theorists. If the images suggested in the use of certain words—individual, emancipation, rational thought, autonomy, and so forth—carry positive, unproblematic connotations, they are likely to lead to the development of a conceptual map that highlights those aspects of our collective cultural territory where it is thought these images can be more fully realized. Other words that put in focus aspects of the cultural territory not highlighted by the liberal maps are likely to be seen as irrelevant or a distraction motivated by sinister forces. Authority, discipline, tradition, and conservative are examples of words that liberal educational theorists are uncomfortable with. Because a serious consideration of the deeper meaning of these words would involve looking at features of our experience that challenge the core assumptions underlying the liberal view of emancipation and social progress, the words tend either to be categorized as part of the repressive and irrational culture or rejected as irrelevant in an era of social engineering and rational self-control. Educational theorists who operate within one of the archetypal forms of educational liberalism appear comfortable only when using a more restricted vocabulary. Unfortunately, this restricted vocabulary exerts an influence not only on the boundaries of educational theory, but also on which issues are put in focus and which should not be looked upon.

The content of vision and understanding, as well as the areas of silence, are a function of an ideological orientation. And as the ideology has its own vocabulary and conceptual grammar, it can be understood as a language system. The language and the mode of political consciousness that characterize a particular ideological orientation are thus different dimensions of the same process. Just as the language that sustained the mechanistic Newtonian world view impeded understanding what David Bohm called the "implicate order" revealed by the new physics, the language of liberal ideology sustains a particular view of the social world (including its future possibilities) while impeding alternative ways of understanding. The language that reproduces the unique conceptual characteristics of an ideological orientation thus must be viewed as distorting communication in order to prevent the emergence of a complex view of social reality that exceeds the explanatory power of the existing ideology. To use Claus Mueller's definition, distorted communication "designates all forms of restricted and prejudiced communication that by their nature inhibit a full discussion of problems, issues, and ideas that have public relevance" (1973, p. 19). Thus, the lexicon of an ideology becomes critical to understanding the areas of discourse that will be distorted and inhibited. In the case of the ideology of liberal educational theorists, the distortion of political discourse reflects not only the vocabulary that is proscribed as ideologically inconsistent, but also the special interests of the cultural subgroup they represent.

The connection between the distorted communication that characterizes liberal educational theory and the use of power can be more fully understood if we consider Michel Foucault's argument that the exercise of power involves "guiding the possibility of conduct and putting in order the possible outcome." The vocabulary that sustains the world view of an ideology, in addition to establishing connotative and metaphorical biases, becomes part of what Foucault in "The Subject and Power," called "the question of government"—the social-cultural-linguistic context in which power relationships "structure the possible field of action of others" (1982, p. 221). Viewed in this way the ideological framework, as well as the vocabulary it designates as appropriate for educational discourse, represent more than the confrontation between enlightened thinking and the forces of oppression. The relationships of power are far more complex and subtle. Again Foucault helps us to overcome the simplistic routines of thinking that must themselves be viewed as masking the exercise of power. The analysis of power relations, he tells us, involves considering the systems of differentiation that determine how power relations will be expressed. These systems of differentiation reflect economic, linguistic, and traditional forms of status and privilege. He also points out that the analysis of power must take account of types of objectives that motivate the participants, as well as the means of application and different forms of advantage that help to determine the outcome (p. 223).

Foucault's multidimensional way of understanding the exercise of power goes beyond the more limited focus of this analysis, but it serves to center the connection between language and power in a manner generally not associated with liberal discourse. The Enlightenment foundations of liberal educational thought contribute to thinking of liberal discourse as on the side of truth and progress, and only engaged in a power struggle for the purpose of liberation. By understanding language as one dimension in the exercise of power, albeit a form of power made more potent by our past tendency not to see the connection between language and power, we can also view the liberal educational theorists as representing a point of view that can be situated both in terms of a cultural subgroup and within a particular epistemic orientation. Consequently, the language itself must be situated within a field of power contested by different social and cultural groups.

The ideals of truth, justice, and progress appear to represent the interests of everybody, but this is an illusion that obscures the way language—which must always be viewed as a specific language—organizes reality according to its own epistemic grammar. There is no one language that represents a common reality, as there is no one conceptual structure of reality. Thus the liberal ideals, in spite of sincere intentions, represent a vision based ultimately upon a particular set of cultural assumptions. In suggesting that liberal educational theorists are contestants within the field of power, I am not suggesting that they can escape from representing a specific set of interests by moving to a more elevated position where they become the spokespersons for humanity in general.

Language always gives expression to special interests, some of which must be viewed as more defensible than others. But the justification of these interests must be made, not just assumed. The issue here is to recognize more fully the connection between language and power and to use this awareness as the basis for expanding the conceptual and lexical bases for a form of liberal educational discourse that is more defensible.

Although Claus Mueller's view of distorted communication implies the possibility of undistorted communication, a careful examination of the way language involves the exercise of power (structures "the possible field of action for others") suggests that power always involves an element of distortion. This can be more easily understood if we start with the relation of words to thought. The Russian poet O. Mandelstam touches on a critical relationship between words and the differentiation of the phenomenological world into thought when he wrote, "I have forgotten the word I intended to say, and my thought, unembodied, returns to the realm of shadows" (cited in Vygotsky 1962, p. 119). The chief point here, as Lev Semenovich Vygotsky put it, is that "thought is not merely expressed in words; it comes into existence through them." Every thought, he continues, "tends to connect something to something else, to establish a relationship between things" (p. 125). In establishing "What Is" through the act of naming, which seems to be one of the primary functions of words, the most basic form of power is exercised. What is not named remains part of the horizon—that is, undifferentiated background of the phenomenological world characterized by silence and inattention. What is named becomes the focus of intentionality, and the object of thought and speech. Beyond this elementary expression of power, the process of naming involves illuminating certain features to the exclusion of others and suggesting relationships between what is named and what is already familiar. The words "society," "social role," and "student" put in focus only a limited aspect of the referent, while other aspects remain embedded and out of focus. What is not spoken thus becomes part of the realm of silence while what is spoken becomes the only "possible field of action."

The use of a conceptual framework that influences the metaphorical and connotative nature of the naming process must also be seen as an expression of power. The conceptual framework or ideology serves, according to Clifford Geertz, as a map of problematic social reality and matrix for the creation of a collective conscience (1973, p. 220). As the symbolic framework that guides interpretation, establishes the ground rules for seeing comparisons and continuities, and provides coherence to the play of metaphorical thought, it represents the most basic though often unconscious strategem in determining the relationships of power.

For example, Joel Spring's statement on the need for a form of education "which will encourage and support non-authoritarian individuals who are unwilling to bow to authority" (1975, p. 131) represents a series of metaphorical images that take on meaning because of the unstated assumptions that underlie the conceptual framework that gives a coherent picture of reality. Spring's image of individual freedom makes sense only within a conceptual framework that posits the reality of an autonomous and self-directing individual, the connection between the autonomous action of the individual and social progress, and the inherent goodness of human nature. At the deeper level of a cultural episteme, it assumes a dichotomous rather than dialectical relationship between the individual and society, revolution and cultural conservatism, and freedom and social determinants. It is also dependent upon a progressive sense of history.

By putting in focus a particular picture of reality, the conceptual framework puts out of focus other ways of understanding. Thus it contests the "possible field of action" at the most basic preconscious level of thought. To stay with the example of Spring's statement, which could be endlessly duplicated in terms of other theorists, the conceptual framework which he acquired as a member of a particular Western language community puts out of focus the dialectical relationship between the individual and the linguistic-cultural milieu that sustains and gives individualism its particular form of expression. In being put out of focus, such a dialectic is delegitimated as worthy of consideration, and in the process a form of control is exercised over the direction of discourse. What cannot be spoken, or is tainted by being put in a conceptual category that carries pejorative connotations, lacks efficacy in influencing the course of action and thought. The idea of emancipation, for example, which is held by many educational theorists working within the liberal conceptual framework, involves a basic assumption about the possibilities of overcoming embeddedness in cultural traditions. When the idea of emancipation is guaranteed by a teleological view of the universe, it becomes an act of treason against progress itself to take seriously questions pertaining to those aspects of a shared culture that are worth preserving. Language that takes account of those aspects of human experience not given legitimate standing is already prejudged. The conceptual categories that organize the boundaries and prefigure the scenarios of what can be talked about, the visions that will guide human action, and the evils to be overcome, thus tend to preempt the liberal notion that the outcome of discourse reflects a purely rational and open process.

As the work of Basil Bernstein and others has demonstrated, class and cultural group affiliations are important determinants in the relationship of power and discourse. "Different speech forms or codes," Bernstein wrote, "symbolize the form of social relationship, regulate the nature of speech encounters, and create for the speakers different orders of relevance and relation" (1975, p. 174). Educational theorists have used his distinction between elaborated and arrested codes as the expression of differences in social class to clarify the role played by schools in maintaining class inequality. Yet Bernstein's analysis of the cognitive patterns and speech forms that characterize the differences between the arrested language code of the working class and the elaborated language code of the middle class can also be used to understand how class and cultural affiliations influence the language and conceptual orientation of liberal theorists of education.

The four archetypal forms of liberal theories of education we shall be examining reflect, for example, the epistemological orientations of a particular group within the middle class. In addition to possessing the lexical characteristics of an elaborated language code, which allows for more of the life world to be symbolically represented, these liberal educational theorists exhibit a set of linguistic and epistemological traits that become particularly powerful in determining the outcome of contending discourses between sociocultural groups. In the premodern world, before the individual and rationality became the ultimate sources of authority, discourse served to reinforce the taken for granted beliefs that were unified into a comprehensive and compelling world view. As Foucault observed, "where the determining factors saturate the whole there is no relationship of power" (1982, p. 221). In this situation discourse reproduces and reinforces the transcendent sources of authority upon which the world view of the culture is based. As all aspects of the life world are saturated, to use Foucault's metaphor, there is no real freedom of choice because the "possible field of action" is determined by the traditional patterns of the culture. In this setting discourse does not play a political role in the sense of creating or responding to new possibilities. "Power," as Foucault put it, "is exercised only over free subjects, and only insofar as they are free."

As a modernizing culture is based on assumptions that give special authority to ideas of individualism, rationality, the progressive nature of change, and so forth, the "possible field of action" is expanded. In the process, power is contested within social relationships, the conflict between various forms of authority, and between modes of technique. In effect, a modern culture that destabilizes the traditional foundations of belief creates the liminal space where, in being "betwixt and between" the established patterns of the past and new relationships and values yet to be settled upon, language takes on special political significance. Language becomes, in the modern context, a dominant factor in the exercise of power that determines the new forms of understanding, sources of authority, and, ultimately, the new social practice (Bowers 1984a).

Within a cultural context where modernization itself is part of the field of power relationships, social groups who use language as an expanded technology of power have a special advantage over social groups who live their culture in a manner that does not involve treating it as an abstract problem to be endlessly reflected upon, rendered problematic, and reified into theory. The power to establish the legitimacy of new names, explanations, and sources of authority involves a partial escape from the embeddedness of tradition. This power is not only an expression of the linguistic characteristics of an expanded language code, as Bernstein has argued, but it is also strengthened by a messianic ideology that is committed to the progressive realization of truth and enlightenment. Liberal educational theorists, as members both of the bourgeois class committed to modernization, and the subclass that subscribes to a unique epistemological code that provides the means of emancipatory thinking, cannot be viewed as representing the universal interests of mankind. In effect their elaborated language code becomes the instrument of partisan thinking and can serve to distort the possibilities of a more complex political discourse involving different cultural groups.

This generalization can be given more substance by using Alvin Gouldner's analysis of the epistemic elements of intellectuals, as well as Edward Hall's distinction between low-context and high-context patterns of thinking. Both Gouldner, the perceptive observer of Marxism who saw himself as an "outlaw" engaged in a demystification process, and Hall, who has used the study of culture to illuminate the patterns embedded in our own natural attitude, help us to see, in different ways, the particular forms of distortion that characterize the world view constituted by the mode of discourse that educational theorists share with other liberal intellectuals. Our task in later chapters will be to suggest ways of overcoming these distortions while preserving the legitimate values and concerns of the liberal tradition of thought.

The recent interest that educational theorists have shown in the question of class has not been extended to include the class and epistemic orientation of intellectuals. This is unfortunate because the pattern of thinking of intellectuals, or what Gouldner has termed the culture of critical discourse, is based on a set of rules ("a grammar discourse") that governs all significant discourse. Gouldner's elaboration of these rules enables us to recognize that the elaborated language code involves something more politically significant than the proclivity, which both Bernstein (1975) and Bourdieu (1971) called to our attention, toward thinking in universalistic rather than context-specific terms. As Gouldner points out, in addition to requiring conformity to specific rules for thought and discourse, these rules serve as the basis for delegitimating other modes of discourse. Serious thought and speech, according to Gouldner, must reflect the following assumptions: (1) assertions must be justified, (2) the mode of justification must avoid invoking any form of authority other than that of theory and empirical evidence, and (3) the acceptance of assertions is to be based on voluntary consent and informed by the power of argument and evidence. The rules of discourse further specify that the language be explicit and universalistic ("one word, one meaning, for everyone and forever") rather than dependent upon tacit and context-specific meaning (Gouldner 1979, pp. 28–29).

In the interests of emancipatory forms of discourse, reliance on the "speaker's person, authority, or status in society" to justify speech claims is forbidden. As a result, the mode of discourse to which intellectuals subscribe "de-authorizes all speech grounded in traditional societal authority, while it authorizes itself, the elaborated speech variant of the culture of critical discourse, as the standard of all serious speech." The ground rules regulating "significant" discourse become, in effect, the expression of power. When speakers who do not conform to these rules are deauthorized, the political process becomes distorted, with the view of reality constructed by intellectuals prevailing over those of more embedded cultural groups. Although the world view of the intellectual, with its special pattern of teleological thinking and its assumptions about the nature of authority and the individual, is associated with our highest values, the ground rules governing discourse preclude a serious challenge by other cultural groups. This does not mean that this mode of discourse is easily or successfully imposed on other cultural groups. Resistance takes many forms, as is recognized by anyone who takes the time to observe the varied rules that govern discourse on the street and in the meeting places outside the halls of government bureaucracy and institutionalized learning.

Edward Hall's distinction between high- and low-context patterns of thinking helps to bring the issue of culture into the consideration of the relationship between discourse and power. What he calls a low-context pattern of thinking shares many of the characteristics of the "culture of critical discourse" described by Gouldner. Whereas Gouldner limited his analysis primarily to explicating the assumptions that give legitimacy to a particular mode of discourse, he did not elaborate on the epistemic characteristics of the deauthorized forms of discourse.

Hall's distinction helps put in focus fundamental and perhaps irreconcilable differences that separate cultural groups. In summarizing the characteristics that separate high- from low-context patterns of thinking, we should keep in mind that liberal educational theorists, in terms of their professional lives, reflect the low-context style of thinking and, in terms of their current ideological biases, cannot represent the interests or world view of cultural groups who possess a high-context pattern of thinking. In later chapters, when the problem of reconstructing the conceptual foundations of liberal educational theory is discussed, we shall return to Hall's distinction, as it helps to clarify a basic weakness in liberal thinking that must be addressed.

According to Hall, one of the functions of culture is to provide a highly selective screen (interpretive framework) that influences what we pay attention to and what we ignore. As there is a danger of taking in too much information and causing what Hall termed "information overload," cultures have developed different ways of coping with this problem. At least five different factors enter into the complex process that governs what will be perceived and what will be ignored: "the subject or activity, the situation, one's status in the social system, past experience, and culture" (1977, p. 86). The rules of governing the influence that each of these factors will have on perception are internalized as part of the tacit knowledge acquired as a member of the language community. This part of Hall's view of the relationship of culture to cognition is part of the conventional wisdom within anthropology. The part of his theory that relates more specifically to our concern with whether the assumptions associated with the liberal view of discourse exclude cultural groups who do not share the same epistemic code has to do with how different cultures work out the balance, in the communication process, between the explicit linguistic code, context, and meaning.

The study of communication in different cultures led Hall to the conclusion that cultures can be identified on a continuum that reflects the emphasis given to these three elements in their form of communication. A culture that has what Hall termed a high-context form of communication is predominantly "one in which most of the information is either in the physical context or internalized in the person, while very little is in the coded, explicit, transmitted part of the message" (p. 91). A culture with a low-context form of communication, by contrast, is one where the information is largely vested in the explicit language code, and context is de-emphasized as a source of meaning and information. Traditional native American cultures have a high-context pattern of communication where context is an important source of meaning, while Anglo-Europeans exhibit a low-context form of communication, with the elaborated language code (in Bernstein's sense) serving as the primary carrier of information. Hall observed that in cultures where context is an important source of information, relationships tend to be more stable and communication tends to be more efficient and satisfying because the participants share a common fund of tacit knowledge learned within a lived context over a long period of time. In effect, high-context "transactions feature preprogrammed information that is in the receiver and in the setting, with only minimal information in the transmitted message." Where an emphasis on change, individualism, and abstract thought weakens the importance of a shared context as a source of information, more of the "information must be in the transmitted message in order to make up for what is missing in the context (both internal and external)" (p. 101).

By showing how different cultural groups utilize embeddedness in context as a source of meaning and information, Hall introduces an important issue likely to be overlooked by theorists who, conditioned by the assumptions of their own low-contexting culture, assume that the explicit language code is not only the primary source of significant information but also the vehicle of a higher form of understanding that can be generalized across cultures. If we compare the high-context form of communication with Gouldner's description of the grammar of critical discourse, irreconcilable differences emerge. A cultural group that fits Hall's definition of high-context pattern of thinking and communicating would not view the shared context of the individual's life world as irrelevant to significant discourse. Because a high-context orientation involves a base of shared knowledge that grows out of unified and long-standing social relationships, it would be unnatural to use a form of communication that "devalues tacit, context-limited meanings," to use Gouldner's phrase. The rules governing the intellectual's mode of thought and communication include using "explicit and articulate rules, rather than diffuse or tacit features of the speech context" (Gouldner, p. 28), which are the very characteristics of the high-context form of communication. The positions are irreconcilable because of the epistemic bias of the intellectual against tacit forms of knowledge and traditional forms of authority not based on explicit rational principles.

Another way to understand the desire of the intellectual to transcend the constraints that context places on the rational constructions of reality is to view it as the Enlightenment goal of freeing man from embeddedness. Yet the nature and degree of the individual's embeddedness exceed what can be grasped by the rationalist mode of thinking. As Ernest Schachtel observed,

> Man is also embedded in the countless patterns of routine, convention, more or less automatic behavior on his own part and the part of others. He is embedded in his family, his home, his work, the circle of his friends, his town, his language, his culture, and his country. These publicly or privately "institutionalized" patterns, while created by man and changeable by him, in a way take the place of the instinctive behavior

in which animals are embedded. The embeddedness function of these patterns plays a large role, psychologically, in the conservative tendencies of man, in his fear of new individual as well as social ways of life. (1959, p. 52)

Whereas in the past, for example, certain religions have held out the possibility of escaping embeddedness and the Enlightenment vision of the fully realized individual assumed the irrelevance of context, today theory is viewed as the vehicle that promises transcendence from the hold of embeddedness. That we can escape entirely and that embeddedness is entirely dehumanizing are two profoundly problematic assumptions.

Power, as was stated earlier, is expressed in delimiting the field of significant discourse. If the field of discourse excludes important aspects of collective human existence, then the political process is skewed in favor of the cultural group who imposes its conceptual categories as the ground rules for defining "What Is." This can be grasped more clearly by using Michael Shapiro's definition of politics as the sanctioned control of what constitutes valued experience. As discourse is an important element in the exercise of control, both in terms of what is affirmed and what is denied as valued, the conceptual categories of the social group that succeeds in establishing its mode of discourse over that of other groups become critically important elements in the political process. The categories themselves must be viewed as part of the political process and should be open to debate rather than given a privileged neutral status. For these categories of thought represent the most forward phase of the political process that determines what issues will be contested through more established and recognized political processes and what aspects of human experience will be judged as too insignificant to be talked about.

Subsequent chapters will involve an examination of how particular views of the purpose of schooling, the style of pedagogy, and the content of the curriculum reflect the constraints imposed by the conceptual categories used by liberal educational theorists. In examining the general characteristics of liberal thought, it should be remembered that the surface interpretation of deep-level assumptions has produced important differences in educational theories. The neo-Marxists, for example, view both the purpose and process of education in a substantially different way from the technocratic followers of Skinner. Yet at the deeper level of conceptual categories a case can be made that their respective theories begin with a shared set of assumptions (Bowers 1984b, pp. 365–91). There are important differences between other traditions within the field of liberal educational discourse. But mapping these differences, as well as commonalities, will not be our main concern. The central concern, as stated earlier, is to challenge the reigning deep assumptions of liberal thought in order to make the language of liberal educational theories more accountable, and thus more sensitive, to the post-modern and post-liberal era we are now entering.

Challenging the assumptions that undergird the foundations of liberal educational thought will involve examining how certain tenets serve to deligitimate other areas of cultural experience as unworthy of discourse. What needs to be put in focus is how liberal educational thought expresses a negative dialectic where exclusion, rather than synthesis, becomes the creative expression of power. Basic to this negative dialectic is a set of assumptions, viewed essentially as unproblematic, that serve as the conceptual starting point for technocratic liberal, neo-Marxist, neoromantic, and progressivist theories of education. These assumptions include the view that education contributes to a progressive form of social change, that the power and authority of the individual must be progressively strengthened either through skill development or consciousness raising (Dewey's ideas represented a serious challenge to this idea), that a critical form of rational thought must replace more traditional forms of cultural authority, and that educated judgment enables the individual to stand for truth and thus above the partisan use of power. These bedrock assumptions not only served to provide a sense of security about how to think about reality, they also established the conceptual boundaries that separated enlightened, progressive thought from the unenlightened and reactionary. By rigidly holding to these core liberal assumptions, recent theories of education have become both more attenuated and divorced from social reality. The educational practices that grew out of Skinner's theory as well as the more extreme educational proposals of the romantic humanists of the sixties remind us of how unexamined liberal assumptions can be extrapolated to the point where they become a caricature of a rich political tradition of thought. Even the conceptual categories of neo-Marxists such as Paulo Freire, who fuse Marx's class analysis with the liberal view of the emancipated individual, fail to address this problem of an increasingly restricted discourse.

Before attempting to identify the issues that must be engaged if we are to formulate a theory of education for the post-modern era we are now entering, it will first be necessary to examine the chief characteristics of the four archetypal forms of educational liberalism. This will be limited to the ideas of John Dewey and Paulo Freire, who have given us the two most significant theories of education in recent years, and B. F. Skinner and Carl Rogers, who represent the more polarizing and contradictory extremes of educational liberalism. Their theories will help us to identify the chief characteristics of the social reality made possible by their modes of discourse; an examination of their discourse will also help us to identify the areas of silence that contributed to distortions in understanding. Subsequent chapters will involve an examination of the nature of our cultural embeddedness in traditions, as well as the contributions that philosophical conservatism (the "Forbidden Faith," as Raymond English termed it) can make to expanding the discourse of liberal educational theory. The ultimate objective of this analysis will be to sketch the outlines of a post-liberal theory of education that will, hopefully, initiate a broader dialogue on the purpose of education in a world that seems bent on realizing Nietzsche's prophecy of a nihilistic end.

2

The Problematic Discourse: A Profile of Liberal Theories of Education

AN important feature of contemporary life is the manner in which experience increasingly exceeds the authority of our language and thus our ability to understand the present. This is not a new problem, as people have always had to deal with the present in terms of language frameworks that reproduced conceptual patterns created in response to an earlier set of social conditions. But the problem of understanding the present, as well as the future, by adopting the rearview mirror perspective of our language frameworks has been exacerbated by the rate of change that now characterizes our culture. In more stable cultures the conceptual lenses acquired from the past required only minor adjustments, as the traditional patterns of daily life remained essentially unaltered. The introduction of computers, genetic engineering, and work robots, as well as the myriad forms of intervention by the state into daily life, to cite only a few of the vast number of cultural experiments we are now undergoing, exceeds the explanatory authority of the conceptual frameworks that sustained discourse in the past. Those who can produce data, establish the superior efficiency of the new technology, and promise greater control and profits, are increasingly filling the conceptual and moral voids caused by the increasing lack of symmetry between our often time-bound conceptual frameworks and new cultural developments.

The discontinuity between daily experience and the authority of our language is further increased when the metaphors of the language become the basis for thinking mythically. Talk that equates change only with progress, rationality only with human betterment, and individualism only with emancipation, can quickly lose touch with the real world, where the complexity of experience seldom fits the simplicity of ideals and where ideals, when carried to an extreme, have a way of turning into new sources of oppression.

Liberal theorists of education, like other groups of liberal thinkers, contribute to the growing disjunction between daily experience and our ability to understand that experience by promoting the very values and beliefs that are accelerating the process of cultural experimentation. These values and beliefs, which reflect what can be called the positive vision of liberalism, serve to legitimate the disintegrating forces of modernization. These same values and beliefs also serve as the main conceptual foundation for the liberal educational theorist's vision of a more ideal society. This ironic situation reflects another facet of the crises in liberal thought, namely, the failure to examine how the ideals of an essentially humane and hopeful vision became reified. In holding this reified vision, the liberal educational theorists failed to examine how their most basic beliefs and values are often used to foster those elements of modernization that are most threatening both to the ecology and to communal well-being.

Before considering more carefully specific liberal theories of education in terms of the disjunctions between the current liberal vision and the process of modernization, the areas of silence created by a restrictive discourse, and the strengths that can serve as a basis for a reconceptualized educational theory to guide us in the post-liberal era we are now entering, we must first juxtapose the key elements of the liberal vision against widely acknowledged characteristics of modern life. This will enable us to avoid blindly accepting the liberal ideals without asking about the possible connection between these ideals and the ongoing series of crises faced by modern society.

As liberalism has at various times been associated with the Enlightenment, humanism, democracy, capitalism, and, more recently, the welfare state (often simultaneously), it is difficult to define liberalism with any real precision (Dunn 1979, pp. 28–29). The problem is further compounded by the widespread tendency to blur the conventional and often erroneous distinction between liberalism and conservatism by labeling the classical variant of liberalism as the expression of conservative values. Adding to the confusion caused by this habit of mislabeling political genres is the popular tendency, found in both the press and scholarly writing, to associate liberalism with a set of beliefs that, in many ways, simplify and distort the complex intellectual foundations of liberal thought. "Liberalism," according to Sheldon Wolin, "has been repeatedly characterized as 'optimistic' to the point of naivete; arrogant in its conviction that human reason ought to stand as the sole authority for knowledge and action; bewitched by a vision of history as an escalator endlessly moving upwards toward greater progress; and blasphemous in endowing the human mind and will with a godlike power of refashioning man and society in entirety" (1960, p. 293). This "vulgar caricature," to use Wolin's phrase, appears nevertheless to contain the very assumptions that guide the thought of current liberal theorists of education, as well as many others who are untroubled by the fact that the source of the current view of liberalism is more likely to be found in the radical democratic rhetoric of the French Enlightenment than in the more ambivalent writings of Locke and Hobbes. As Dunn laconically observed, "dispositionally, liberalism has little regard for the past" (p. 29); this observation surely applies to liberal educational theorists who ignore their own genealogy.

Our task here is not to set the historical record straight; rather, it is to identify the key assumptions of the contemporary liberal vision and to suggest why these assumptions must be viewed as problematic. By clarifying the problematic nature of these assumptions—which provide the background horizon for thinking about individualism, rationality, and progress—it will be easier to recognize the assumptions and foci of liberal theories of education that might otherwise escape critical scrutiny. The problem to be overcome here is the hermeneutical one of understanding, in the sense of clearly recognizing and exercising critical judgment, when there is a close symmetry between the beliefs the reader takes for granted and the position being studied. When this situation occurs, the assumptions that have not been made explicit and problematic are likely to remain hidden in the shared horizon that characterizes the natural attitude.

Limiting the discussion to key beliefs that have become increasingly problematic is not intended to suggest that all aspects of liberalism are being challenged, or that it no longer represents a viable political option. Nor is it meant in any way to diminish the legacy of liberal achievements. Protection of the individual's civil liberties, the right to form opposition parties for the purpose of challenging governmental policy, the use of law rather than force as the means of settling disputes, the ability to mobilize the power and resources of government for the purpose of dealing with social problems, and a concern with redistributing resources for the purpose of realizing greater equity in areas of education and health care— these are all solid achievements that deserve only to be strengthened. The problem lies more with the increasing disjunction between the current intellectual foundations of liberalism and the social and ecological problems we now face.

In the past the liberal way of thinking about individualism, rationality, and progress provided a coherent, compelling, and enlightened set of political options. Today, however, the traditional liberal formulation of these beliefs contributes to conceptual uncertainty and increasing strife between contending social groups who attempt to manipulate the policy agenda of government for their own ends. The prognosis for the future of liberalism is varied and often pessimistic. Many intellectuals have simply sided with Marx's view that liberalism is the self-serving ideology of a now moribund class. Other observers, such as Theodore Lowi, see its flaws leading to a degenerate form of "interest-group liberalism," where the political process becomes the arena for "giving to each according to his claim, the price for which is a reduction of concern for what others are claiming" (1979, p. 55). John Dunn, the English political theorist, communicates a deeper sense of doubt:

> There seems every reason to doubt the possibility of a comprehensive and coherent *modern* philosophy of liberalism; and perhaps more disturbingly (though perhaps also consequently) there seems little reason to believe that the more attractive values of liberalism enjoy any privileged relation to the historical process. Indeed the question has now become not one of whether History is *committed* to liberalism or to some more splendid and transcendent apotheosis of liberalism—but rather one of whether History is likely to continue much longer even to tolerate it. (1979, p. 54)

Others, such as Daniel Bell, Benjamin Barber, and William Sullivan, see the contemporary state of liberal thought as no less flawed but have responded to the challenge of attempting to reformulate its conceptual foundations.

The disjuncture between core liberal beliefs and the contemporary world seems to be widening in a way that makes the liberal position increasingly untenable, particularly in the social-ecological arena where the crisis appears to be exacerbated by the implementation of the more progressive liberal beliefs. The liberal view of individualism serves as the best example of this problem. Individualism and liberalism are nearly synonymous terms; in fact it would be impossible to think of liberalism without considering the individual as the basic social unit. This is not to suggest that the contemporary view of individualism has existed in unaltered form throughout the history of liberal thought. In its present form, however, individualism means being free, distinct (unique), self-responsible in a moral and rational sense, and capable of continual self-development (growth). The phrases "individual thought," "self-realization," "emancipation," "self-discovery," "individual choice," and so on, clearly reflect a view of the individual as the basic social entity, capable of self-formation and direction, and as the ultimate source of authority. These phrases are integral to the discourses of humanistic psychology and counseling, education, art, and (ironically) the business community who view the individual as the basic element of the "market."

The idea of the socially autonomous individual, essential to the liberal prescriptions for continual emancipation of the individual (an idea that is interesting for its lack of a self-limiting principle), has been seriously challenged by such divergent thinkers as Marx and Durkheim. Marx, following Hegel, insisted that thought is a social capacity, while Durkheim saw the anomic form of individualism (which has surprising affinities with the view of individualism as an unending quest for self-expression and realization) as the expression of a social pathology. More recently, cultural linguists, having established the connection between the symbolic aspects of culture and "individual" thought, provide a way of understanding "individualism" itself as the expression of a particular cultural orientation. The work of cognitive psychologists has recently strengthened our understanding of the connections between language and our conceptual schemas; at the same time they have reinforced the work of George H. Mead, Alfred Schutz, and others who combined symbolic interactionism with phenomenological sociology to establish a dialectical view of the "individual" as an intersubjective being. These intellectual developments, which now span decades of cumulative effort, represent a highly complex and powerful conceptual framework that denies the legitimacy of the contemporary view of the autonomous individual. Yet this alternative body of theory appears to have had little influence, with the exception of Dewey and Skinner (the latter basing his challenge on research with rats and pigeons), on the liberal view of individualism.

The growing schism between how the "individual" is being understood in the more linguistically oriented social sciences and psychology and the view of the self-determining individual that is to be further emancipated through the adoption of liberal theories of education reflects a growing crisis in the theories that guide educational practice. But the crisis extends beyond the area of theory. The view of the individual as engaged in an inner quest for meaning (Rogers), emancipation (Freire and Giroux), and the maximization of pleasure and avoidance of pain (Skinner) easily lends itself to a more material pursuit of self-interest, exploited by commercial interests which have made the consumer ethic the ultimate goal of individual self-realization. This view of the self-directing individual treats freedom as unconditional, positive forms of power as an expression of individual agency, and authority as centered in individual judgment. As the individual is made the epicenter of the social world, the prospects of a healthy civic life become increasingly problematic. By not emphasizing the common aspects of social and personal life, liberalism—particularly in its educational variant—has undermined the forms of expression that characterize freedom, power, and authority in healthy communities. Instead of treating self-reflection as an aspect of membership in an interdependent community, the claims of community are vitiated by the liberal tendency to make self-determination the ultimate test, and to fall back on utilitarianism as a way of mediating between different definitions of what constitutes the interests of the individual. As Daniel Bell stated the problem facing liberal society;

> Any society, in the end, is a moral order that has to justify (in the sociological jargon, to legitimate) its allocative principles and the balances of freedom and coercions necessary to facilitate or enforce such rules. The problem, inevitably, is the relation between self-interest and the public interest, between personal impulses and community requirements. Without a public philosophy, explicitly stated, we lack the fundamental condition whereby a modern polity can live by consensus (and without it there is only continuing conflict) and justice. (1976, p. 250)

With the emphasis on individual self-determination (which collectively is expressed in interest group politics) the moral claims of the community that might serve to channel the expression of individualism become increasingly attenuated. And with the atrophy of this part of the individual-community dialectic, votes and opinion polls become the primary basis for determining social consensus. The degree of support for education, the nature of an equitable allocation of resources in society, the role of government in regulating the affairs of everyday life, the extent of environmental damage we will tolerate in the name of profits and scientific inquiry, and the share of the public treasury we will entrust to the defense establishment are public policy issues settled on the basis of those groups who combine self-interest with the new technologies of power.

Beyond the vital issues surrounding how to reconcile the contemporary liberal view of individualism with what Bell called the needs of a "public household" (those aspects of community life that cannot be fulfilled by individuals acting alone), there are other signs of the growing disjuncture between the vision embodied in the core beliefs of liberalism and social and ecological realities. The multifaceted nature of the liberal view of individualism, for example, appears to be generating contradictory pressures that threaten the survival of the more worthy elements. The abstract view of the individual as essentially free and potentially self-determining (the view that is generally found in emancipatory theories of education) is increasingly contradicted by anthropological evidence and the growing understanding that "human nature" is modified in each historical period—to put it in Marxian terms. The possessive view of individualism which underlies both the contemporary idea of property rights and the market economy generates, according to C. B. Macpherson, "class differences in effective rights and rationality, yet requires for its justification a postulate of equal natural rights and rationality" (1962, p. 45). It has also led to a degree of consumerism that habituates the individual to the treadmill of technological and market innovation.

To take another example, the remissive aspect of the self-realizing individual involves a different form of contradiction between romantic vision and recent social developments. The shift from a view of individualism that found the source of authority in a shared belief system, such as Puritanism, where flaws of character and the achievement of success were judged as individual attributes, to a view of the individual continually seeking new forms of expression has led to a basic change in the locus of authority. John Carroll, an Australian sociologist, has argued that the modern view of individualism, which celebrates the values of self-expression, discovery, and pleasure, has actually led to a decline in the authority of the individual and a concomitant rise in the authority of institutions, both public and private, to control and regulate the life of the individual (1977, pp. 29-30). The remissive form of individualism, in effect, relativizes the communal foundations of a shared sense of moral authority, with the consequence that individual judgment reflects what is perceived as useful, fulfilling, and pleasurable. With the increasing emphasis on individual interpretation, on overcoming the hold of traditional values, and on the authority of subjective judgment, the idea of "obedience" to the dictates of a fixed set of moral principles or traditional beliefs appears (mistakenly) as the anachronistic belief of a more authoritarian era. Yet it is this subjectivizing of authority that undermines the ability to establish a common ground, a consensus on the authority of moral principles, for resisting modern forms of authoritarianism. The problem, as Hannah Arendt put it, is that living "in a political realm with neither authority nor the concomitant awareness that the source of authority transcends power and those who are in power, means to be confronted anew, without the religious trust in a sacred beginning and without the protection of traditional and therefore self-evident standards of behavior, by the elementary problems of human living-together" (1961, p. 141). As authority rests on the shifting sands of individual experience, the authoritarianism expressed in legislated meanings, rules, and prescribed behaviors becomes a more dominant characteristic of modern life. In effect, the remissive form of individualism replaces the traditional problem of authority with the modern quest for freedom and in the process abdicates any claims on authority to those who possess the technologies of surveillance and image formation.

The realm of political individualism involves a similar erosion of past liberal achievements. Ideas of consent and representation were based on a recognition of the rights of the individual. Similarly, the liberal ideal of limited government reflected a central concern with safeguarding individual liberties. Although the progressive nature of political individualism has been substantially tarnished by the increasing tendencies to use the political process to attain private economic interests, the values of consent, representation, and constitutional guarantees, when compared to alternative political models that blur the distinction between the individual and the state, must remain as the basis of any reconceptualization of liberal principles. Yet ironically the main threat to the basis of representative government comes from the growing dependence upon the liberal ideal of basing decisions on a rational process itself. Since the time of Bacon and Descartes, the dominant view of rationality has increasingly become associated with power, instrumental problem-solving, and the establishment of objective knowledge. Reflection as the source of understanding has given way to a more active and teleological form of rationality where power is expressed through the application of technique. As Jürgen Habermas as well as others have pointed out, the increasing reliance on purposive rationality creates a crisis of legitimation where traditional forms of cultural authority must give way to positivistic forms of knowledge and, it must be added, to the social class whose interests are served by the new epistemology. As the authority of traditional belief systems is supplanted by the cognitive claims of purposive forms of rationality, the intersubjectively held conceptual framework of the individual that previously served as the basis of authority becomes increasingly marginalized. Habermas observed that the new form of rationality, with its "'scientific-technical process of creation' introduces a 'total cutting off of previous history' and a 'change in the identity of man'" (1973, p. 125). In the place of belief systems that cannot be justified in accordance with the conceptual ground rules that recognize only empirical forms of knowledge, "short lived synthesis of isolated pieces of information, which have taken the place of global interpretation, secure the authority of science *in abstracto*" (p. 84). Thus the conceptual foundations that supply the sense of meaning necessary for the individual's participation in the democratic process become increasingly supplanted by a reductionist mode of inquiry that recognizes only the objective plane of understanding and instrumental value.

The liberal's Promethean attitude toward rationality as the new basis of authority that frees us from the embeddedness of tradition stands in sharp contrast to the more ambivalent record of achievement. Perhaps a more accurate way to think about the reliance on rationality as the only legitimate source of authority is to view it, along with the liberal assumptions about individualism and progress, as a form of cultural experimentation. But unlike a scientific experiment there are no controls, gathering of data, or careful observation of the consequences that follow the introduction of new ideas and technologies into the culture. The assumption has been that the cultural context is largely irrelevant to the dictates of rationality and that the introduction of new ideas and techniques automatically represents a progressive development. The view of society as something to be engineered has further conditioned us to ignore questions about the cultural consequences of new technologies and abstractly formulated ideas. But the spread of rationality, particularly the purposive-rational variant, introduces doubts about the final outcome of the cultural experimentation that characterizes modern-liberal society. The rapid rate of technological and ideological change, along with the nihilistic orientation which is fostered by the liberal view of a context-free form of rationality, puts the culture on an uncharted trajectory.

For example, the substitution of rationalization, in Max Weber's sense, where explicit, abstract, and calculable rules and procedures are substituted for tacit forms of traditional knowledge, has introduced sharp and discontinuous changes into the evolution of the work place as well as other areas of social life. The separation of mental and manual labor and the expansion of the role of government thus represent cultural experiments that are surrounded with uncertainty about long-term consequences. Max Weber's use of such terms as "fateful," "an iron cage," and the "apparatization" of man reflected his deep concerns about the Faustian trade-off of obtaining greater freedom and mastery of nature through the increased rationalization of the world. The rise of the modern state is equally problematic in terms of whether it can coexist with more traditional values and patterns of community life. As an increasingly interlocking system of bureaucratic institutions that bases authority on the rational knowledge of experts, the state continually expands its power through legislation and the control of discourse. The power of the state, as Anthony Giddens observed, is further increased through its capacity to gather information on all aspects of daily life. This storage of information represents, in a sense, the "data base" for increased surveillance and supervision of conduct (1981, p. 5). Jacques Ellul identified similar developments in the area of modern technology, which appear to be a direct outgrowth of core liberal beliefs. Driven by a concern with rational calculation, predictability, efficiency, and transportability across cultural contexts, modern technology—in both its mechanical and social forms—introduces a continuing stream of innovations into the culture that often severs the normal continuities between change and tradition. The development of new technologies out of scientific knowledge, which is an accelerating process, represents the best and most alarming example of the liberal tendency to introduce innovations without concern for the long-term consequences for disrupting the cultural fabric that sustains everyday life. The synthesizing of new chemicals, which now threaten to poison both our water supply and atmosphere, and the new developments in the area of genetics serve as examples of how scientific and technological developments have exceeded our political capabilities as well as our ability to grasp the moral and cultural consequences. But as long as these developments can be given legitimation by the liberal conceptual framework, we interpret them as signs of progress, even though the environmental evidence (which is easier to grasp than the evidence of cultural disruption) suggests that the products of the new knowledge are doing irreversible damage to the ecosystems, at least when measured by the time frame of humans. The ideas of purposive rationality, progress, and a form of individualism that must become increasingly rootless in order to adapt to an accelerating rate of change thus provide a set of conceptual lenses that put out of focus the unstable and experimental nature of our culture.

Because of our inability to examine the darker side of our highest values, we have failed to recognize what Nietzsche attempted to bring to our attention over one hundred years ago, namely that the values and beliefs we associate with progress (and even the notion of progress itself) represent the "inner logic" that fosters the growth of nihilism. Basically, nihilism involves a loss of meaning and a relativizing of all forms of authority in one's life. As everything becomes viewed as equal to everything else, the subjectivism of personal experience becomes the final refuge. In place of deeply held commitments, a recognition of the claims authority makes on us, and a shared sense of meaning, nihilism leads to a form of cultural and spiritual exhaustion where the individual feels a sense of alienation, meaninglessness, and powerlessness. In order to escape the existential-cultural void created by nihilism, the individual, according to Hubert Dreyfus, seeks self-realization through various forms of "experience" (1981, pp. 507–8).

The causes of nihilism are complex, with roots deep in Western patterns of thought. While recognizing the danger of oversimplifying the explanation of the cultural forces that foster nihilism, it is possible to identify how the liberal view of individualism, rationalism, and progress contributes to nihilism. For instance, the view of the autonomous individual faced with the continual challenge of achieving self-realization locates authority entirely within the individual, and in the process relativizes all other forms of cultural authority. At the same time the liberal view of the rational process, which is characterized by an emphasis on critical reflection and a theoretical understanding, separates the individual from the ongoing embeddedness in the life world of cultural practice. This mode of thought according to Dreyfus, objectifies by setting the world over against the knower, decontextualizes in order to allow for generalizing theory across contexts, and elevates explicit forms of knowledge (which involves separating knowledge from context) over implicit and tacit forms of understanding (pp. 510-11). The relativizing effect of critical inquiry, as well as the objectifying and decontextualizing nature of theoretical forms of knowledge, strengthen the authority of individualism and at the same time erode the sense of meaning and efficacy of what Michael Oakeshott called the "practical knowledge" that characterizes the cultural embeddedness of most human activity (1962, pp. 8-12). Given the power of the idea of progress in shaping the projective consciousness of the modern liberal, it is not surprising that the growth of nihilism has not been recognized. The idea that change is inherently progressive leads automatically to viewing those beliefs and values that contribute to change—individualism and critical reflection—as signs of progress. The development of technology is similarly viewed as a manifestation of progress, even though it often involves the destruction of traditions that serve as the underpinnings of personal memory so necessary to orientating oneself in time. To destroy that past in order to control the future, or to at least make it "cost effective," becomes in effect the moral obligation of the progressive individual. That the idea of progress involves a grossly oversimplified understanding of the nature of our embeddedness in tradition and that it contributes to the sense of rootlessness that characterizes nihilism does not seem to matter. As an image, it serves more as a conceptual and moral compass that confirms that change, experimentation, and innovation involve a clear sense of ontological direction. But it has not helped in recognizing the cultural basis of the ecological crisis or the connections between higher values and the varied manifestations of individual malaise.

The conceptual crises of liberalism suggested by this brief overview of unresolved social-environmental problems raises disturbing questions about the power of discourse to depoliticize the very language that exercises such a powerful influence on the categories of thought that determine which issues will be recognized and which ignored. The depoliticizing of language occurs as reified ideas and values are allowed to influence the focus of political attention while remaining themselves safely insulated from the critical scrutiny and negotiation that characterize the more democratic manifestation of the political process. The result is a narrowed discourse where the dialectic between language and life-world context, which should lead to the reconceptualization of language as experience deepens understanding, is displaced by a form of communication that confuses conceptual formulas for social vision, the manipulation of clichés for analysis, and moral pronouncements for direct action. This form of discourse, when carried to an extreme, becomes a world of its own, requiring that analysis conform to established intellectual formulas and a continuing reiteration of moral prescriptions. All ideologies, to varying degrees, exhibit this tendency to depoliticize key elements of their own linguistic and conceptual categories. By fostering the illusion that their own conceptual foundations have objective and thus universal standing, ideologies insure that the political process will operate within fixed boundaries and in accordance with established rules of thought and discourse. Technocrats, for example, assume that measurability and efficiency represent a culture-free starting point for thinking about the problems of social change; similarly, Marxists assume the progressive nature of revolutionary change and the efficacy of abstract theory. Liberal educational theorists are also captives of their own discourse where, in a quite literal sense, the vocabulary and conceptual categories interact on each other in a manner that establishes the boundaries of approved thought and social vision.

For our purposes it is important to examine more carefully the various discourses that characterize liberal educational theorists in order to determine their understanding of the crisis facing modern society, as well as the question of whether their interpretations of liberalism leads to an adequate theory of education. Of particular importance will be these theorists' views on individualism, the rational process, and nature of change. Although contemporary liberalism is far too complex to be understood solely on the basis of these three ideas, they nevertheless seem crucial to understanding the major sources of conceptual confusion that characterizes the liberal position. The view of individualism that one holds, for example, has important implications for how community is viewed and for what is seen as the nature of authority and where it is ultimately located. The view of the rational process also relates to the problem of authority, but equally problematic is the relationship between rational thought and context (which involves the dimensions of temperal, spatial, cultural, and psychological embeddedness). The view of change is critical in terms of the standing that will be given to tradition; when change is identified with progress, for instance, the complexity of tradition tends to be simplified to the point where it is viewed as a source of constraint that needs to be transcended. The particular formulation given to the nature of individualism, rationalism, and change also has profound implications for how a theory of education will be conceptualized, including the nature of the curriculum, pedagogy, and the connections that will be seen between the educational process and society.

As liberalism has been translated by educational theorists into distinct traditions of thought, the analysis of the conceptual underpinnings of the liberal discourse in education will be limited to the views of John Dewey, Paulo Freire, Carl Rogers, and B. F. Skinner. These theorists represent the main educational varieties of liberalism: the scientific-democratic, the neo-Marxist-existentialist, the neoromantic, and the techno-behaviorist. While these four theorists do not represent the entire spectrum of liberal theories of education (where, for example, does one place Joel Spring or Maxine Greene?), they nevertheless appear to have developed the most comprehensive theories of education that reflect the major archetypes into which the educational versions of liberalism have been fragmented. They also represent, on the surface level, four distinct discourses on the nature of education, society, and the human condition. An examination of their ideas, epistemological categories, and vocabulary, which constitute the symbolic dimensions of their discourse, will provide useful insights into the problem of reconstituting the liberal discourse in education in a manner that addresses the problems of modernization. In effect, the conceptualization of a post-liberal theory of education must build upon the strengths of existing liberal theories of education while, at the same time, avoiding their limitations. In order to emphasize the constructive intent of the analysis, we shall begin with a profile of the educational theories of John Dewey and Paulo Freire, as both have developed powerful theories that contain elements that must be retained in any formulation of a post-liberal theory of education.

John Dewey

The time span of Dewey's work, as well as the range of his intellectual interests, make it difficult to summarize his views. Yet there is an identifiable center that enables us to recognize that regardless of whether Dewey is writing on education, aesthetics, or the more traditional philosophical issues, his analysis, like the spokes of a wheel, is always directed toward bringing us back to the central task of reconstructing our way of thinking so as to be more in harmony with what he understood as the process of modernization. For Dewey, it was not modernization that was problematic, but rather the old ways of thinking and acting that prevented us from experiencing the growth that represented the promise of modernization. Thus the discourse that Dewey operated within, which he both strengthened and helped to redirect, represented an attempt to modernize our way of thinking across the entire range of human activity. In order to obtain a clearer picture of how his understanding of modernization established the boundaries and determined the conceptual structure of his liberal discourse, it will be necessary to focus specifically upon what he understood as the crisis posed by modernization, as well as the key aspects of traditional ways of thinking that needed to be reconstituted (i.e., the nature of the rational process and individualism).

Dewey's understanding of temporality served as the metaphysical underpinning of his view of modernization. Time, for Dewey, was like the ceaseless flow of a river that carries us toward a continually receding horizon. The movement presses forward in a manner that gives experience, in both its temporal and spatial dimensions, a directional quality of unending novelty. George Santayana referred to the directional quality that Dewey's sense of temporality gives to all aspects of his thinking as the "dominance of the foreground" (Schilpp 1951, p. 251). Dewey himself expressed this sense of time when he said that we "live forward." Modernization, as he viewed it, involved this same notion of moving into the future; but he also understood modernization as moving into an expanding horizon of possibilities that could be realized only as people were prepared to constantly adjust their way of thinking to the continual changes in the circumstances of social life. Thus modernization could not be approached in a passive manner; instead, it carried moral obligations for active engagement and set a broad agenda for reconceptualizing the foundations of social life. Dewey's seemingly timeless intellectual efforts were directed toward working out the conceptual implications of aligning the social world to the progressive movement of modernization.

What Dewey associated with being modern (and progressive) deeply influenced the political priorities embedded in his discourse and, in the case of the scientific method and democracy, helped to give them special standing in the realm of the unproblematic. Choices about whether we should use the scientific method as the model of thinking and democracy as the basis of determining the outcome of political issues were simply not arguable. Anticipating Hanna Pitkin's (1972, pp. 200–201) insight that membership in a language community involves the tacit acceptance of thought patterns that prefigure the scope and focus of the individual's more explicit level of political involvement, Dewey directed his energies to politicizing the conceptual foundations of the larger language community that, in his view, unconsciously accepted a whole series of political norms that could not be justified in terms of the modern world view. While attempting to politicize the conceptual foundations of this larger language community in order to bring them into the modern world, as he viewed it, Dewey remained largely unaware of how his own thinking was directed by the conceptual conventions of the language community to which he belonged.

The crisis of modernization, as Dewey understood it, was represented in the unresolved state of mind about whether the power of the scientific method should be used to establish the basis of authority or whether the older epistemological systems (both philosophical and religious) were to retain their dominant status in determining social affairs. The premodern view of reason, as Dewey tirelessly reminded us, assumed that the changing nature of experience was not the source of knowledge. Instead, the rational process was viewed as a spectator relationship to a "transcendent, absolute, or inner reality," and its purpose was to contemplate fixed essences, eternal truths, and moral absolutes. With the scientific revolution of the sixteenth and seventeenth centuries the modern view of the rational process began to emerge, and with it came a new understanding of the significance of experience as the source of a new form of instrumental knowledge. As Dewey summed up the essential difference that separated the new from the old way of viewing the source of knowledge, intelligence is "an organizing factor within experience" and reason "experimental intelligence." Thus the "test of ideas, of thinking generally, is found in the consequences of the acts to which the ideas lead, that is, in the new arrangements of things which are brought into existence" (1960, p. 136). "The world of modern science," which he saw as the *sine qua non* of the new era, "is an open world, a world varying indefinitely without the possibility of assignable limit in its internal make-up, a world stretching beyond any assignable bounds externally" (1957, p. 54). The crisis of modernization, in his view, would only be overcome as the patterns regulating conceptual and social activity were reconstructed in a manner that took account of this "open world" of changing experience.

Dewey's attempt to bring the discourse of philosophy, education, and politics (not to mention aesthetics and religion) into the modern era involved a wide-ranging attack on traditional ways of thinking. What he was attempting to achieve was a way of understanding how authority could be determined in a world with no fixed reference points beyond the notion of growth itself (which he acknowledged as the only moral end). For our purposes of understanding the unique conceptual characteristics of the linguistic regularities that Dewey wanted to see established, we will turn more directly to his view of putting education and liberal ideology on the ontological footings that remained after the scientific mode of thought had completed the task of demythologizing the foundations of belief. The problem for Dewey was to formulate a way of understanding that made authority conditional upon the consequences of an experimental method of inquiry. Thus he turned away from viewing education as the process of learning a fixed body of knowledge, the individual as an independent source of moral and rational authority, and liberalism as involving a fixed commitment to the values of individualism, competition, and the negative state.

Having rejected the premodern view, as he saw it, that located authority in the rational apprehension of what is fixed and enduring, Dewey argued that the only reliable source of authority we could have is the scientific mode of inquiry. As he put it, "science has placed in our hands the means by which we can better judge our wants, and has aided in forming the instruments and operations by which to satisfy them" (1960, p. 45). Authority thus became equivalent to the exercise of power in solving the ongoing problems of social life. As one observer (Damico 1978) has noted, by relating authority to successful problem solving, Dewey laid the groundwork for a new understanding of both the individual and social dimensions of freedom. The authority of the scientific method, if it is to be demonstrated in the broadest possible way, "issues from and is based upon collective activity, cooperatively organized" (p. 92). Thus, authority is strengthened as inquiry becomes a cooperative activity. Similarly, as "individual freedom stands for the forces by which change" (i.e., successful problem solving) "is intentionally brought about" (p. 94), individuals experience greater freedom as they come under the social control of cooperative inquiry. Freedom then becomes associated with a socially shared instrumental capacity for solving collective problems, rather than with the existential view that locates the individual in the liminal psychological space apart from society.

Dewey's understanding of the connectedness of knowledge and experience, as well as his deep belief in the power of the scientific method to resolve disputes pertaining to the worth of ideas and values, led him to assign formal education a central role in the reconstruction of the conceptual basis of social life. While he viewed all aspects of social life as educative in function, he wanted schools to perform the special mission of providing the "purified medium of action" that would insure that only those elements of the past that strengthened the cooperative application of creative intelligence to social problem solving would be passed on to the young. By teaching students to utilize the mental habits of experimental inquiry—careful observation of the actual interconnections of problematic situations, formation of hypotheses for guiding future action, and learning from the consequences of testing ideas in the context of ongoing experience—Dewey saw schools overcoming the separation between the narrow and sterile spectator form of learning of traditional schools and the social capacities needed in a modern society. In teaching the mental habits associated with experimental inquiry, the schools would be contributing socially as well as individually to the "reconstruction or reorganization of experience which adds to the meaning of experiences, and which increases ability to direct the course of subsequent experience" (1916, p. 89). Dewey's view of education as increasing the "power of subsequent direction or control" within the context of the social world led him to emphasize the natural connection between education and politics. But before we examine how the unity of education and politics led Dewey to a reformulation of liberalism, it will be necessary to focus more directly upon his view of the individual.

"Individuality," as Dewey wrote in *Individualism Old and New*, is at first spontaneous and unshaped; it is a potentiality, a capacity of development" (1962, p. 168). The form individualism takes is thus dependent upon preexisting patterns of behavior and habits of mind that characterize the society into which one is born. Thus, individuality reflects a community orientation; it is not self-shaping or autonomous. The argument that individuality is shaped and formed "only through interaction with actual conditions" could be substantiated by considering the influence of membership in a language community on thought and disposition, the social nature of experience, and the stake that everybody has in solving the ongoing problems that threaten the well-being of the larger community. Thus Dewey challenged the idea of the autonomous individual on the grounds that it was based on an erroneous understanding of the nature of freedom.

The problem of individual freedom was not a matter of escaping from social control in order to exercise greater inner self-direction (as is associated with the idea of the self-determining individual) but of acquiring a form of power that involves an increased capacity to reorganize experience. For Dewey, a recognition of the social nature of the individual leads to understanding how the fostering of interdependence increases the effective power of individuals. As he put it, "there is always a danger that increased personal independence will decrease the social capacity of an individual. In making him more self-reliant, it may make him more self-sufficient; it may lead to aloofness and indifference. It often makes an individual so insensitive," he warned, "in his relations to others as to develop an illusion of being really able to stand and act alone—an unnamed form of insanity which is responsible for a large part of the remedial suffering of the world" (1916, p. 52). The schools could foster the growth of "effective and creative individuality" by strengthening the capacity for communicating, cooperative decision-making, and the use of experimental intelligence in dealing with collective needs. In the process, schools would be nourishing the intellectual and social traits essential to the growth of a more democratic form of social life.

Dewey's attempt to modernize the conceptual foundations of liberalism reflected his basic belief that education and politics should be understood as the social dimension of the scientific method of thinking. The old liberalism, which he identified with John Locke, Adam Smith, and John Stuart Mill, put forward "ideas as immutable truths good at all times and places." While Dewey found certain elements of the traditional liberal position worth preserving (the concern with liberty, the development of inherent capacities of the individual, and the importance given to freedom of thought and expression), he was nonetheless adamant in his opposition to what he considered to be the core assumption of the liberal position, that is, the idea that as autonomous individuals pursue their self-interest the entire society would benefit. According to Dewey, this was the "Achilles heel of early liberalism." Individuals, acting on their own and relying upon myriad forms of authority to justify their ideas and values, would instead create unsolvable conflicts and undermine the possibility of cooperative action.

A modern view of liberalism, Dewey held, must recognize the growing interdependence of social life and the power that comes from utilizing the scientific method as the basis of the problem-solving process. This meant viewing liberalism as a method of intelligence, as a process of association and collective action, and as an ongoing process of education. As stated earlier, for Dewey the scientific method was to become the new basis of authority in questions pertaining to the validity of ideas and the worth of values; in effect, it was to be the touchstone of authority for establishing consensus within the community. It was also to be the basis for expanding the individual's freedom of thought and action, since Dewey viewed the method of intelligence as contributing to growth in social capacities essential for a more participatory form of involvement in the community. He also believed the potential of the scientific method to be fully realized in situations involving the widest possible form of collaborative effort. In effect, the importance of cooperation to increasing the efficacy of the scientific method was the warrant for his view of liberal society as a form of "associated behavior" that involved a new form of individualism. This view of the power of shared intelligence led Dewey to recommend fundamental structural changes in society. "The only form of enduring social organization," he wrote in *Liberalism and Social Action*, "that is now possible is one in which the new forces of productivity are cooperatively controlled and used in the effective liberty and the cultural development of the individuals that constitute society" (p. 54). But even this process of social planning, which Dewey saw as the highest expression of democracy, was to be continually adjusted through the process of experimental inquiry. This was to be the key to a forward-living, participatory society.

Paulo Freire

As Paulo Freire's educational ideas have strong existentialist and Marxist elements, an explanation is required of why he is included in a discussion of liberal theories of education. On the surface, it would seem that Freire is being miscast, since he clearly opposes both the competitive form of individualism and the free market forces of a capitalistic economy essential to the mainstream of liberal thinking. But these are characteristics of classical liberalism, and thus do not provide a basis for excluding Freire as a liberal educational theorist. Freire is not, however, committed to the structural or elitist streams of Marxist thought (the dictatorship of the proletariat) that clearly break with traditional liberal views about the dignity and empowerment of the individual. His Marxism could more appropriately be labeled as a form of democratic humanism, an ideology which would be scorned as a form of revisionist liberalism in those countries that rely upon a more scientific Marxism as the basis of their social organization. At a deeper epistemological level, which is the real starting point of his theorizing, Freire uncritically accepts the most basic premises of liberal thought: locating authority within the individual, participatory democracy as the form of governance, the progressive nature of change, a secularized society, and a continual process of emancipation to be achieved through critical reflection. He is clearly closer to the liberalism of Dewey than he is to the educational views of Lenin and Makarenko (both of whom faced the question of reconciling Marxist principles, educational practice, and the political, economic, and social requirements of a society in the throes of revolutionary change). Thus, Freire will be treated as representative of the neo-Marxist-existentialist stream of liberal educational thought.

A profile of Freire's theory of education must begin with what he sees as the fundamental problem of our epoch. His analysis of the problem, and the theory of education he advances for dealing with it, reflect how the use of an established discourse shapes the theorist's vision to preestablished conceptual patterns (albeit revolutionary in nature) and fosters predictable areas of silence. As a set of lenses, Freire's lexicon—domination, emancipation, praxis, dialogue, limit situation—provides a different angle of political and educational vision, but the background horizon that gives his theory both a sense of depth and its unique configuration remains nearly identical to that of Dewey.

Freire does not refer to modernization, but he does address himself to what he views as "the fundamental theme of our epoch," the various forms of domination that serve to dehumanize the individual; the widespread existence of domination, in turn, suggests the challenge of this epoch—liberation (1971, p. 93). Domination, according to Freire, is caused by an unjust social order, and is expressed in many forms. Economic domination involves sheer exploitation that reduces the individual to an object that is to be taken account of only as part of the calculus of profits. But domination, regardless of whether it is rooted primarily in economic, political, or cultural exploitation, has the effect of limiting the consciousness of individuals in a manner that causes them to adopt a passive attitude toward the conditions of their existence. They think within the conceptual categories given them by their oppressors, they speak the language that both reinforces their "limit situations" and prevents them from conceptualizing how human beings ought to live, and they act in a subservient manner in order to insure survival at a biological level. The form liberation is to take, which Freire sees as having both political and educational implications, is determined by his views of what it means to be human, of the nature of the rational process, and of the connection between humanization and progress.

Freire's opposition to all forms of cultural invasion reflects his deep commitment to people participating in authentically democratic forms of cultural development, yet his discussion of what it means to be a human being moves to an ontological level that, while supposedly free of cultural bias, is in fact heavily oriented toward a Western existential view of the individual. To be human, for Freire, is to be free; and this freedom is expressed, in part, in the relationship between the individual and language. Freire correctly argues that language involves the codes that will determine the patterns of both thought and action. But his view of fully humanized individuals posits a relationship in which individuals invest language with meaning through their critical reflection and action. To quote Freire on what human freedom means: "Human existence cannot be silent, nor can it be nourished by false words, but only by true words, with which men transform the world. To exist, humanly, is to name the world, to change it" (p. 76). False words can be understood here to mean words prescribed by others, as well as those words that involve a passive, spectator relationship to the world. Human freedom thus involves speaking a "true word," one that involves the individual as a reflective, acting being who, in the process of investing the world with intentionality and meaning, helps to transform it.

Although Freire's ontology locates freedom in the intentionality of the individual, he is not advocating a view of the individual as basically competitive and solitary in nature. As non-oppressive forms of communication involve dialogue with others, there is an inherent communal, and thus social, dimension that must develop if individuals are to realize their fullest human potential. Dialogue involves mutuality, trust and openness, and a willingness to participate in a shared learning process. The form of individualism implied by monologue—isolated, distrustful, prescriptive, rigid, and authoritarian—stands in sharp contrast. While Freire clearly understands the relationship between certain forms of communication and dehumanization, it is not entirely clear that his own position avoids the danger of viewing the individual as essentially autonomous in nature—a perennial problem in liberal theories of education.

A dehumanized form of existence involves heteronomy—that is, living a life dictated by external forms of authority. Fully humanized individuals, on the other hand, achieve emancipation from "living submerged" and from colonized states of existence, and they accomplish this as they assume full responsibility for the conditions of their existence. The justification for locating authority within the individual (a condition that Freire sees as leading to a natural state of dialogue and communion with others) is the human capacity to exercise critically reflective thought. Yet since Freire views the individual's existential situation as continually precarious, the warrant for the individual's authority must be continually renewed by a dialectical progression in which an action leads to critical reflection, critical reflection in turn to a new action, and so on. The fundamental importance that Freire assigns to critical reflection in the continual struggle to maintain an emancipated, and thus human, form of existence can be seen in the following statement:

> Men, however, because they are aware of themselves and thus of the world—because they are *conscious beings*—exist in a dialectical relationship between the determination of limits and their own freedom. As they separate themselves (through critical reflection) from the world, which they objectify, as they separate themselves from their own activity, as they locate the seat of decisions in themselves and in their relations with the world and others, men overcome the situations which limit them. . . .
> As critical perception is embodied in action, a climate of hope and confidence develops which leads men to attempt to overcome the limit-situations. (1971, p. 89)

Freire's view of man as in continual danger of being submerged by external forms of authority reveals a way of thinking about time that is not dissimilar to Dewey's position. Just as Dewey located the individual in a space-time framework that involved a linear progression of overcoming problematic situations, Freire, using a somewhat different vocabulary, expressed essentially the same view. "As reality is transformed," he wrote in *Pedagogy of the Oppressed*, "and these situations are superseded, new ones will appear, which in turn will involve new limit situations" (pp. 89–90). By locating authority in the critical reflection of the individual, Freire's ontology gives legitimate standing only to the present act of demystification (decoding the limit situation) and to future actions. He referred to problem-posing education as "revolutionary futurity." The power of critical reflection thus orientates the individual toward the future, or as Freire put it: "Problem-posing education . . . affirms men as beings who transcend themselves, who move forward and look ahead, for whom immobility represents a fatal threat, for whom the looking at the past must only be a means of understanding more clearly what and who they are so that they can move wisely [and] build the future" (p. 72).

Given the "dominance of the foreground" in Freire's position (to use the phrase Santayana ascribed to Dewey's sense of temporality), the past becomes reduced to the "mythical remnants of the old society" that continually threaten to inhibit the continual process of revolutionary change (p. 158). While writing on the specific problem of a literacy program in Guinea-Bissau, Freire referred to the importance of searching for the authentic past of the people. But the study of the past is legitimated on the grounds that it gives back to the people "the right to make their own history" (1978, p. 20).

One of the most striking characteristics of Freire's theory is the lack of ambiguity about the nature and method of liberation. It stands, in his view, clearly juxtaposed to domination as the other theme of our epoch. It is, in fact, a vision uncomplicated by any reservations that might arise from considering the darker side of the historical record in this area or from examining the complex interplay of power in the language-thought process. The elimination of dehumanizing oppression involves surmounting the "limit situation" that reduces individuals to objects and prevents them from speaking and acting authentically. According to Freire, the only form of political action that liberates must be pedagogical in nature. In effect, education that involves dialogue in problematizing the limit situation is fundamentally political (in the positive sense) in that it involves the practice of freedom. Education is thus seen as a process of critically reflecting on the conditions of embeddedness, as well as a means of forming new conceptual foundations for decision-making and action.

The starting point of an emancipatory form of education is the immediate life world of the individual. What must be learned is how the assumptions and values embedded in the patterns of everyday existence condition (and thus limit) the individual's thought and behavior. Yet as the individual who must transcend the conditioning process is often submerged to the point where daily experience is lived at the taken-for-granted level, it is necessary for the educator (also termed coordinator and co-investigator) to document the existential situation of the learner. This documenting process (as opposed to bringing in a curriculum that is foreign and irrelevant to the learners) enables the learners to obtain distance from the social conditions that they have interiorized into their natural attitude, thus allowing them to recognize the patterns of their existence. Through dialogue, which involves all the participants engaged in the learning process, the cultural codes that underlie the learner's existential situation can be identified in terms of thematic elements and rendered problematic. In this process of decoding, according to Freire, "men exteriorize their view of the world," and as they begin to think about (or decode) the relationship between themselves and their physical-social existence, they will begin to recognize the commonality of their condition. The sense of empowerment that accompanies the transition from passive acceptance to critical awareness of the taken-for-granted beliefs to which they have been conditioned in turn enables them to relate "speaking the word to transforming reality." But this process of transcending limit situations does not mean that the individual's freedom is assured from that point onward. As mentioned earlier, as limit situations are overcome, "new ones will appear," and the process of consciousness-raising must again be reenacted.

Carl Rogers

The discourse of Carl Rogers represents a powerful example of the romantic-humanist stream of liberal thought. It is a discourse characterized by a profound faith in the essential goodness of human nature. It is also a discourse that involves a limited vocabulary, as well as reliance upon conceptual categories that organize reality in a manner that eliminates contradictions, ambiguities, and the tragic element in life. If we accept, at face value, the metaphorical images that serve as the connecting links in Rogers' theory of education, it would seem that we have achieved an absolute symmetry between our thought and the highest values. Although many other educators share with Rogers the same language affiliation, and thus the same way of understanding education, society, and the human condition, one has a profound sense of unease that this discourse obstructs an understanding of the complexity of the world we live in. The vocabulary is simply too limited to put in focus those elements of human experience that exist as part of the historical record but do not fit the view of the individual as inherently free, resourceful, and virtuous. The reality illuminated by this discourse suggests that the desire to believe has prevailed over the will to understand.

The individual is the epicenter of Rogers' universe. Accordingly, Rogers understands the crisis of modern society in terms of how the individual's freedom and natural goodness are inhibited by conservative forces; he sees the solution to social problems in terms of freeing the individual's potential for ameliorative thought and action; and he conceives of the immensely difficult task of education that balances the nurturing of wisdom, knowledge that involves an historical perspective, technical skills, and personal imagination and courage, in terms of the teacher's ability to facilitate the student's powers of individual self-direction. Before we look more closely at how Rogers conceptualizes the nature of individualism, the rational process, and the progressive nature of change, it is important to establish more fully the way in which his understanding of the crisis of modernization relates to his view of education. In the opening paragraph of *The Freedom to Learn for the 80's,* Rogers states that "schools, generally, constitute the most traditional, conservative, rigid, bureaucratic institution of our time, and the institution most resistant to change" (p. 1). The groups that support schools, with all these negative characteristics, represent the conservative forces in society, and thus are responsible for the renewed emphasis on basics and discipline. In contrast to the static universe that he attributes to the conservative's position, Rogers understands the essential characteristic of modernization to be constant change; this, in turn, requires the maximization of individual freedom. If we are to survive, he warns, we must make the goal of education "the *facilitation of change* and learning." More specifically, he states, the goal is "to free curiosity; to permit individuals to go charging off into new directions dictated by their own interests, to unleash the sense of inquiry; to open everything to questioning and exploration, to recognize that everything is in a process of change—here is an experience I can never forget" (p. 120).

In attempting to define the form of freedom appropriate to the modern world, Rogers identifies it as an "inner thing" that is located within the individual and that has to do with "the realization that 'I can live myself, here and now, by my own choice.' . . . It is the discovery of meaning within oneself, meanings that come from listening sensitively and openly to the complexities of what one is experiencing. . . . The free person moves out voluntarily, freely, responsibly, to play her significant part in a world whose determined events move through her spontaneous choice and will" (p. 276). Rogers' view of freedom involves replacing an externally directed moral code, as well as the expectations of others, with an inner sense of direction where the individual's own feelings, choices, and self-worth are valued as the highest expression of being.

Given this view of the individual, which emphasizes the equal value of all forms of experience, it is not surprising that Rogers does not give special significance to rationality as a source of knowledge. The real problem is not that of acquiring a fixed body of knowledge or of exercising a form of rationality that increases one's power of prediction and control. Rather, it is a matter of the quality of the person's involvement in what Rogers termed the "learning event." In contrast to what Rogers viewed as a truncated form of left brain activity, authentic learning is self-initiated and involves the whole person. Whole-person learning "combines the logical *and* intuitive, the intellect *and* the feelings, the concept *and* the experience, the idea *and* the meaning" (p. 20). Only this form of learning, according to Rogers, involves the development of the whole person, including masculine and feminine capacities.

The powerful metaphorical images Rogers uses to designate individual growth—"freedom" as self-direction, "being real" as discovery of the inner authentic self, "valuing" as trusting one's own feelings, "learning" as self-initiated discovery—reflect the connection in his thinking between the growth of the individual and the nature of progress. Growth in personal discovery and wholeness is never-ending, and thus progress remains a continual possibility. Yet progress is to be understood on the level of individual development, rather than as the impersonal evolution of institutions or the unfoldment of historical forces. The constraints on progress are thus understood by Rogers as constraints on the individual's growth toward "wholeness"; a list of these constraints would include theories, institutions, and social practices that are based on assumptions that do not take account of the individual's powers of self-direction.

In the area of formal education, the antiprogressive practices and beliefs would include viewing the teacher as the possessor of knowledge and the student as the recipient, the textbook and lecture as the method of transmitting knowledge to passive students, and the teacher as the source of power for organizing the learning of the student. "Person-centered education," on the other hand, is progressive in that it is based on the assumption that "decision-making power is in the hands of the individual or individuals who will be affected by the decision . . . [and that] each person regulates the modes of feeling, thought, behavior, and values through her own self-discipline" (pp. 189–90). The progressive teacher

is thus a facilitator of the student's self-directed learning, providing resources that will further stimulate the student's natural curiosity and a
supporting atmosphere for students as they learn to trust their own
thought processes and decision-making abilities.

B. F. Skinner

The argument that Skinner's ideas on education and society
reflect a particular mutation within the liberal tradition of thought seems
to run against the grain of common sense and moral decency. As the
author of a popular tract intended as a final requiem for the liberal ideas
of freedom and dignity, Skinner would appear, at first glance, to be out of
sympathy with liberalism. Yet as his ideas represent the antithesis of the
philosophical conservative position, which we shall later examine, we are
forced to reconsider his connections with liberalism. His rejection of the
liberal idea that the individual must be viewed as essentially free and
morally responsible, while a transgression of a basic liberal canon of
belief, does not mean he has abandoned all aspects of liberal thought. The
belief that change, when guided by rational thought, represents a progressive movement into the future is fundamental to his position. One can
even make the case that the primitive pleasure-pain psychology that
underlies his theory of operant conditioning has its roots in the psychological theories of such earlier liberal thinkers as Thomas Hobbes and
Jeremy Bentham. The fact that Skinner signed the "Secular Humanist
Declaration" may also help locate his ideological affiliation. But the real
case for viewing Skinner as a liberal thinker, albeit one with a rational-
technicist orientation, will be made in subsequent chapters, where the
analysis of our embeddedness in tradition and the nature of philosophical
conservative thought will demonstrate more fully that Skinner represents
a special stream within the discourse of liberalism. For now it is important
to summarize his ideas on the crisis of modern society, as well as on how
the nature of individualism and rationality must be reconceptualized if
further progress is to be assured. This will enable us to see how the
vocabulary and the conceptual categories essential to his theory serve to
establish a somewhat different set of boundaries for serious discourse and
illuminate what he regards as the chief reference points in human experience.

The crisis facing modern man, according to Skinner, is fundamentally
a conceptual one and results from the failure to recognize the causal
nature of human behavior. Damage to the ecology, the threat of nuclear
annihilation, and widespread crime and violence are commonly seen as

the failure of people to act more rationally and to base their lives on a sounder set of values. While Skinner concurs on the list of problems facing society, he sees this tendency to place the blame on the failure of mental and moral capacities as an antiquated, prescientific way of thinking. Social problems will not be solved by changing attitudes, increasing people's sense of responsibility, or appealing to their initiative and increased rational capacities. By attempting to alter the inner states of the individual—a sense of morality, a capacity for rational thought, a sense of responsibility, and so forth—we insure that the behavior contributing to social problems will likely continue. The way to alleviate the causes of the social problems is to change the behavior of people, and this can be achieved, according to Skinner, through the development of a technology of behavior (1972, p. 3).

The irony of Skinner's position is that we will begin to solve our social problems as we change our way of thinking about the individual. Instead of the idea of the individual as a rational, moral, and free being, we should think of these inner states as forms of behavior shaped by the contingencies of reinforcement in the environment. To quote Skinner: "Freedom is a matter of contingencies of reinforcement, not the feelings the contingencies generate" (p. 35). Similarly: "Good things are positive reinforcers. . . . To make a value judgment by calling something good or bad is to classify it in terms of its reinforcing effects" (pp. 89-90). And finally, a more lengthy passage:

> Perhaps the last stronghold of autonomous man is that complex "cognitive" activity called thinking. . . . Rather than suppose that it is therefore autonomous man who discriminates, generalizes, forms concepts of abstractions, recalls or remembers, and associates, we can put matters in good order simply by noting that these terms do not refer to forms of behavior. . . . It is always the environment which builds the behavior with which problems are solved, even when the problems are to be found in the private world inside the skin. (pp. 184-85)

In Skinner's view, the individual is neither free nor rational, and in continuing to use this archaic metaphorical language we put out of focus the external forces that shape behavior. Individuals, like other organisms, are very simple in that they act to free themselves of harmful and aversive effects. When all the metaphorical trappings are stripped away from our way of thinking about ourselves, it becomes a simple matter of observing how our behavior is "shaped and maintained by its consequences" (p. 16). Behaviors are followed by consequences, and when the consequences lead to the behavior being repeated, they act as reinforcers. In effect, the environment not only "prods and lashes," to use Skinner's words, "it *selects*." Understanding human behavior thus becomes a matter of observing the relationship between behavior and the contingencies of reinforcement. Although Skinner's theory eliminates the traditional view of the autonomous individual, it does retain a notion of the person's individuality by emphasizing the different patterns of reinforcement schedules that make up the individual's experience, as well as differences in what Skinner termed "genetic susceptibilities to reinforcement" (p. 190).

Skinner's reductionist theory does not leave all of the liberal vision in shambles. In spite of his attempt to explain rational thought as a behavior under the control of external contingencies of reinforcement, he nevertheless relies upon the use of a liberal-sounding argument (presented in a highly rational manner) to make the case that we can progress only as we apply our knowledge of science and technology to the problem of designing the reinforcement schedules necessary for producing the behaviors we desire. The agents of progress are to be a group of people who understand how behavior is a function of reinforcement and who will take an experimental approach to the problem of designing a new environment in which human behavior can be efficiently predicted and controlled. By viewing culture "like the experimental space used in the analysis of behavior" (p. 145), it will be possible to free individual behavior not only from the random and often contradicting patterns of reinforcement that have evolved over time, but also from the illusions associated with traditional beliefs (including the notion of the autonomous individual). In effect, the tasks of this new class of "cultural designers" will be to emancipate individual behavior from cultural patterns that are not rationally and experimentally designed; another way to understand this task is to see it as the desire to replace tradition with the certainty of scientific knowledge and the efficiency and predictable control of modern technology.

Concluding Remarks on Discourse and Conceptual Maps

The vocabulary and conceptual categories that enable a discourse to establish what Foucault termed a "regime of truth" exert a powerful influence on what issues will be perceived as problematic, what questions are appropriate to ask, and what solutions are considered acceptable. The discourse, in effect, serves as a conceptual map that brings order to the flow of experience by prescribing what should be given attention and what should be ignored. E. F. Schumacher gave a personal account of how a map controls what we experience as real:

On a visit to Leningrad some years ago I consulted a map to find out where I was, but I could not make it out. From where I stood, I could see several enormous churches, yet there was not a trace of them on my map. When finally an interpreter came to help me, he said, "We don't show churches on our maps." Contradicting him, I pointed to one that was very clearly marked. "That is a museum," he said, "not what we call a living church. It is only living churches that we don't show." (1979, p. 1)

The concealments and distortions of perception caused by our conceptual maps are not as easy to detect as when we use a street map, since the former provide the patterns of symbolic order (meanings, images, relationships, definitions, values) that will be imposed on experience. As our conceptual maps provide the interpretative framework used to bring order and meaning to the external world, they become the basis of our natural attitude and thus their influence on thought and discourse is seldom recognized.

The theories of Dewey, Freire, Rogers, and Skinner can be understood as variations on the "regime of truth" that characterizes the archetypal discourses of educational liberalism. As such, their vocabularies, metaphorical images, and conceptual categories provide a conceptual map for reading the terrain of human experience. Their liberalism was not concerned with justifying the more traditional liberal agenda of expanding the civil liberties of the individual or, in its more recent mutation, of using the resources of government to ameliorate the conditions of the socially and economically disadvantaged. As these liberal goals were mostly taken for granted, the liberal educational theorists turned their attention to illuminating a different set of concerns. Although differences in emphasis led to the development of distinct and even conflicting liberal theories of education, all four theorists used common generative metaphors as their conceptual starting point. Perhaps the most basic of these generative metaphors is the image of emancipation. As part of the conceptual bedrock of modern liberalism, emancipation, as Jeremy Shapiro pointed out, refers to the belief "that human beings have the capacity to act freely and create the future through the use of their rationality and agency, and yet are held back, both individually and collectively, by their immersion in the past and in nature" (1976, p. 147). Dewey understood the shared reliance upon the method of intelligence as emancipatory in nature, while Freire viewed emancipation in terms of raising consciousness. For Rogers, the goal of emancipation is achieved as individuals learn to trust their own emotional and intellectual responses; Skinner, on the other hand, did not view the individual as either rational or responsible, yet argued for emancipation by assigning to an elite group of "cultural designers" the task of rationally organizing the reinforcement schedules in the social environment in a manner that would free people from the accumulated control systems embedded in the past. A second generative metaphor common to all four theories of education is the notion that knowledge is power. With the exception of Rogers, they view knowledge as explicit, instrumental, and the absolute source of authority. Even for Rogers, who values other ways of knowing, critical reflection is the primary basis for locating authority in the judgment of the individual. Finally, a third generative metaphor that underlies these liberal theories of education is the image of change as linear and progressive. Since education involves empowerment (for Skinner empowerment is limited to "cultural designers" like himself), the process of change can be both accelerated and controlled through education. In effect, this generative metaphor makes education synonymous with progress.

As the vocabulary essential to the discourse of educational liberation is also essential to the expression of modern consciousness, many readers are undoubtedly wondering why the obvious is being challenged, much less even being discussed. The idea of empowering individuals and controlling the future must appear to them as the last hope against the forces of darkness that we never entirely escaped, and that are now threatening to engulf us. But before we genuflect before the altar of progressive ideas and values, we need to go back to the example of Schumacher's map by asking whether the conceptual map that modern liberalism makes available to us is not similarly flawed in concealing from view important aspects of our life world. To put it another way, what does the "regime of truth" that characterizes the diverse discourses of liberal theories of education conceal from us? Does it force us to adopt a rigid prefigured position that prevents learning from the anomolies that do not fit the liberal paradigm? Again, we come back to the central thesis that liberal theories of education involve a discourse that both facilitates and restricts, and that if the promise of a liberal understanding of education is to be strengthened, it will be necessary to confront those areas of human experience that modern liberalism either distorts or conceals.

The conceptual drift that accompanies the language of the liberal educational theorists clearly favors modernization; these writers leave the reader with the impression that if the full promise of this dawning epoch remains unfulfilled, it is because atavistic forces have prevented organizing social experience in accordance with basic liberal principles. What is needed is the full implementation of liberal theories of education—which would vary according to the various streams of liberalism. What is put out of focus by the conceptual bias in the language of liberal educational theorists is the problematic nature of modernization itself, and more specifically, the way in which the generative metaphors of liberal thought—i.e., individualism, rationality, and progress—when taken to the extreme have contributed to the crisis. Although Dewey warns against increasing the independence of the individual and Freire dissents from an atomistic view of individualism by stressing the mutuality of dialogue as the only legitimate form of communication, the four interpretations of liberal principles reflect a common emphasis on a rational mode of thought as the primary means of empowerment. It is this mode of thought, in the form of the scientific method for Dewey and Skinner and critical reflection for Freire and Rogers, that is to become the new basis of authority.

What is put out of focus is the relativism fostered by this view of individual empowerment. By connecting the idea of rationality with the notion of self-direction, liberal views of education make morality, commitment to communal goals, and the authority of tradition contingent upon the judgment of the individual. Each of the educational theorists assumed that critical reflection (where Skinner would stand on this issue is more problematic) would elevate individual judgment to a level where consensus would form the basis of a moral community, but such an assumption reflects the dominance of romantic vision over a clear recognition of the adversarial, fragmenting, and relativizing nature of critical reflection. As Alasdair MacIntyre has argued, rational thought gives the appearance of elevating moral decision making, but actually serves to strengthen the cultural tendency toward the emotivism of subjective judgment (1984, p. 24). The relativism that characterizes the liberal position also has implications for how to reconcile individual self-direction with the more complex demands associated with membership in a community. William Sullivan (1982) noted that "modern liberalism isolates the act of free volition, the will as self-assertion, and emphasizes the individual struggling against constriction" (p. 163). The classical notion of "a common *paideia*, or moral civic cultivation," on the other hand, "rested on the assertion that growth and transformation of the self toward responsible mutual concern is the realistic concern of public life" (p. 168). The relativizing of communal authority and shared moral commitments, which accompanies the liberal view of individual empowerment, is an issue that these liberal educational theorists ignore. It would not be entirely incorrect to argue that they do not recognize the problems associated with the relativism of their respective positions because of the *telos* that underlies their thinking. As they viewed it, history is moving in a progressive direction, and its forward movement is assured as decisions are based on individual reflection.

The distortion of understanding caused by their "escalator" view of history also leads to other areas of silence and even, in some instances, to adopting a hostile stance toward considering certain issues as worthy of consideration. Connecting rationality with empowerment and emancipation leads to silence on the issue of whether rationalism is to be exercised within a framework that recognizes self-limiting principles. It is difficult for the liberal to think of limiting the processes of empowerment and emancipation, especially when one thinks within a dichotomous framework, but when rationality becomes the *modus operandi* of technology and the bureaucratic state it is easier to recognize the need for traditions of thought that will provide the bases for subordinating rationality to other concerns. Another set of issues that the liberal educational theorists fail to recognize relates to the experimental attitude that underlies modern liberalism. Dewey made experimentalism the highest form of human activity, while Skinner referred to culture as "experimental space." Yet as John Berger, the British art critic and Marxist, has pointed out, experimentation can only be undertaken by people who are sufficiently affluent that they can survive the reversals of failed experiments (1979, p. 206). People who lack the margin of safety necessary for experimenting with the foundations of existence would tend to view liberalism as wasteful and reckless, perhaps even life threatening. And if we adopt the perspective of the environmentalist or social worker, instead of Third World societies, we see that experimentation with new chemicals and technologies is producing evidence that the margins of our own cultural survival are thinner than traditional liberal thinkers recognize.

In addition to the conceptual drift of the discourse of these theorists, which leaves important issues unaddressed, there are other areas of experience, worthy of serious attention, that they proscribed. The emphasis on emancipation and change, which is guaranteed as progressive by the *telos* embedded in their patterns of thinking, leads to viewing tradition as a source of constraint. In Dewey's thinking, tradition is associated with prereflective habits, with a spectator view of knowledge where the status quo is incorrectly assumed to have enduring qualities, and with a form of ontological misunderstanding that reflects a prescientific way of thinking. Tradition fares little better in Freire's thinking, as the dialectic of reflection-action-reflection, and so on, serves as the engine of progressive emancipation from the "specters" and "cultural remnants" of the past. The extreme subjectivism of Rogers and the equally extreme technicist orientation of Skinner reduce tradition more to the status of total irrelevance.

The irony is that while the focus of these theorists' discourse was on empowering the individual (to be achieved by conditioning in Skinner's scheme of things), they did not address the way in which the individual is embedded in tradition. By viewing tradition in adversarial terms, they disclosed how little they understood about the individual. In effect, their respective liberal visions reflected that they had not fully grasped that individualism, emancipation, and change are metaphors reflecting earlier conventions of thought that segmented reality into distinct entities abstracted from context. The result is a distorted view of the individual's powers of origination and of the emancipatory potential of the rational process. In effect, their theories are not adequately grounded in an understanding of the many ways in which the individual is a bearer of tradition. As a result of separating the individual from embeddedness in context, the liberal educational theorists tended to represent tradition as the force of darkness that continually threatened to pull the individual backward. Education was to be the means for the great escape. A fuller understanding of the nature of tradition, as well as the complexity of the individual's embeddedness, would have perhaps led to a more qualified interpretation of education as an emancipatory activity and to greater sensitivity toward those traditions that education should help to preserve.

Lastly, the "regime of truth" established by Dewey, Freire, Rogers, and Skinner, for all its emphasis on the power of rational thought, imposed a reign of silence on the need to focus the power of critical reflection on the bedrock assumptions of modern liberalism. Questions pertaining to human nature, progress, modernization, scientific method, individualism, and the nature of power were not asked because of the epistemological habits embedded in their language orientation. Further, the inability to ask questions can also be laid at the door of the liberal bias that conservatives are a self-serving, reactionary lot who have not had anything important to say about the human condition. Thus the literature that might have helped them to adopt a more reflexive stance toward their own unexamined assumptions, like the buildings not represented on the official map given to Schumacher, was viewed by liberal thinkers as undeserving of recognition.

Identifying aspects of experience ignored by the discourse of liberal educational theorists is the first step toward revising and expanding the conceptual possibilities of the discourse. The second step is to explore more fully the two domains that appear the most promising in terms of providing a more adequate basis for preserving the traditional liberal ideals of civil liberties, as well as for reformulating those aspects of liberal thought that strengthen the nihilistic tendencies in modern society. The first domain of human experience that needs to be illuminated and given linguistic legitimacy as part of a theory of education is the phenomenon of our embeddedness in tradition. This will be the focus of the next chapter. In the following chapter we shall turn to the literature of conservative thinkers in order to obtain a new vantage point for considering those aspects of liberal thought that need to be reformulated. After the case has been made for broadening the discourse, we shall then return to the task of utilizing the theoretical foundations established by Dewey and Freire as a basis for a post-liberal theory of education.

3

De-Centering Individualism: The Nature of Embeddedness and Tradition

GIOVANNI SARTORI'S observation that "what is unnamed either remains undetected, or tends to be forgotten" (1978, p. 5) is a good starting point for identifying a major weakness in liberal theories of education. The conceptual habits reflected in the liberal discourses summarized in the previous chapter, which involve the *telos* of progressive change and rationality as the basis of emancipation, also assume the possibility of the autonomous, self-directing individual. Although Dewey and Skinner held divergent and in some ways dissenting positions from the more orthodox view of modern liberalism, they shared other liberal assumptions that located authority within the individual. This took the form of experimental inquiry for Dewey, while for Skinner only a group of cultural designers possessed the ability to engineer a more progressive form of social existence. Although their educational theories emphasized different liberal concerns, they nevertheless shared the assumption that education should empower people to transcend their embeddedness in traditional patterns of thought and behavior. In one sense Sartori's statement does not apply: tradition was not accorded in their theories the status of non-being; rather, it was identified as something to be overturned in favor of more rationally based and progressive ideas. Yet in another sense his observation illuminates a basic deficiency in the liberal discourses we have examined: namely, the way in which the emphasis on empowerment of the person puts out of focus the complex network of relationships that constitute the person's embeddedness, as well as how the temporal aspect of embeddedness can be understood as a tradition.

Just as political and educational elements of liberalism survived the demise of laissez-faire liberalism, they are also strong enough to endure in an intellectual environment that acknowledges the complexity of the person's embeddedness and the equally complex nature of tradition. In fact, the argument being advanced here is that liberal traditions, particularly in education, will only survive as they are strengthened by a discourse capable of addressing issues put out of focus by the teleological view of individualism. The liberal's juxtaposition of the metaphorical image of time (with its underlying *telos*) and individualism led to the myth of emancipation from embeddedness in habituated social routines and from the authority of historical forms of understanding. Given this orientation toward transcendence as the means of self-realization, the individual becomes the basic social unit, and the communal aspect of life recedes to the point either where it is no longer part of serious discourse or, as in the case of Dewey and Freire, where it represents an unresolved dilemma— namely, how does one reconcile the authority of critical reflection, which fosters the capacity for individual dissent from group norms, with communal forms of authority?

As Sullivan pointed out, the challenge facing liberalism is the renewal of a sense of social and moral relationships essential to the interdependent community (1982, p. 207). A recognition of the many ways the person is actually embedded in interdependent relationships, as well as of how individuals experience the authority of a shared language and cultural norms as the natural attitude toward everyday life, should lead to a recognition that the keystone of liberal educational theories should not be the autonomous individual but, instead, the individual as a social-cultural being. If this latter metaphorical image of individualism represents more fully the complexity of the individual's embeddedness in the cultural-linguistic world, as well as elements of existential individuality, the development of an educational theory will not have to overcome the conceptual impasses that exist when the starting point is the atomistic, self-directing individual.

Besides confronting the issue of the alienation of the individual from a sense of membership in a "public household," to use Daniel Bell's phrase, which is caused in part by people believing the ideologically derived idea that they are self-determining beings rather than looking to experience itself as a basis of understanding their own individuality, a post-liberal theory of education must also address the problem of nihilism. As Hubert Dreyfus tells us, nihilism involves a loss of seriousness and meaning, with the result that nothing is experienced as having authority with us (1981, p. 508). In effect, everything becomes relative in a way that makes authority contingent upon the judgment of the individual. The cultural forces contributing to the relativizing of the foundations of our belief system, including the shared forms of authority that are experienced as the individual's source of power, can be traced to traditions of thought emerging out of Western approaches to philosophy (Rosen 1969; Mac-Intyre 1984), to the extension of the scientific mode of thought into everyday life, and to the liberal view of the autonomous individual. The reformulation of educational theory will most certainly not reverse the relativizing tendencies in our culture, as the causes are more deeply rooted; but it will help to eliminate the appearance that educational theorists are blind to the problem of nihilism in modern society and that their quixotic mission is to promote the very values and ideas that contribute to the problem.

Identifying the various dimensions of the individual's embeddedness is a relatively straightforward task, since the weight of contemporary scholarship makes it exceedingly difficult to maintain the liberal idea of the autonomous individual. But getting people, particularly liberal academics, to take seriously the temporal nature of our embeddedness (i.e., tradition) is fraught with greater risk. Even though we are all bearers of tradition, the modern liberal's ideological bias tends not only to put out of focus the way in which experience is based on tradition, it also requires as a sign of liberal orthodoxy that tradition be viewed as a source of constraint to be transcended. Because of this longstanding antipathy, the mere mention of the word tradition tends to evoke a hostile response. In spite of the categorical responses that will be engendered, and the possibility of misinterpretation by readers conditioned to organizing ideas and experience according to the conceptual pattern dictated by the liberal *telos*, it is necessary to bring a discussion of tradition into any reconsideration of a liberal theory of education. It must be kept in mind, however, that the discussion of tradition—how we reenact traditions, how we are implicated in their endurance and their change, and how our relationship to traditions has political implications—is not to be interpreted as advocating that we embrace specific traditions or that we passively accept them. That would get us into the realm of ideology, and it is this ideological perspective on tradition that has prevented us from understanding what can best be described as the phenomenology of tradition, that is, how we experience it as a source of meaning. There is a certain irony in the fact that liberals who think of tradition as backwardness and associate it with politically reactionary positions are, within the context of their own lives, dependent upon the reenactment of numerous traditions in order to sustain the social and conceptual patterns upon which their natural attitude is based. In effect they have no words in their ideologically prescribed vocabulary for acknowledging how their own lives are embedded in the reenactment of traditions, but they possess the vocabulary (which is derived from a tradition) for announcing the end of all traditions and proclaiming the need for individuals to create their own future.

To reiterate, the purpose of examining the nature of tradition is to provide the linguistic and conceptual basis for expanding the parameters of the discourse on education. As long as liberal theory treats any attempt to understand tradition as collaboration with reactionary forces, it will remain conceptually limited, excessively romantic, and awkwardly silent on the vital question of what aspects of our past we need to conserve. Lastly, an understanding how experience involves reenactment of traditions will help to de-center the idea of the individual as a potentially free agent whose full empowerment is contingent upon complete emancipation.

Embeddedness

To recognize the embeddedness of the individual as an aspect of the human condition is not the same as accepting what Freire termed the condition of being "submerged in the historical process." Being submerged involves, according to Freire, a "semi-intransitive state of consciousness" where individuals "cannot apprehend problems situated outside their sphere of biological necessity." Alienated and powerless, they tend to accept fatalistically the social conditions of existence, and their struggle is reduced simply to biological survival (1973, p. 17). Freedom, he tells us in *Pedagogy of the Oppressed*, "would require them to eject this image and replace it with autonomy and responsibility" (1978, p. 31). While Freire's appeal for individual autonomy appears to conflate being "submerged" with being embedded, thus echoing the idea of individual transcendence that Shapiro found as a core assumption of modern liberalism, there is a critically important distinction between the two that Freire does not acknowledge.

As we shall clarify more fully in the subsequent discussion, embeddedness involves interdependencies that are both supportive and restrictive; it could also be understood as the social-cultural-physical milieu that provides the context as well as the symbolic patterns that make communication with others possible. To think in the dichotomous categories of either being oppressed or being free, a polarity which characterizes this stage of Freire's thinking, is to confuse legitimate concerns about social injustice with an inescapable aspect of the human condition. What Freire should address is the particular forms of embeddedness (the structural and ideological elements) that contribute to poverty and stunt the development of human potential, while at the same time recognizing that social reform—even when genuinely revolutionary—will not eliminate individual embeddedness. The important distinction observed by Freire's view of emancipation, which is shared by other liberal educational theorists with the exception of Dewey and, more recently, of Maxine Greene, is not embeddedness versus freedom, but whether the symbolic order that determines the form of embeddedness (the economic and political system, ideology, linguistic foundations of expressive culture, and so forth) nourishes the sense of meaning, order, and general fulfillment of all members of society or whether it fosters more exploitive relationships. Thus to argue that individuals must be understood within the context of their embeddedness—that is, as social-cultural beings rather than as autonomous, self-directing beings—does not involve ignoring Freire's concern with the problems of exploitation and self-alienation encompassed in his image of being "submerged." Hopefully, by acquiring a deeper understanding of the intersubjective connections that characterize embeddedness, it will be possible to place recommendations for educational and social reform on sounder conceptual footings.

If the image of the autonomous, emancipated individual can be understood, in part, in terms of the failure of liberal theorists to recognize the metaphorical nature of language, then we might ask how the image of the individual as a social-cultural being reflects both a more accurate understanding of embeddedness as a characteristic of the human condition and a concern with the empowering potential of formal education. To put it another way, what does the image of the individual as a social-cultural being put in focus that is obfuscated by the image of the individual as the center of moral and rational authority and free from the constraints of embeddedness? At a common-sense level, part of the answer would involve identifying the individual's phenomenological world: patterns of routines, social conventions, relationships with friends and family, work roles, movement through social spaces, and so forth. But it is possible to identify at a more theoretical level those aspects of interpenetration and interdependency that must be considered as an inherent aspect of the individual. Rather than understanding the individual as inhabiting a social and physical environment (the common-sense view of individual interaction with others), we must take account of how the social-cultural-linguistic world is internalized into a self that involves cultural shaping while retaining important elements of individuality. Heidegger's statement "Man speaks" suggests the common sense view of the individual as the *source* (author) of expression who moves about social space interacting with others—sometimes in a self-determining way and at other times in inauthentic (heteronymous) ways. But after clarifying that speaking is an aspect of our humanness, Heidegger also makes another statement that de-centers the individual as a rational self-directing being. This statement, "Language speaks," can partly be understood in terms of what he termed the "presencing element in language" as we follow in thought "the speaking of language" (1975, p. 193). While Heidegger's concern here is with the ontological foundations of language, the control that language exerts over thought and speech can be explicated more easily by turning to the insights of cultural linguists and, more recently, the work of political scientists concerned with the connection between language membership and political participation.

The traditional idea of how the atomistic individual uses language as a tool of expression was expressed in John Locke's statement that "words . . . come to be made use of by Men as *the signs* of their *Ideas*" (Aarsleff 1982, p. 63). But this view of the individual *using* language is reversed by Edward Sapir who argued that "the 'real world' is to a large extent unconsciously built up on the language habits of the group. . . . We see and hear and otherwise experience very largely as we do because the language habits of our community predispose certain choices of interpretations" (1949, p. 69). This view of language as a "symbolic guide to culture" serves to de-center the individual as an autonomous, self-directing agent; instead of the individual speaking a "true word" and "transforming the world," to quote Freire, the individual's thought patterns as well as discourse are influenced in the most profound ways by the epistemological categories embedded in the language. For example, Clyde Kluckhohn gives as an example of how language interpenetrates the individual's experience the different ways in which the speaker of English and the speaker of Greek experience the nature of time. While speakers of English view themselves as moving through time, the Greeks, he notes, conceive of themselves as stationary, and "of time as coming up behind them, overtaking them and then, still moving on, becoming the 'past' that lay before their eyes" (1972, pp. 111–12).

If further support is needed to buttress the argument that the individual's powers of origination are considerably less than assumed by the liberal educational theorists, we can turn to Michel Foucault's analysis of discursive practices. "Discoursive practices," according to him, "are characterized by the delimination of the field of objects, the definition of a legitimate perspective for the agent of knowledge, and the fixing of norms for the elaboration of concepts and theories" (1977, p. 199). A close reading of this statement locates the exercise of power in the interplay of the discourse itself; thus, it is not the individual who defines the legitimate perspective, fixes the norms for what can be talked about, or designates what is to be excluded. The authority of the discourse, which sets the limits on thought and determines both the method of application and the subjects against which power is to be applied, is exercised not by "rational individuals" but by the technical processes of institutions and patterns of social interaction. "We should admit," Foucault wrote, again excluding the individual as a source of authority, "that power produces knowledge . . . that power and knowledge directly imply one another, that there is no power relation without the correlative constitution of a field of knowledge, nor any knowledge that does not presuppose and constitute at the same time power relations" (1979, p. 27).

The process of socialization into membership in a language community, or to a discourse (to use Foucault's term), involves individuals becoming embedded, both in terms of the symbolic interaction that sustains their interpersonal world and the conceptual categories that enable them to think and express themselves. But it is a form of embeddedness where the traditional boundaries separating the individual from society break down. As Hanna Pitkin put it, "One insight that the model of language membership suggests, then, is that the customary distinctions between the individual and society, between the self and some larger whole to which it belongs are not fixed, mutually exclusive categories. Rather, they concern different aspects of, different perspectives on, a single reality. Society is not just 'outside' the individual, confronting him, but inside him as well, part of who he is." But Pitkin also recognized the need to recognize the all-important element of individuality. "Who an individual is," she wrote, "both distinguishes him from all others and relates him to them" (1972, p. 195). The point that language is the source of individual empowerment and expression, as well as the instrument that binds the individual to the conceptual categories that make mutual understanding possible, was particularly important to Pitkin. As she emphasized, the dual function of language does not involve a contradiction. To strengthen her position, she quotes Hannah Arendt's observation that language possesses the "twofold character of equality and distinction"—equality in the sense of sharing a language system that enables communication to occur, and distinction in the sense that individuals, without it, would not need to speak or act in order to make their individuality understood (p. 195). The element of individuality can also be understood in terms of the mannerisms that accompany the expression of intentionality, what Ward Goodenough (1981, pp. 32–33) terms the "idiolect" of the speakers (their own versions of the language they speak) and the rational-interpretive activity that occurs mostly within the conceptual boundaries laid down by the language.

The view that "thought is not merely expressed in words, it comes into existence through them" suggests another way of understanding embeddedness (Vygotsky 1962, p. 125). Although the individual continually alters the meaning of words through the poetic imagination that characterizes metaphorical thinking, the social origins of the language used to formulate thought point to the individual's dependency upon the complex communication processes that make up the social world. The primacy given to the word (which is generally socially derived) by Vygotsky is accorded equal significance in the sociology of knowledge of Alfred Schutz, Peter Berger, and Thomas Luckmann, as well as in the symbolic interactionism of George H. Mead and Erving Goffman. As our purpose here is not to provide an analysis of these positions *per se*, but to use them in order to shed light on the many layers of the individual's embeddedness, it will suffice to identify a few key insights of both positions.

Although the sociology of knowledge uses a somewhat different vocabulary from that of anthropology, it nevertheless addresses the same basic question of how the individual acquires the cognitive maps essential to sustaining the world view of individuals who collectively make up society. But the sociology of knowledge helps to illuminate the role of communication in sustaining both the objective and existential dimensions of meaning. As Berger and Luckmann put it, "The most important vehicle of reality-maintenance is conversation. . . . If this is understood, one will readily see that the great part, if not all, of everyday conversation maintains subjective reality. . . . At the same time that the conversational apparatus ongoingly maintains reality, it ongoingly modifies it" (1967, pp. 152–53). Definitions and categories of thought are thus shared with new members; and for those who have already acquired the recipe knowledge (and in the process modified part of it through misinterpretation and reflective thought), conversation is the medium for both mutual reinforcement and negotiation. The omnipresence of conversation (Mead viewed thinking as an internalized conversation with the Other) is a source of meaning and support for the individual; it also provides the means for the more personal dimensions of expression. The alternative to conversation is silence, which is the logical outcome of carrying the liberal view of the autonomous individual to the extreme. Although silence can be seen as a refuge from the pressures of the social world, and thus as providing the temporal and social space essential for renewal, it can also involve for many people loneliness, anxiety, and alienation. Too much silence at the wrong time appears to be inimical to the individual's development.

Another important insight of the sociology of knowledge is that the world of daily life is, to cite Alfred Schutz, not entirely a private one but from the outset intersubjective in nature, "shared with my fellow man, experienced and interpreted by others; in brief it is a world common to all of us" (Wagner 1973, p. 163). By viewing the individual as an intersubjective being, Schutz is strengthening the linguists' arguments for de-centering the privileged status that modern liberalism has accorded to the idea of the autonomous individual. But his explanation of how the intersubjective is constituted and sustained through every day communication with others also adds to our understanding of why embeddedness cannot simply be viewed as a "limit situation" from which the individual is to be emancipated. The social world into which the individual is born, according to Schutz, is experienced "as a tight-knit web of social relationships, of systems of signs and symbols with their particular meaning structure, of institutionalized forms of social organization, of systems of status and privilege, etc." (p. 80). Through conversation with others these "trustworthy recipes for interpreting the world" are internalized into consciousness and experienced as part of the individual's natural attitude. Although Schutz viewed the individual more as a recipient than an originator of the symbolic basis of the natural attitude (it "is only to a very small extent of his own making"), he nevertheless recognized the unique aspects of a person's individuality in terms of the function that imagination and intentionality play in relating the world of others to one's "own context of experience."

Embeddedness involves living in different language environments that create a dialectical tension between socially dictated patterns and subjective meanings. With regard to the more coercive aspect of language, Berger and Luckmann observed that it forces us "into its patterns." For example the language of architecture, with its spatial grammar, provides the objective conditions for the experiencing of "place," which is in part the sense of "dwelling" within enclosed space (Norberg-Schulz, 1980, pp. 5-9; Bachelard, 1969). Individuals are also forced "into its patterns" as they move through the different language systems that characterize social space; not only must different parts of the personality be exhibited in the communication process, but body language and conceptual codes must be continually adjusted. The dialectical nature of this process has been carefully studied and documented by Erving Goffman (1971). As an example of the reciprocal nature of culturally prescribed patterns and subjective meaning that characterizes the individual's embeddedness in a language environment, Goffman describes what is involved in the simple act of one individual passing another:

> Thus, in driving and walking the individual conducts himself—or rather his vehicular shell—so that the direction, rate and resoluteness of his proposed course will be readable. In ethological terms, he provides an "intention display." By providing this gestural prefigurement and committing himself to what it foretells, the individual makes himself into something others can read and predict from; by employing this device at strategic junctures—ones where his indicated course will be perceived as a promise or warning or threat but not as a challenge—he becomes something to which they can adopt without loss of self-respect. (p. 11)

Through his studies of the protocols that govern interaction in other social settings Goffman illuminated how the most basic aspects of human existence involve a tacit knowledge of the appropriate language systems. As George H. Mead pointed out much earlier, communication involves an ongoing "conversation of gestures." Without a recipe understanding of what the gesture was intended to mean, the dialectic of pattern and meaning would break down, and individuals (used here in the liberal sense of being literally free and self-determining) would have to negotiate the most elementary rules for governing human interaction. Instead of being able to rely upon information encoded in the language systems that both regulate and facilitate communication, thus giving social life the essential element of predictability, individuals would be continually negotiating the meaning of such basic moves in the language game as eye contact, body language, and the proxemics of social spacing. Without the tacit knowledge of what Goffman called the "ground rules that provide the normative basis of public order," communication would be characterized by a Hobbesian state of existence.

This brings us to considering individual embeddedness from the point of view of culture. In one sense culture is the most inclusive category for understanding the individual as a social-cultural being, as it encompasses language systems, patterns of social interaction, belief systems, social structures, forms of economy and politics, and so forth. All the forms of individual embeddedness discussed up to this point, as well as others that have not been dealt with, can be understood as an aspect of culture. For example, Clifford Geertz's definition of culture encompasses the broadest possible symbolic boundaries of human activity. For Geertz, the concept of culture "denotes an historically transmitted pattern of meanings embodied in symbols, a system of inherited conceptions expressed in symbolic forms by means of which men communicate, perpetuate, and develop their knowledge about attitudes toward life" (1973, p. 89). What is important about viewing embeddedness in terms of culture, aside from the element of being largely handed down from the past—an issue that will be examined in the next section dealing with tradition—is that the form of knowledge that enables us to perform in ways that are culturally congruent is learned at an implicit or tacit level. It is this aspect of culture that is especially pertinent to illuminating the modern paradox of embeddedness.

Contrary to the liberal view that associates power, control, and self-direction with a form of rationality that recognizes only explicit forms of knowledge, most of our knowledge is actually tacit in nature (Douglas 1975). Unlike our more explicit and conceptual forms of knowledge that reflect the cultural episteme embedded in language patterns, the forms of knowledge we rely upon to negotiate our way through everyday life generally cannot be made explicit. As opposed to symbolic-explicit forms of knowledge, tacit knowledge is more functional; if the individual fails to perform correctly, there are real social consequences—like failing to communicate, in Goffman's sense, the right message to the people that one is passing on the sidewalk. Perhaps the best example of this tacit knowledge is the way in which the individual learns the language systems—verbal, spatial, behavioral—of the community. In contrast to the liberal view of rationality, the recognition of the individual's "cultural knowledge" as a form of tacit understanding reverses the privileged status traditionally accorded to rationality by emphasizing the controlling influence of culture. It is not an ideological issue involving a depreciation of the value of rationality, but rather an acknowledgment that despite our most rational efforts to be independent thinkers we cannot escape the epistemological categories of our language or consciously transcend all the tacit knowledge we apply in response to the requirements of different cultural contexts. As Edward Hall pointed out, as long as everyone follows the same cultural rules, we tend not to be aware of the system of controls we are under (1977, p. 43). Patterns of social spacing, thinking in shared categories (including thinking of ourselves as "individuals"), and the taste of food—to cite just a few examples—are experienced as part of our natural attitude, and thus they represent the embedded world of meaning that is continuously reinforced as we communicate with each other.

The extent of individual embeddedness, which involves issues related to the individual's sense of meaning, to predictability, and to the transmission of the recipe knowledge built up over generations of social experience, raises questions in terms of the liberal perspectives on education that were outlined in the previous chapter. By locating authority in either the rational process (Dewey, Freire, and Skinner) or in the emotive-rational responses of the individual (Rogers), these theorists reflected the idea that education should contribute to emancipation. Yet a careful examination of their discourses reveals a common silence on what constitutes the limits of emancipation. For Skinner, culture is like "experimental space." As the epistemological underpinnings of his discourse can cope only with the observable and explicit, overcoming the constraints of embeddedness (culture) is simply a matter of rationally organizing the contingencies of reinforcement. Rogers' ideal of individuals regulating their own "modes of feeling, thought, behavior and values through . . . self-discipline" involves viewing the individual through a set of ideological lenses that completely puts out of focus the intersubjective nature of culture. Similarly, by starting with an existential view of the individual rather than a sociology of knowledge interpretation, Freire juxtaposes emancipation against embeddedness. Instead of a form of education that empowers people to conceptualize alternatives to specific forms of social injustice, Freire leaves the image that embeddedness, in all its complexity, represents the "limit situations" that must be made explicit and transcended through revolutionary action. Finally, as acknowledged earlier, Dewey possessed a view of the individual as social in nature, yet his emphasis on scientific problem-solving, as well as his ontology of change, put out of focus the limits of using scientific knowledge as a basis for understanding culture. In effect, none of these discourses recognizes the consequences of carrying emancipation beyond a certain limit. Nor do they acknowledge the tension between explicit and tacit forms of knowledge; this is important both for putting into perspective the cultural bias of different views of rationality as well as for understanding how to make explicit selected aspects of the natural attitude. An acknowledgment of the individual's embeddedness may help to clarify fundamental issues relating to how education is to reconcile individuality with membership in a community. Embeddedness, in one sense, provides a model for understanding community, but it also confronts the educational theorists with distinguishing between a language community, which is an inevitable aspect of embeddedness, and the political community that requires a sense of individual responsibility and communicative competence.

Lastly, by not incorporating into their theories an understanding of the nature of individual embeddedness, the liberal educational theorists lost sight of the fact that one aspect of embeddedness (regardless of whether we are talking about linguistic, cultural, or behavioral forms) is duration. Cultural practices exist over time; an acknowledgment of duration (or the past as an aspect of temporality) leads to understanding the individual's relationship to tradition. As each of the liberal educational theories is based on a metaphorical image of tradition that represents it as an historical force that threatens to submerge the individual and as a threat to the rational process, it is imperative that we turn next to an examination of the temporal dimension of embeddedness. Perhaps this will lead to expanding the conceptual possibilities of a post-liberal discourse, as well as to admitting a more complex view of the prospects of emancipation.

Tradition

The language of the four liberal theories of education discussed here reflects a deep ideological bias against tradition and in favor of the present and the future. This bias is clearly reflected in the following statement of Freire:

I cannot permit myself to be a mere spectator. On the contrary I must demand my place in the process of change. So the dramatic tension between past and the future, death and life, being and non-being, is no longer a kind of dead end for me; I can see it for what it really is: a permanent challenge to which I must respond. And my response can be none other than my historical praxis—in other words, revolutionary praxis. (1985, p. 129)

Aside from Freire's own commitment to revolutionary change, what is interesting about this statement is the manner in which the tension between the past and future is metaphorically represented. The temporality of culture and human existence, according to Freire's conceptual categories, can be understood in terms of "death and life, being and non-being." With temporality neatly segmented into exclusive categories of either death or life, Freire understandably declared himself to be on the side of life and history—which he understood as a state of 'becoming.' Although Freire observed that it is the "essence of humanity that men and women create their own existence, in a creative act that is always social and historical even while having its specific, personal dimensions" (p. 129), he clearly views the past as providing little more than the context and source of obstacles that must be transformed. But the recognition of the historical dimension of temporality is not the same as acknowledging it as a source of legitimate authority in people's lives.

Freire's conceptual tilt toward the future (similar to Dewey's "dominance of the foreground") is shared by the other liberal educational theorists concerned with either individual empowerment or a more rational organization of society. Given the conceptual biases of their discourse, there is a serious possibility that any attempt to think against the grain of current thought by taking the nature of tradition seriously will be met with hostility, disbelief, and a great deal of confused thinking as the old schema for organizing reality is imposed on a new way of understanding. Yet the risk must be taken if educational theory is to be freed from the modern myths that by destroying (or ignoring) the past we can control the future. To free educational theory from this myth does not mean, however, that the concern with improving the human condition through education should be abandoned in order to fulfill the phantasies of reactionaries who want to revert to past social patterns and beliefs. Rather the purpose is to ground theory by taking account of tradition as a third dimension of temporality that tends either to be ignored entirely (Rogers) or to be viewed pejoratively (Dewey, Freire, and Skinner). In effect, the task is to take seriously Anthony Giddens' argument that the space-time dimensions of social action must be incorporated into social theory and that the analysis of duration, or what over time has become constituted as substantive tradition, not be prejudiced by ideologies with a strong teleological orientation (1981, pp. 90–108). Stated more bluntly, we should understand what tradition is before we develop an educational or social theory that attempts to eliminate it; tradition may be more complex and more integral to our lives than modern ideologies suggest. Indeed, its absence—or reduced presence—may be an early warning sign that a totalitarian ideology is emerging, one that will attempt to legitimate itself by restructuring memory through the invention of spurious traditions (Hobsbawm & Ranger 1983, pp. 1–15).

Before we attempt, then, to clarify how the past lives in the present without necessarily being a source of oppression, we should keep in mind a distinction between tradition and traditionalism. As Jarvslar Pelikan expressed it, "tradition is the living faith of the dead, traditionalism is the dead faith of the living" (1984, p. 65). Traditionalism has to do with reactionary responses to the circumstances of the present, where the dead traditions of the past are seen as the patterns into which the present must be forced. This is definitely *not* what is being suggested here. Nor is any attempt being made to assume an ideological stance, such as a cultural conservative might take, in which tradition is to be accorded a privileged position. The issue is a more neutral one of asking about the nature of traditions and how they enter into our lives, rather than of attempting to make a judgment about whether they are good or bad. The latter is a vitally important question to raise about specific traditions, particularly when we become aware of their disjointedness with the times, but to ask about whether traditions are good or bad in the abstract (or in general) is to exhibit a gross misunderstanding of the nature of tradition. Worse yet, it suggests that one has already adopted the *a priori* stance of an ideology that requires a formulaic way of thinking about tradition.

The relationship between ideology and tradition is an interesting one, particularly when the ideology denigrates tradition in order to strengthen a belief in progressive change. Aside from the political implications of proscribing the dimensions of human experience essential for obtaining historical perspective, the spectacle of ideologues urging emancipation from all tradition involves considerable irony. The ideologue's clothes, behavioral mannerisms, patterns of thought and speech, even the epistemological characteristics of the ideology itself, manifest patterns that have roots in the past. That an ideologue is in fact a bearer of tradition, while the ideology itself presents a vision of reality that omits the embeddedness of the human condition, should lead to a greater sensitivity to the possible disjuncture between the life world and the explanatory power of an ideology. Because the discourses of the four archetypal liberal theorists of education exhibit a strong tendency to separate the explanatory framework from the phenomenological ground of existence, the following attempt to explicate the nature of tradition should be seen as an attempt to overcome this disjuncture. At the same time it represents an attempt to initiate a true dialectic where critical reflection on the possibilities of a more humane social world is informed by an understanding of the cultural and existential nature of the life world.

Hannah Arendt's observation that "the authority of the living [is] always derivative" is a good starting point for understanding how the past lives in the present. Or to make the same point somewhat differently, "no generation, even those living in this present time of unprecedented dissolution of tradition, creates its own beliefs, apparatus, patterns of conduct, and institutions" (Shils 1981, p. 38). These statements are not meant to imply that individuals (as well as whole generations) do not innovate, reinterpret, forget, and in other ways alter the cultural traditions they inherit from the previous generations. The statements simply point to the incontrovertible fact that individuals or even a whole generation of people cannot, in spite of their revolutionary efforts, create their own culture. Our limited capacity to innovate in a manner completely divorced from the past suggests that a natural starting point for illuminating how the past lives in the present would be a phenomenological description of our life world—with special attention given to our embeddedness in traditional cultural customs, social patterns, institutions, and linguistic conventions. Yet in being an integral part of our life world, living traditions are difficult to make explicit; we take them for granted—like the cultural rules that govern how we write on paper (or computers) from left to right and top to bottom—and, as Hall pointed out, we become aware of being controlled by the past only when the received cultural practice produces undesirable results or is challenged by more suitable practices. The experience of tradition is similar to Arendt's observation about authority: "Since authority always demands obedience, it is commonly mistaken for some form of power or violence. Yet authority precludes the use of external means of coercion; where force is used, authority itself has failed" (1961, pp. 92-93). The authority of traditional practices—linguistic, behavioral, moral, institutional, and so on—does not involve a sense of external imposition; rather it is experienced as part of the natural order of social life. Traditionalism, like authoritarianism, involves the sense of being coerced by an outside source of power.

Although a phenomenological description of any aspect of the life world would yield a rich set of practices that could then be analyzed for the purpose of making explicit how traditions are reenacted in the present, that approach would be inappropriate to our more immediate task of clarifying the nature of tradition and how a recognition of tradition should be incorporated into educational theory. A more straightforward explanation of the nature of tradition will achieve this end and, in the process, help to demonstrate Heidegger's point about the power of language to reveal within the realm of the natural attitude what previously had been concealed. A more explanatory approach to understanding tradition may also help to illuminate the metaphorical nature of language by revealing how tradition, as a metaphor shaped by the ideology of the Enlightenment, has been associated in the writings of liberal educational theorists with those aspects of human experience that should more properly be labeled as traditionalism. By introducing a new set of references for giving meaning to the word tradition, perhaps we will be able to see that the inclusion of the word into a discourse concerned with emancipation from ignorance and social injustice does not involve a contradiction or a retreat into a reactionary position.

There appears to be a growing recognition that tradition is far more complex than suggested by the image that equates it with the "dead weight" of the past. In recent years Hannah Arendt, Hans-Georg Gadamer, Anthony Giddens, and Alasdair MacIntyre have all attempted to present a more balanced view of the nature of tradition; and Arendt and Giddens recognize tradition as an essential aspect of individual memory and thus see it as a counterpoint to the centralizing of power by the state. Yet perhaps the most important and exhaustive examination of tradition has been carried out by Edward Shils in his book *Tradition.* Instead of addressing the problem of how to incorporate a deeper understanding of tradition into social theory, which is the case with the other thinkers, Shils attempts to identify the many ways we live in the grip of the past, as well as how traditions change from within and from without. It is the thoroughness of his examination of the dynamic nature of tradition that illuminates the ground of our existence and puts in focus the distortions caused by the ideologies of the Left and the Right. Because of the exhaustive nature of Shils' analysis, the following will represent only a brief overview of his insights into the nature of tradition; while the discussion will put in focus issues that need to be incorporated into any discourse of the emancipatory purpose of education, it should not be viewed as an adequate substitute for a careful reading of his work.

The definition of tradition that Shils uses includes "anything which is transmitted or handed down from the past to the present" (p. 12). This definition sets aside the question of whether the transmissions from one generation to the next were rationally selected or whether their effects were beneficial or not. It is not so much that these questions are unimportant as it is a matter of obtaining a more comprehensive understanding of the nature of tradition before ideologically based judgments are allowed to be made. Indeed, the transmission of tradition from one generation to the next includes far more than most ideologies are prepared to acknowledge: "material objects, beliefs about all sorts of things, images of persons and events, practices and institutions . . . buildings, monuments, landscapes, sculptures, paintings, books, tools, machines. In effect it includes all that a society of a given time possesses and which already existed when its present possessors came upon it and which is not solely the product of ecological or physiological necessity" (p. 12).

As this view of tradition encompasses historical continuity in all areas of our conceptual and material culture, it is important to identify significant aspects of the individual's relationship to tradition. Although the individual is inescapably embedded in tradition, not all individual thoughts or performances are controlled by tradition or add to what is transmitted to the next generations. As Shils observed, "an action ceases to exist once it is performed" (p. 12). But the action may contain elements that reproduce patterns inherited from the past and, in the process of reenactment, may contribute to transmitting them to the next generation. Making rational judgments, expressing feelings, and speaking to others are examples of acts that possess both transient and reproductive elements. Besides identifying certain characteristics of human action that are quite separate from tradition, Shils also noted that behaviors and thought patterns that endure for a short period of time often do not become part of tradition. They are examples of what he called a fashion; although they have many of the elements essential to a tradition, they fail to endure over what Shils viewed as the three-generation minimum required for the formation of a tradition. For example, as we know from recent experience, certain fashions of speech unique to a whole group of people not only fail to survive the generation that produced them but are replaced within that generation by a rapid succession of metaphorical fads. On the other hand, recent changes in linguistic conventions that eliminate gender distinctions show every sign of becoming part of the traditions individuals will experience as part of their natural attitude.

Contrary to the view that separates the autonomous individual from tradition and treats the latter as a forced imposition of the past on the present, Shils points out that traditions can only exist as individuals sustain them. As this point is crucial to understanding the misconception underlying the liberal assumption about emancipation from tradition, it is important to quote fully Shils' observation:

Traditions are not independently self-reproductive or self-elaborating. Only living, knowing, desiring human beings can enact them and modify them. Traditions develop because the desire to create something truer and better or more convenient is alive in those who acquire and possess them. Traditions can deteriorate in the sense of losing their adherents because their possessors cease to present them or because those who once received and re-enacted and extended them now prefer other lines of conduct or because new generations to which they were presented find other traditions of belief or some relatively new beliefs more acceptable, according to the standards which these generations accept. (pp. 14–15)

Although this view correctly brings out the connection between human agency and tradition, it does not seem to distinguish clearly between traditions that are sustained through conscious choice and traditions that are transmitted at the level of taken-for-granted belief. In spite of this shortcoming, which should not be passed over lightly, Shils succeeds in overcoming the static view of tradition as a monolithic juggernaut that threatens to force the present into the patterns of the past. "In no society," as Shils points out, "could life be lived entirely under the domination of tradition; no society could survive only from the stock of objects, beliefs, and patterns presented" (p. 27). The changing circumstances of a society and of individuals involve a continual disjunction between tradition, which represents answers formulated in response to circumstances in the past, and the novel and problematic elements of the present. Thus Shils argues for a view of tradition that involves a tension between the persistence of tradition ("tradition is like a plant which repeatedly puts down roots whenever it is left in one place for a short time") and the need to adopt innovative responses to current problems. Here Shils is not arguing what ought to be the case, but acknowledging that the starting point of human action involves an embeddedness in traditions of thought, technologies, institutions, and sources of legitimation. To put it another way, he is saying that intelligence (the source of innovation) and memory ("the vessel which retains in the present the record of experiences undergone in the past") are both essential elements in the problem-solving process. Intelligence without memory would be directionless and likely to commit the mistakes of the past; memory without intelligence would be unable to recognize the novel elements in experience and conceptualize adequate responses to present circumstances.

Shils' analysis of how the thread of tradition is interwoven into every aspect of the life world serves as a powerful antidote to those ideologies that provide only the conceptual lenses for seeing change. In what amounts to a beginning inventory of how the past lives in the present, Shils provides the basis for future phenomenologically oriented investigations that are essential to grounding ideological prescriptions. His inventory of how traditions endure includes the monuments, buildings, layout of physical space (including roads, dwellings, and cities) coins, artistic works, documents, and records that we daily interact with. At the more conceptual level are the traditions related to technologies, crafts (in both the folk culture and work place), inventions, scientific investigation, storytelling, scholarly publications, and so forth. There are also the traditions of the family, of education, of political, economic and legal systems, of ceremonies and sports, and of the rules governing social interaction. The technology of printing that makes possible the communication of ideas pertaining to the need to overthrow the past represents a thread of tradition that goes back to earliest attempts to leave a written record of human thought. The idea of revolution itself arises out of a distinct tradition of thought. Even such new technologies as the computer incorporate traditions that in turn were built on previous traditions; the thread of tradition that connects the computer keyboard with the typewriter goes beyond that to the printing press, which in turn grew out of the previous technology and its supporting ideological traditions. Shils' inventory of how contemporary culture remains in the grip of the past hopefully will serve to awaken many readers to recognize that time has a more substantive dimension than just the present and future. That he was able to write about tradition in a manner that will appear new and insightful to many readers serves as a reminder of how the conceptual categories of modern (primarily liberal) ideologies often distort our ability to recognize the most basic elements of our phenomenological world.

Besides providing an introductory inventory of our dependence on tradition, Shils examines the dynamics of how traditions change from within as well as from without. Again he avoids treating human agency and tradition as being dichotomous and oppositional. He sees the relationship as one of tension that involves both a base of support and a source of challenge. As Shils put it, "The existence of tradition is at least as much a consequence of limited power to escape from it as it is a consequence of a desire to continue and to maintain it. . . . Traditions are indispensable; they are also very seldom entirely adequate" (p. 213). Although it is not our purpose here to summarize the full range of Shils' insightful observations on the dynamics of change, it is important to point out that he locates the agency for change (in terms of endogenous factors) in the workings of human imagination, including the desire to improve on traditions, changes in moral sensitivities, applications of critical thought, charismatic leaders, and ideologies that are overtly opposed to tradition. The process of change, which tends to occur with increasing unevenness within a society, often reflects the conflict between social groups with different political, economic, and religious interests. Yet even in this case, when the traditions embraced by one social group are imposed on others or used for exploitive purposes, the political process aims at transforming traditions that are structurally and conceptually at the root of the problem and not at overturning all tradition. As Shils points out, even though a desire may exist for a complete revolution that will allow society to begin afresh, it is impossible to dispense wholly with traditions and to eliminate entirely the influence of the past, short of creating a new language, a new conceptual basis for technology, and a new epistemology for organizing the life world.

Shils concludes his examination of the nature of tradition by returning to an important theme in Max Weber's thinking: the relationship of modern rationalism to tradition. This relationship is also important to liberal educational theorists, though for very different reasons. Whereas Weber expressed deep concern about both the form that rationalism was taking in the Western process of modernization and its spread into more areas of cultural life, liberal educational theorists have tended to view rationalism as part of the emancipatory process and thus have adopted an uncritical stance toward it. More recent educational theorists, such as Henry Giroux, have become concerned about the instrumental mode of rationality that underlies the elaboration and spread of mechanical and social technologies, but they have introduced considerable confusion into the discussion by arguing that technicism is an expression of a conservative ideology (Aronowitz & Giroux 1985). Shils reestablishes the connection that Weber saw between rationalism and modernization by treating the desire to bring more social life under the predictive control of rationalism as an "anti-tradition tradition." In the process he juxtaposes the spread of rationalism with the loss of empowering traditions and the curtailment of individual agency and thought, concerns that echo Weber's earlier warnings.

In the sense that all belief systems are concerned with explanation, prediction, and exercising control over the events of daily life, they should be understood as the expression of rational thought. Thus we are not discussing rationalism in general, but a particular form that has evolved from early Jewish theology, the bureaucracies of Rome and the early Catholic church, and more recently from the Enlightenment traditions that secularized the modern foundations of knowledge. This purposive form of rationalism attempts to systematize all action, increase prediction and control through the use of measurable data, and delegitimate all forms of traditional authority not originating in data-based theory. It is, ironically, a tradition of thought that is against all tradition—except those elements that have instrumental value for solving a current problem in social engineering. As Shils points out, the early liberal formulation of this view of rationalism emphasized the freedom of individuals to exercise rational authority over the conduct of their own lives (and thus transcend the grip of tradition); in more recent times this view has given way to the belief that "rationalization by government is the best way of doing it since government is capable, so it is thought, of bringing everything into one unified, rational scheme" (p. 288). The assumptions of this anti-tradition tradition include the belief that all human experience can be explained in terms of variables that can be known and scientifically manipulated, that all knowledge is explicit and amenable to observation and experimental testing, and that experts are the guardians of the only true epistemological tradition—and thus are the only legitimate sources of authority.

Shils views the unchecked spread of this mode of rationality as a threat to substantive tradition as well as a source of totalitarian government that will, because of its use of rationalization as a means of legitimation, be more difficult to challenge. Yet he also sees tradition as surviving the nihilistic onslaught of rationalization. Tradition, as discussed earlier, is too complex, tacit, and foundational to the interpretive frameworks that guide the lives of people to be completely eradicated. But parts of tradition can be lost (e.g., the de-skilling of the worker caused by the separation of mental and manual labor, the loss of moral traditions caused by subjectivist and situation ethics, the loss of civil liberties caused by growth of the power of the state). Shils suggests that once it has receded from regular usage, a tradition cannot be deliberately restored (p. 329). Although this may be an overstatement, his observation puts in focus an aspect of our cultural experience that is, in different ways, both exceedingly resilient and exceedingly fragile. Often times, in our desire to propagate rationalism in order to be more modern, we fail to examine our traditions and thus end up overturning the more fragile and worthwhile tendencies in our culture, while strengthening the more dehumanizing ones. The progressive displacement of a liberalizing education by a "manpower" approach to determining the nature of the curriculum serves as a recent example of how the modern mode of rationalism is blind to the nature of tradition and thus to critical questions about cultural continuity and change.

In addition to the desire to rationalize all aspects of social life, Shils views the unqualified version of continual emancipation as equally injurious to tradition. The Enlightenment provided the philosophical justification for the modern idea of emancipation and, in the process, introduced a profoundly appealing image of human possibilities. Indeed, the drive for emancipation has succeeded in overturning dead and stultifying traditions and replaced them with new traditions—the achievements of the feminist movement being a recent example. But the image of emancipation, as Shils points out, is a metaphor that grossly oversimplifies our understanding of individualism, the power of critical rationality, the nature of tradition, and the unpredictable consequences that follow the introduction of new ideas and technologies into the culture.

As a metaphor dependent upon a background ideology, emancipation has become disconnected from its earlier, more limited historical focus and is now viewed as applicable to all aspects of the human situation, including the individual's entire social-cultural embeddedness in tradition. The metaphor not only carries into the present the biases of its parent ideology, it also reproduces the assumptions about individual empowerment that characterize the more recent stages of modern consciousness (i.e., the autonomous individual; the progressive nature of change; and rationality as the source of human agency, control, and authority). The result is a powerful image that obscures the complexity of social change, our actual ability to rationally control the direction of social change, and the enduring nature of tradition. But it is the manner in which the idea of emancipation forces our view of tradition into a conceptual formula, which itself derives from a tradition of thought, that is important to our discussion of the liberal view of the emancipatory potential of education.

The point is not that emancipation from specific social conditions is undesirable (indeed it is necessary to the renewal and transformation of living traditions) but that the term is often used as a metaphysical category, with the assumption that it can be achieved existentially by overturning all traditions and thus all forms of authority not centered in the rational judgment of the individual. In effect, its use in this sense fits Zijderveld's definition of a cliché, a term that serves as a badge of ideological affiliation rather than a word that possesses real explanatory power for understanding the world we live in. The following observation by Shils sets the context within which specific acts of emancipation must be achieved:

> A society is a "trans-temporal" phenomenon. It is not constituted by its existence at a single moment in time. It exists only through time. It is temporally constituted. It has a temporal integration as well as spatial integration. To be cut off from the past of one's society is as disordering to the individual and to the society as being cut off from the present. *Anomie* has a temporal dimension. (p. 327)

This is an aspect of the human-social condition that is trans-ideological. By calling attention to this "fact" of social existence, Shils is urging that the tension between the idea of emancipation and an understanding of tradition be restored—particularly in the thinking of social and educational theorists. The presence of this tension means avoiding the categorical declarations about the oppressiveness of all traditions, which in turn can be used to justify a form of socialization that fosters a collective amnesia toward the past. On the other hand, maintaining the tension involves a recognition that the context of reform may contain elements of tradition that deserve to be continued. The task of incorporating this sense of balance and complexity into the metaphorical image of emancipation will involve disconnecting it from the earlier liberal ideological frameworks that ignored the individual's social-cultural embeddedness, the tacit nature of cultural knowledge, and the influence of language on rational thought.

Concluding Remarks

Aside from Dewey, who incorporated important aspects of the individual's embeddedness into his theory while at the same time adopting the Enlightenment tendency to simplify tradition by recognizing the rational process as the only legitimate source of authority, the other liberal educational theorists appear to separate the individual from cultural embeddedness, theory from common sense, and emancipation from tradition. Their views on education, which have profound implications for both teaching and curriculum, reflect the power of language to enforce conceptual habits, even when the conceptual habits are contradicted by the force of everyday experience. Embeddedness in the language processes and lived traditions that make up the social-cultural world represents the foundation of daily existence; embeddedness is not an epiphenomenon of ideology but the ground of existence that ideology (theory) must take into account.

The metaphors of liberal thought appear to reproduce the biases and silences of the ideology out of which they are derived. In effect, the old conceptual schemas continue into the present, controlling the current discourse in terms of conceptual categories formulated in response to past debates. Individualism as a metaphor of many faces, as witnessed by the different streams of liberal thought in education, cannot be easily reconciled with the view that "language speaks," as the latter locates the controlling authority within language itself. Similarly, the metaphorical image of rationality, including both the instrumental (Skinner) and critical reflection (Freire) variants, rules out the tacit forms of cultural knowledge that connect the present with the past, provide a sense of meaning, and insure the cohesiveness of the life world in a manner that cannot be reproduced through explicit forms of knowledge. In effect, the generative metaphors of liberalism reflect the anthropocentrism of modern Western society where men and women are, to quote Michael Harrington, pro-claimed "as the lords and ladies of the universe" (1983, p. 8).

Aside from the liberal traditions that provide the rationale and institutional support for protecting civil liberties (which, it must be emphasized, are not being challenged here), the canons of modern liberalism lead to a view of social reality that not only fails to address the most basic problems facing modern society but now even threatens the very civil liberties that are part of the liberal tradition itself. In order to see how the omissions—those elements that are not part of the discourse—of educational liberalism contribute to the crisis we now face, it may be useful to summarize Michael Harrington's observations. As a democratic socialist, Harrington views the crisis of modern society as basically spiritual in nature and traces the causes back to the patterns of thought that have evolved over the last three hundred or so years. Harrington's attempt to center the problems of meaning, social integration, and transcendence (both individual and communal) is important because his analysis of the conceptual roots of the crisis reflects an ability to think beyond the boundaries of traditional ideological categories. By using a more complex discourse that transcends the conceptual restrictions of current ideologies, he serves as a model for thinking about the challenges and prospects of educational theory. In addition, there are two other reasons for summarizing Harrington's view of the current crisis. The first is that part of the solution to the problems he identifies may be found in a deeper understanding of how we are embedded in a social-cultural world; this understanding, in turn, could lead to correcting basic misconceptions in our guiding ideologies and serve to mitigate the more extreme causes of cultural nihilism. The second reason for taking Harrington seriously, beyond the power of his arguments, is that his views could have been expressed by a philosophic conservative. The opening of his discourse to issues that have long been a concern among philosophic conservatives points to the path to be pursued in the next chapter, namely, the contribution that philosophic conservatism can make to a reconstructed liberalism.

To summarize Harrington's much more complex argument, the rise of science, rationalism, and atomistic individualism led to a secularized world where religion no longer provided the source of authority essential to basing the life of the community on a coherent set of moral assumptions. With the de-centering of religion that followed the adoption of successively more progressive forms of liberalism, Harrington identifies six crises that he says we find ourselves facing at the present: (1) "a crisis of legitimacy in the late capitalist" (and mature communist) "society, as one of the prime motives for noncoerced obedience and acquiescence in the social order begins to disappear"; (2) "the economic consequences of the shift from the 'Protestant ethic' to compulsory hedonism of un-planned and irresponsible growth"; (3) "the appeal of totalitarian move-ments as substitutes for religious solidarity"; (4) "the loss of the philo-sophic and 'common sense' basis for responsibility before the law as various determinisms occupy the territory once held by religious doctrines of free will and/or moral responsibility"; (5) "the decline in the sense of duty toward unborn generations"; and (6) "the relativization of all moral values and a resultant crisis of individual conscience" (p. 8).

A close reading of Harrington's concerns as well as his prescrip-tions—using the promotion of the community, moral incentives, and democratic participation as the main criteria for determining national policies (pp. 217-18)—leads to a rejection of the liberal view of the individual as self-directing and a self-sufficient source of fulfillment, rationalism as the source of guiding authority, and emancipation as the progressive stripping away of external forms of authority, responsibility, and embeddedness. Although Harrington's final formulation of how to deal with the "humdrum nihilism of everyday life" does not overcome the tension that exists between a community (which involves transcendent forms of authority) and democratic participation (which locates authority within the individual), he is nevertheless reaching for a deeper, more hermeneutical understanding of community. In the process he is urging a major shift consistent with the previous discussion in this chapter, namely, that the individual be understood as embedded in a social-cultural world.

Yet in understanding the forms of control that culture, including language and tradition, exerts over the individual, and in determining how these control processes can be used to strengthen the bonds of community, it is important that we avoid the overly deterministic position represented in the following statement by E. P. Thompson: "We are *structured* by social relations, *spoken* by pre-given linguistic structures, *thought* by ideologies, *dreamed* by myths, *gendered* by patriarchal sex norms, *bonded* by affective obligations, *cultured* by mentalities and *acted* by history's script" (quoted by Harrington in *The Politics at God's Fu-neral*, p. 20). Although Thompson's statement may be more valid than the view of the self-directing individual central to the theories of Freire and Rogers, it nevertheless eliminates the dialectic between human imagi-nation and the material-symbolic context of cultural existence. The latter represents the "what is" of human existence, and while human imagina-tion cannot entirely escape the influence of the symbolic patterns inter-nalized from the existential relationship of embeddedness, it possesses the power to pose the question of "what ought to be" and thus to problematize the context of human existence.

Education involves acquiring both implicit and explicit forms of knowledge, with the two processes often occurring simultaneously. Thus education strengthens both embeddedness, including the complex process of bonding the individual to a social-cultural context, *and* the powers of human agency essential for reconceptualizing the more detrimental conditions of that embeddedness. The two processes, however, can never be separated as clearly as the liberal theories of education presented earlier assume. Before we turn to the task of formulating a more adequate theory of education, it will be necessary to address what has become a source of near intellectual paranoia among liberal theorists of education—namely, the suggestion that conservative views on education and society should be taken seriously. This fear has resulted in a restriction of the discourse of liberal educational theorists and led to the awkward position of their being incessant advocates of change while maintaining a silence on the question of what aspects of the cultural heritage ought to be conserved. Sorting out the forms of conservatism that should be taken seriously from those that are simply reactionary ideological stances and identifying conservative issues that must be addressed by liberal educational theorists will be our next tasks.

4

Varieties of Conservatism

IF we view an ideology as performing the same function as the map Schumacher used in Leningrad to get his spatial bearings, we can more easily recognize a second major limitation in the thinking of liberal educational theorists. Schumacher recalled how the map identified certain features of the terrain but also left him confused, because other visible features were not included on the map. An ideology is like a conceptual map in that it provides the reference points for orientating ourselves in terms of the social and temporal dimensions of existence; but it may also omit references to certain aspects of our life world or shape our perceptions according to the biases that existed at the time of the map's (the ideology's) origin. Liberal educational theories, as reflected in the ideas of Dewey, Freire, Rogers, and Skinner, emphasize education as the means of fostering social change, but are embarrassingly silent on the equally important question of what should be conserved. It is almost as though the ideological map puts in focus what is socially and individually problematic and ignores the rest.

But the problem goes much deeper and reveals a major conceptual flaw of liberalism. The following statements are important for what they reveal about liberalism's escalator view of history, which can in part be explained by its emphasis on empowerment of the individual ("technocratic elites" in Skinner's scheme) and the assumption that change is progressive. For Dewey, "experience is the result, the sign, the reward of that interaction of organism and environment which, when it is carried to the full, is a transformation of interaction into participation and communication" (1958, p. 22). In contrast to the doing, undergoing, and reconstructing that characterize experience (guided, of course, by scientific intelligence), the authority of past achievements, in Dewey's view, was a potential source of alienation from the method of intelligence. In a series of statements that reflect a basic confusion about the difference between a living tradition with maintenance of the status quo and the oppression of the present by the dead authority of the past, Dewey sets up the dichotomy between romantic escapism into the past ("inert conservatism") and a form of life that involves "intelligence as an organizing factor." "Man differs from the lower animals," Dewey wrote, "because he preserves his past experiences. What happened in the past is lived again in memory. . . . Thus the primary life of memory is emotional rather than intellectual and practical." But, according to Dewey, memory is a form of escapism, a "vicarious experience in which there is all the emotional value of actual experience without its strains, vicissitudes and troubles" (1960, pp. 1–2).

Dewey is not alone in confusing the conserving of worthwhile aspects of the cultural heritage with passivity, escapism, or—even worse—the reactionary maneuvering of privileged social groups. Although Skinner's approach to the promise of science led him in a direction that would have been abhorrent to Dewey, he nevertheless expressed the same attitude toward the past. "Old days," he wrote in *Beyond Freedom and Dignity*, "are called good old days, when the inherent dignity of man and the importance of spiritual values were recognized. Such fragments of outmoded behavior tend to be 'wistful'— that is, they have the character of increasingly unsuccessful behavior." Yet the past was not to be entirely eliminated in Skinner's more engineered world, which was also to be based on "experimental analysis." Man's "achievements in science, government, religion, art and literature remain as they have always been, to be admired as one admires a storm at sea or autumn foliage, or a mountain peak, quite apart from their origins and untouched by a scientific analysis" (1972, p. 203). Rogers treats the conservation of past cultural achievements as a form of indoctrination that undermines democracy in the classroom, involves authoritarian teachers who mistrust students, and requires that the authority of tradition be maintained through the use of fear and bureaucratic controls (1983, pp. 185–87). In contrast to the person-centered education which he advocates, Rogers associates conserving traditions as part of the educational process (which reflects his exceedingly naive understanding) with "the most traditional, conservative, rigid, bureaucratic institution . . . the institution most resistant to change" (p. 1). Freire's view of the dialectic of conservatism and change—a view which in fact eliminates any authentic dialectic—is perhaps best summed up in the following statement:

> In these complex societies we sometimes find ourselves living very much submerged in time, without critical or dynamic appreciation of history, as if history were flying over us, commanding and relentlessly

regulating our lives. This is a fatalism that immobilizes, suffocates, and eventually kills us. History is nothing like this. History has no power. As Marx has said, history does not command us, history is made by us. History makes us while we make it. Again, my suggestion is that we attempt to emerge from this alienating daily routine that repeats itself. Let's try to understand life, not necessarily as the daily repetition of things, but as an effort to create and re-create, and as an effort to rebel, as well. (1985, pp. 198–99)

Here Freire is speaking about the human situation in general, and his notion of a non-alienating praxis applies to all cultures and not just to specific colonized situations.

Another example of how liberal ideology, with its biases against tradition, imposes a secular version of the struggle between the forces of light and darkness on the complexity of life is the following statement by Giroux who urges us to have a commitment "to a radical transformation of the existing society *in all its manifestations*" (italics added). What is required at this time, according to Giroux, is a radical pedagogy "informed by a passionate faith in the necessity of struggling to create a better world. In other words, radical pedagogy needs a vision—one that celebrates not what is but what could be, that looks beyond the immediate to the future and links struggle to a new set of human possibilities" (1983, p. 242). Although Giroux suggests that the radical transformation of society ("in all its manifestations") is partly justified by an "obligation to the past," he presumably is thinking of revolution as a memorial to those individuals and social groups who were victims of past forms of social injustice. This is about as close as he comes, except for urging that an historical perspective is essential for developing a radical critique, to suggesting that there is anything in society that is worth conserving.

A careful reading of these liberal educational theorists yields surprisingly few references to past cultural achievements that are not interpreted within a teleological framework. It could be argued, at one level, that liberal educational theories, which reproduce the unexamined epistemological categories of the past, represent one of those interesting anomalies in Western thought—namely, an ideological tradition that urges that all traditions, in the name of individualism and progress, be transcended. We refer, of course, to the tradition of teleological thinking. But aside from the reification of this aspect of liberal thought, there is a more basic question of why liberal educational theories, failing to recognize the more problematic aspects of society and to politicize issues of social justice, must be understood within the much larger context of a culture that includes enriching and life-sustaining traditions. The music, literature, art, architecture, technology, social mores, oral folk traditions, and institutions (including, in our case, the constitutional framework that protects civil liberties from the extremists of both the Left and Right) of a culture cannot simply be categorically judged as oppressive or relegated—albeit with an attitude of reverent respect—to a museum for the curious. As noted in the previous chapter, our embeddedness in the living traditions of a culture far exceeds what most of us are able to recognize, particularly given our conceptual biases. Many of these traditions of belief, social practice, and artistic expression are an integral dimension of experience, which even individuals committed to revolutionary change take for granted. For example, both Marx and Lenin led personal lives that were rooted in conventional practices that sharply contrasted with their writings on the need for revolutionary change; their adherence to the cultural conventions of family life, their tastes in art and literature, and their dependence on technologies that provided a modicum of convenience all reflected a culturally conservative life style (Lilge 1977, pp. 566-68). More recently, Freire expressed a similarly conservative tendency when he recalled that, in addition to writing on the need to recognize that "history has no power," he "spent sixteen years in exile, with Elza helping me to survive by looking for things that tasted like home cooking." As suggested by Freire's recollection of this sixteen-year quest to recover the familiar experience of earlier traditions, we are deeply and often unconsciously bonded to our culture. The ability to recognize that we are dependent on, that we cherish, and that we are spiritually nourished by our cultural heritage should not disqualify us from being able to speak out forcefully on those aspects of the culture that must be resisted and transformed. To put it more succinctly, any liberal discourse that aims to bring about improvement in the human condition must give attention to those aspects of cultural experience that ought to be conserved. This may seem obvious to many, but it is not part of the thinking that underlies the archetypal forms of educational liberalism.

An important question that needs to be asked concerns the inability of liberal educational theorists to relate theory to the continuities in our own phenomenological world. Theory should meet a test that takes account of the theorist's own life style; if the originator of the theory values certain traditions—in music, food, literature, social relationships, and so forth—then the theory should be qualified accordingly. This would involve grounding theory so that it represents more accurately the complexities of the life world. But this, interestingly enough, is not a test that is met by any of these liberal educational theorists. Skinner's own life has an inner dimension that cannot be explained entirely by "contingencies of reinforcement"; Dewey must surely have experienced moments of contemplation that did not lead to reconstructing experience according to the canons of scientific intelligence; and the call for revolutionary praxis that characterizes the theories of Freire and Giroux must surely stand in sharp contrast with the cultural traditions that underpin and sustain their own daily lives. Why liberal educational theorists have not recognized the distorting effects of their conceptual map (ideology) is a particularly important issue for those of us concerned with maintaining the liberal achievements of the past, while confronting the conceptual foundations of current dehumanizing practices.

There are several possible explanations for the lack of balance in liberal educational theories between a legitimate concern with cultural renewal and an equally legitimate (and necessary) concern with preserving substantive traditions. A partial explanation relates to the manner in which theory, as viewed by Western intellectuals, has tended to devalue both culture as the ground of experience and implicit forms of knowledge. Gouldner observed that as a speech community intellectuals represent reality at a theoretical level by utilizing a discourse that is "characterized by speech that is *relatively* more *situation-free*, more context or field 'independent.'" This speech community thus values expressly legislated meanings and devalues tacit, context-limited meanings. Its ideal is "'one word, one meaning' for everyone and forever" (1979, p. 28). Insofar as liberal educational theorists share the episteme of Western intellectualism, we might be able to account for their tendency to write about the human condition in general. On the other hand, the increasing recognition of differences in cultural world views, the more hermeneutical understanding of individual embeddedness, and the progressive awareness of how language reproduces in thought elements of the unconscious history of culture—all these represent relatively new forms of understanding that assuredly will have an effect on future formulations of liberal thought. Hopefully, they will lead to a form of theory that reflects a greater awareness of context and of the problems of embeddedness and cultural relativism.

A second explanation, which goes beyond the liberal educational theorist's penchant for using a highly abstract and decontextualized language that transforms the desire to eradicate social injustice into a secular theology, has to do with the long history of our more political metaphors, as well as with the equally longstanding conceptual habit of binary thinking. Metaphors, such as progress, democracy, liberal, radical, science, and so forth, have become associated with being modern and enlightened. Even when these terms are used to mask dehumanizing political regimes, they carry with them an aura of legitimacy, truth, and social justice. On the other hand, other terms in our political lexicon have been stigmatized with a different set of connotations. Terms such as conservative and tradition have a long history of being associated with anti-modern, anti-progressive, and anti-scientific values—in a word, with reactionarism. The habit of thinking in dichotomous categories has strengthened this tendency to view whatever is labeled as liberal as the opposite of conservative, of tradition as the opposite of modern, and so forth.

Although we are now witnessing a greater willingness on the part of many people to identify openly with political terms that in the past were associated with being a political pariah (e.g., conservatism), we still see traditional political categories being maintained in the lexical distinctions that misrepresent the traditions of political thought they are supposed to designate. For example, to refer to James Watt, the former Secretary of Interior, as a conservative obscures the fact that his political beliefs are in fact rooted in classical liberalism. Because of the misuse of our political lexicon—which includes the rigid categories into which the terms have been placed—the people who wanted to preserve the forests from economic exploitation were unable to identify themselves with the political term that best describes what they were attempting to achieve—the *conserving* of the natural environment. They persisted in labeling themselves liberals (the ideology that upholds individualism, a free-market economy, and utilitarianism) even though their commitments were basically conservative (to the sanctity of the natural environment, the preservation of the heritage for future generations, and the priority of the general good over the interests of the individual).

This misunderstanding for our most basic political labels can be seen in educational theory, for example, in what Giroux associates with conservatism. The reactionary influence of conservatism in education, according to him, is reflected in the scientific management movement, behaviorism, positivism, "capitalistic rationality," and instrumentalism in all its educational manifestations (including the view that knowledge is objective) (1983, pp. 43–44). On the other hand, he labels educational practices that empower people, promote democratic social arrangements, and insure social progress as radical—the current metaphor for a commitment to the goals of the Enlightenment. Anybody who is familiar with the ideas of conservatives, such as Robert M. Hutchins or T. S. Eliot, however, would find considerable irony in Giroux's attempt to equate conservatism with the most extreme forms of cultural modernism. Common sense would suggest that beliefs and activities concerned with the preservation of substantive traditions would be associated with conservatism, and that beliefs and activities that promote social change, profitability, and the spread of the purposive rational mode of thought would be associated with liberalism. An understanding of the history of the two main ideological traditions in the West (along with various mutations and reversals of positions) would support this common sense way of understanding what conservatism stands for.

Giroux's conceptual errors, however, are not unique, nor is the penchant for labeling traditional liberal values as conservative limited to American educational theorists. Writing on "The Production of Conservative Educational Ideologies," Ken Johnston, an Australian Marxist educational theorist, stated that "central to the ethic of the new conservatisms are the encouragement of competition, the stress on personal responsibility, and the belief that personal effort in the market deserves adequate reward" (1981, p. 10). Johnston, however, is concerned more with uncovering the "economic determinations" that create ideologies than with the equally interesting question of whether deliberate conceptual misrepresentations can be used to serve moral ends (or whether these misrepresentations should be viewed as symptoms of deeper educational deficiencies that ought to concern all educators interested in the goal of emancipation).

Yet there is another question that is raised by the persistent habit of using conservatism as the catch-all label for the more selfish and mindless forces in society. The conceptual map that leads Dewey to associate conservatism with fixed values and ideas, Rogers to see in it only the voice of authoritarianism and rigid resistance to change, Skinner to associate it with noble illusions that are impeding the full development of a science of behavior, and Freire to equate it with a banking approach to education that fosters passivity in the face of domination—such a conceptual map creates a major problem that can only be understood by returning to the earlier discussion of how language can influence the conceptual boundaries of a discourse.

By using conservatism to designate the darker side of human nature and social practice, the term becomes, along with sexism, racism and fascism, a pariah metaphor. And like these other terms, it carries connotations deeply repugnant to most educated people. Especially among liberal educational theorists, including the neo-Marxists who are attempting to fuse Marx's class conflict model with liberal assumptions about the progressive nature of critical thought, the term conservatism is viewed abhorrently. Aside from anthologies of educational thought that provide an obligatory coverage of the entire spectrum of educational ideas, references to conservatism occur only as a means of identifying a reactionary social group or of placing (erroneously) the values and institutions of classical liberalism within an ideological framework.

The desire to maintain as much distance as possible from whatever is viewed as a pariah tends to take priority over a clear understanding of the object of this distancing gaze. This is exactly what has happened within the discourse of educational liberalism; the result is that liberal educational theorists have cut themselves off from giving serious attention to the issues, insights, and cautionary warnings that have preoccupied conservative thinkers from the time of Edmund Burke.

Conservatism, like liberalism, encompasses a diverse range of voices. Some clearly represent that of the soured reactionary, while others, less shrill, give expression to the desire to continue with established values and social patterns. There are even conservatives that fit the stereotyped image represented in the writings of liberal educational theorists. But beyond these groups are others who are attempting to find in tradition alternative ways of living that avoid the more dehumanizing social forces of modernization. There are also highly sensitive, concerned, and reflective individuals who have enriched our political understanding by challenging the ideas and values of those who have been, over the last two hundred years, apostles of social progress. These conservatives have even made fundamental contributions to insuring that certain aspects of the liberal tradition be permanently protected against shifts in popular mood. Given the deep hostility that most liberal educational theorists feel toward conservatives in general, there is considerable irony in the fact that some conservative thinkers have given us the most penetrating analysis of the forces that restrict human imagination and potential. The tendency of liberal educational theorists to lump all conservatives together had prevented them from sorting out those who view our times through a different set of lenses from those who are simply fearful of new ideas, social change, and exposure of privilege. Thus the ideas that would enable liberal educational theorists to obtain perspective on their own assumptions, as well as force them to defend their ideas and values in the face of serious criticism, have simply been ignored.

A statement by Merleau-Ponty illuminates how the past can enrich the present—if we have an ear for the questions that have been asked over time. It also suggests how the thought within a discourse can be strengthened by a dialogue that engages the traditions of both liberal and conservative thought. Historical understanding, Merleau-Ponty observed, "only presupposes the possibility that we have a past which is ours and that we can recapture in our freedom the work of so many other freedoms. It assumes that we can clarify the choices of others through our own, and ours through theirs, that we adjust one by the other and finally arrive at the truth" (1964, p. 204). A dialogue would not only represent a broadened discourse on questions about education, government, and other aspects of the cultural experiment that we know as modern society, but it would also provide liberal theorists insights into the world view of the social groups they alternately view as in need of emancipation or as in possession of a form of culture that is superior to the dominant one. With the exception of Skinner, liberal educational theorists have a strong populist orientation that uses the "people" as the source of ultimate justification for their reform proposals. Understanding the people, and what it is they want to conserve as well as change, requires a deeper understanding of the dynamics of human existence than can be acquired from the root metaphor of liberalism, which is perhaps best symbolized by the solitary individual standing on an escalator that moves continually higher in the scheme of things.

In order to initiate a dialogue and thus begin the task of overcoming the intellectual apartheid that separates the two discourses, it is first necessary to identify four different types of conservatism. As we will see, no single idiom or vision adequately represents what conservatism stands for. There are many different types of conservatism, some even appearing in the guise of the radical. Yet as our purpose here is to expand the discourse of liberal educational thought to include issues of concern to conservatives, it is not necessary to work out a complete taxonomy of the various forms of conservatism. Following in the footsteps of Clinton Rossiter and Raymond English, without adopting entirely their schema, we shall focus on the following general types of conservatism: temperamental or instinctive, cultural, economic, and philosophic. Whether neo-conservatism, the label given in the 1970s to an important group of former socialist and liberal intellectuals who began to work out in the pages of *Commentary* and *The Public Interest* a synthesis of liberal and conservative principles, should be included as a distinct category of its own is not an issue that will be argued here. Although the neo-conservatives often arrived at a different set of answers, their approach to social issues involved the same reflective level of thought that characterizes the tradition of philosophic conservatism stretching from Peter Viereck to Edmund Burke. The more important task is to lay out a rough geography of conservatism in order to bring into sharper focus the conceptual limitations of the liberal educational theorist, and to identify the issues that must be considered in formulating a post liberal theory of education.

Temperamental Conservatism

Temperamental or instinctive conservatism is rooted in the psychological processes of the individual and thus should not be viewed as the creation of an ideology. It reflects a basic orientation of all human beings to find security and comfort in the familiar and thus has undoubtedly influenced our attitudes toward ideologies, particularly the more modern ones that promise continual change. The desire to conserve the familiar reflects, in part, the psychological bonding that is part of our embeddedness in a social-linguistic-cultural environment. Self-concept, the conceptual habits reinforced through language usage, and established associations with traditional sources of meaning (including the culturally defined sources of fear and disorientation) serve as a powerful "flywheel," to use William James's metaphor, for continuing to live within established patterns. It is, in fact, a prereflective form of conservatism that exists in all of our lives. The proclivity to feel at home with the familiar provides the continuity and security that enables us, in varying degrees, to be innovative and to take risks in other areas of our lives. The concept in the sociology of knowledge that best describes the experience of temperamental conservatism is the "natural attitude," the sense of "taken-for-grantedness" toward the routines and patterns of meaning within which everyday life is embedded.

Because of the difficulty of being aware of our own natural attitude, we often are not aware that our attitudes, moods, and thought patterns reproduce tradition. Even when we hold an intellectual commitment to a life of continual social change, important areas of our life will be based on patterns that conserve traditional routines. For example, the radicals of the academy may urge people to resist all social routines that oppress the full realization of their subjectivity, and at the same time live personal life styles that adhere to specific conventions of dress, food, body language, epistemic patterns, tenure, and scholarship (i.e., the use of footnotes, margins, notation system, and so forth). Temperamental conservatism, as an integral part of our phenomenological world, is expressed in the unnoticed routines of daily life. An ideology may politicize certain aspects of the life world—the more explicit psychological, social, and economic issues—but except in its most totalitarian expression, it cannot take account of all the multiple ways in which actions and thoughts reinforce the "flywheel" of temperamental conservatism.

Yet this form of conservatism is more than the phenomenological baseline that precedes and generally endures in the face of disruptions caused by ideologies that rationalize all aspects of experience. According to Raymond English, there is a less cheerful side to this form of conservatism, which is often manifested in a "cowardly human impulse to cling to the known and the accustomed" (1952, p. 399), an impulse reflected in the lines of Hamlet: "And makes us rather bear those ills we have/Than fly to others we know not of." It thus becomes, for some, a conservatism of the paranoid and the traumatized. Although Rossiter, himself a staunch philosophical conservative, rejects this form of conservatism on the grounds that it fails to discriminate between what deserves to be continued and what must be changed, this psychological dimension of temperamental conservatism requires fuller recognition and understanding—and not just for the purpose of bringing the recalcitrant more fully under the rational control of the state.

Temperamental conservatism confronts liberal educational theorists with a basic dilemma. That liberal educational theorists generally have not taken this dilemma into account may help explain why the people who are to be the object of the emancipatory process have not responded to their potential emancipators with greater enthusiasm. The Marxist explanation that the people's state of false consciousness prevents them from recognizing the hegemonic forces of oppression, and that their conservatism is only a symptom of the deeper crisis, has far less explanatory power than its proponents claim. Like appeals for emancipation, the false consciousness argument may be taken seriously by the oppressed with regard to a limited political agenda (i.e., sexism, the need for worker participation in the work process, and so forth) while other aspects of their life world will remain firmly anchored in temperamental conservatism. The proclivity of the liberal educational theorists to articulate the problem of emancipation in sweeping terms that make few concessions to the importance of conserving meaningful traditions appears elitist and reinforces the popular conception that theorists lack the kind of practical wisdom learned from experience. To reach the people it is intended to persuade, the liberal argument may have to acknowledge that the desire to cling to the familiar and meaningful is not always the expression of cowardice or indifference in the face of reactionary forces. In addition to inviting the liberal theorists to be more self-reflective about whether they are prepared to adjust their own lives to the white-heat demands of their theory, a less categorical view of this form of conservatism may lead to a more focused discussion of educational objectives.

Cultural Conservatism

The second type of conservatism also poses a problem for liberal educational theorists, but in a different way. Temperamental conservatism involves forms of knowledge (common sense and the tacit understanding of cultural rules) that liberal theorists have either overlooked or viewed as inferior to more theoretical forms of understanding.

It also goes against the grain of the teleology in liberal thinking; embeddedness in familiar patterns of daily life seems not only an obstruction to social progress but it lacks the appeal of a moral vision. Cultural conservatism, on the other hand, is consistent with the canon of liberal thought which upholds the right of self-determination. Interpreted in a larger framework, the principle of self-determination means the right of a cultural group to find its own way, to struggle against being culturally and economically colonized, and in some instances (this is where the rub comes) to reject most of what liberals themselves believe in order to avoid being Westernized (colonized again). The use of terms such as authentic and indigenous, which are quite appropriate, make even culturally conservative liberation movements sound like epitomes of liberal values. Cultural conservatism can simultaneously be both in harmony and out of harmony with liberal principles. The pursuit of cultural self-determination can lead to strengthening the power of the community over the individual and to reinforcing consensual and traditional, rather than adversarial and individualizing, forms of authority.

Cultural conservatism is nearly as widespread a phenomena as temperamental conservatism and is expressed not only in terms of nationalistic movements but also by cultural groups who attempt to maintain their identity and heritage while being citizens of a larger society. Even cultural groups who are more conscious of their religious commitments—Jews, the Amish, the Hopi Native Americans, and so forth—can be identified with this form of conservatism. By keeping traditions alive through teaching the language and customs of their primary culture, such groups give people a depth of identity denied by the more depersonalizing and anomic characteristics of modern society, and lend culture a significance not recognized in the liberal educational theories. The ideas of Dewey, Freire, Rogers, and Skinner locate authority in either the individual or a variant form of the rational process. When relating the individual to the whole, these theorists think in terms of social membership in a group. But they do not tend to think of the individual in a manner that takes account of the myriad forms of cultural bonding. Even Dewey, with his emphasis on the scientific method of problem solving as a source of empowerment, failed to recognize the power of culture to influence conceptual, psychological, and social processes.

Aside from the more self-conscious (and strident) expressions of cultural relativism, the role of language in reproducing the patterns and rules for the symbolic ordering of the universe makes it one of the most powerful sources of cultural conservatism. Freire, the theorist most aware of the controlling nature of language, represents the individual as capable of escaping the forces of domination through critical reflection (conscientization); although he must continually renew his freedom through the exercise of critical reflection, the individual, in Freire's view, is the sole source of authentic authority and self-direction. But this view of empowerment makes sense only if one assumes that culture has no power or, to paraphrase his statement, that "history has no power." The irony is that such a view of a teleological universe, of the rational process (in its many liberal variations), and of nature of individualism is a reflection of the cultural mythologies embedded in the metaphorical nature of our language. As stated earlier, language reproduces in the present the unconscious history of the past; and even though imagination, critical reflection, and metaphorical thinking both modify and extend this epistemic heritage, the individual cannot escape entirely from participation in a culturally conservative process.

Cultural conservatism, in an ironic way, serves as a challenge to liberal educational theorists to become genuinely radical thinkers. This is quite different from the current practice of associating radicalism with modernizing values and assumptions that equate change with progress, personal authenticity with freedom, and critical reflection with enlightenment. If language makes us participants in the process of cultural reproduction, perhaps the challenge of being radical thinkers will involve investigating the roots of our current crisis—which may lead to the recognition of the origins and current problematic nature of modern thought itself. As culture lives in us largely at an unconscious level, we really do not have the option of being for or against cultural conservatism. The real option, which comes from being the kind of radical thinker that examines the foundations of our belief systems and institutions, is the more limited one of identifying those traditions that can no longer be justified and those essential to maintaining the civilizing achievements of the human community. Empowerment may have more to do with the recovery and renewal (as well as the selective rejection) of traditions than with furthering the myth that the individual, through getting in touch with the authentic self, exercising rationality, or utilizing a technology of behavioral control, can become the absolute source of authority in the universe. The debate is really within the framework of cultural conservatism and not a debate where liberalism stands on the outside making categorical distinctions that represent itself as progressive, humane, and enlightened, and cultural conservatism as the embodiment of the forces of darkness.

Economic Conservatism

Although economic conservatives may share the temperamental conservative's sense of security in familiar routines, the routines themselves are legitimated by a set of beliefs that promote change within the culture. What economic conservatives want to conserve are the privileges, possessions, and power made possible by this set of beliefs. Yet while they want to conserve the positive achievements, the belief systems that underlie their position should not be understood as conservative. The intellectual lineage of economic conservatism goes back to classical liberal thinkers, the positivistic traditions of French sociology, and to social Darwinism. Its great thinkers include John Locke, Jeremy Bentham, Adam Smith, Auguste Comte, Herbert Spencer, and Frederick Taylor. Its critics are Edmund Burke, Samuel T. Coleridge, Alexis de Tocqueville, C. S. Lewis, T. S. Eliot, and Michael Oakeshott— all conservative thinkers who were alarmed by the nihilistic tendencies of the doctrine of modern progress advanced by the interpreters of the classical liberal position.

Economic conservatism, as a category, is important to our discussion of the need to reconceptualize the foundations of liberal educational theory only in the limited sense of clearing up the misuse of our political categories. The practice of labeling as conservative the economic and technological juggernaut that has emerged from the fusion of classical liberalism, positivism, and technicism tends to eliminate the possibility of taking seriously any conservative thinker. Most liberal educational thinkers show little evidence of having read the writings of conservative thinkers; for example, the positivistic orientation of most political science departments has undermined the opportunities to learn about the liberal-conservative debates that characterize the actual history of political thought. Liberals simply use the term conservative as a catch-all to critique current forms of extremism—whether the extremism of the technocrat or that of the Moral Majority. Such mislabeling, in turn, often represents for their readers a process of primary socialization into the taxonomy of political thought. When writers as prominent as Stanley Aronowitz and Henry Giroux associate technicism in education with conservatism, they are socializing readers (and in some cases simply reinforcing stereotypes) to powerful misconceptions that will carry on into the future as part of the conceptual map of the political terrain. In addition to contributing to the further deterioration of political discourse, the association of the economic marauder and the messianic technicist with conservatism cuts off the one area of social and political thought that provides the basis both for an effective critique and for strengthening the more positive achievements of cultural and political liberalism.

As I made this argument in a journal article that went entirely unnoticed (1980b), I will repeat the essential outline only for the purpose of putting in focus the need for a dialogue between liberal and conservative thinkers. The argument is that the continuities between technicism (in both the market place and the cultural sector, e.g., schooling) and the traditions of Enlightenment thought create a dilemma for the critic of technicism. If the traditions of thought that underlie technicism—a synthesis of utilitarianism, positivism, and Taylorism, along with the liberal view of progress and individualism—represent the current legacy of the Enlightenment revolt against tradition, then the critics of technicism must be able to identify themselves with other traditions of thought if they are to avoid promoting the very ideas they want to criticize. The dilemma is reflected in the thinking of both Freire and Giroux, but it can also be seen in Rogers' criticism of the "conservative right" (which upholds the competitive individualism of the free market) while he celebrates the progressive nature of an anarchistic form of individualism. In the thinking of Freire and Giroux, the unrecognized dilemma can be seen in their rejecting capitalism and instrumental thinking as exploitive, while at the same time basing their arguments for an emancipatory form of education on the same canons of liberal-Enlightenment thought that support the social practices from which people are to be emancipated. For example, the assumption that emancipation will free people from the authority of the past involves the same teleological view of reality that enables the capitalist and the technicist to assume the progressive nature of their own innovative practices. To put it another way, the followers of both Freire and the technicists reject the authority of all substantive traditions—except the tradition of emancipation. The difference is that the Freireian point of view involves consciousness-raising, while the technicist relies upon an instrumental mode of thinking. In addition, by locating authority within the critically reflective capacity of the individual, both Freire and Giroux strengthen the same relativizing view of the individual as atomistic, the rational process as instrumental, and ethics as emotive—all essential to the anomic tendencies of a technicist society. To quote Bell again, "man's self-conscious will to destroy the past and control his future" underpins the emancipatory vision of Freire and Giroux (as well as Dewey, Rogers, and Skinner); it is also essential to the modernizing vision of the neoclassical liberals they criticize.

By lumping all forms of conservatism together as intellectually and morally reprehensible, the liberal educational theorists are forced to find within the liberal-Enlightenment traditions of thought a basis for critique. Their success is largely limited to using a "radical"-sounding set of context-free metaphors (emancipation, consciousness raising, resistance, authentic choice, critical intelligence, and so forth) that reinforce the Enlightenment myth of progress. Although the rhetoric encourages people to think critically about the circumstances of their lives, it fails to address at a deeper level the meaning of authority, community, and tradition within the context of modernization. If these aspects of human experience remain unaddressed or are represented as the concern only of the social reactionary, consciousness-raising will surely strengthen rather than ameliorate the anomic form of individualism in which meaning becomes increasingly a matter of subjectivity. Ironically, it is the rootless and remissive form of individualism that is required by both the neoclassical liberal entrepreneur and technicist. Basic to innovators is an ideology that denigrates the importance of memory and equates change with progress.

In a very important way, the pattern of thinking of the neoclassical liberals presents a challenge to liberal educational theorists that will not disappear by attempting to label them as fundamentally different. The intellectual kinship survives, as do the social problems that are the outgrowth of Enlightenment assumptions. The challenge is to obtain perspective on the Enlightenment vision of progress and freedom by thinking against the grain of liberal assumptions. Weighing liberal assumptions against the implications of temperamental and cultural forms of conservatism is an important first step. In effect, these forms of conservatism challenge liberal educational theorists to ground their theory and prescriptions in the life world. Yet there is still a fourth general category of conservatism that involves a long history of thinking against the grain of liberal assumptions. This tradition is known as philosophic conservatism, and it provides an alternative perspective for recognizing the assumptions of the liberal position. In a sense, it provides an alternative conceptual map that helps put in focus the assumptions that limit the discourse of liberal educational theorists.

Philosophic Conservatism

As Raymond English noted, commenting on what he viewed as only a symptom in American political thought, we have no identifiable political philosophy that goes under the banner of philosophical conservatism (p. 394). There have been thinkers—James Madison, Clinton Rossiter, Reinhold Niebuhr, and Peter Viereck, as well as others

—who have challenged liberal assumptions on intellectual grounds and who have laid out pieces of an alternative argument on the prospects of improving society. But the pieces do not represent a coherent statement, nor should they be viewed as a platform around which people with more strategic interests will rally. What is important about philosophical conservatism is an ability to think against the grain of current orthodoxies and, more importantly, to explore dialectically—without the intellectual safeguards of a teleological framework that guarantees the historical rightness of one position over the other—the tension between reason and experience, the individual and the community, tradition and social change, and human perfectability and frailty. Philosophic conservatism represents more of a reflective stance toward the commonwealth, as opposed to the more activist posture of the social reformer calling attention to social ills and organizing reform movements. Yet the more reflective stance of philosophic conservatism should not be interpreted as a form of retreatism into a mediative state of inaction. People deeply concerned with the problem of social reform and the crisis of modern society have given serious attention to the questions asked by the philosophic conservative. Some, like Robert Heilbroner, Michael Harrington, and Anthony Giddens, have had a long interest in the explanatory power of Marxism and a deep commitment to a form of democratic socialism. Others like Daniel Bell, John Carroll, and Hannah Arendt are less easily classified in terms of current political labels; but they share a common interest in clarifying the conceptual foundations of current political action. What is interesting about these thinkers is that they do not draw back from recognizing the importance of the questions that philosophic conservatives have asked since the time of Burke; in effect, they demonstrate that the concern for addressing issues of social justice is not compromised by recognizing the relevance of philosophic conservatism to the current debate. They also demonstrate a point this book is attempting to make—that the discourse of the liberal educational theorist must be broadened if we are to understand the nature of current social and educational problems.

Most philosophic conservatives understand society in terms of a root metaphor that is substantially different from those of liberal theorists. As Rossiter put it, "society is a living organism with roots deep in the past. . . . Society cannot be static. . . . A community cannot stand still; it must develop or decay" (1962, pp. 27–28). And as R. I. White observed, conservatism attempts to discover "the order which inheres in things rather than to impose an order upon them; to strengthen and perpetuate that order rather than to disperse things anew according to some formula which may be nothing more than a fashion; to legislate along the grain of human nature rather than against it" (quoted in Rossiter, p. 29). The root metaphor here is of an organism that must be understood in terms of its geneology, history, context, and unique characteristics—including its capacity to be renewed and evolve. An example of how this root metaphor can be used to underpin fundamental political and social reform can be seen in Gandhi's Satyagraha campaign in India and Nyerere's attempts to base reform in Tanzania on *ujamaa*. The following statement by Nyerere clearly reflects the power of the root metaphor that is so central to the thinking of philosophical conservatives. "We, in Africa," he wrote, "have no more need of being 'converted' to socialism than we have of being 'taught' democracy. Both are rooted in our past—in the traditional society that produced us" (quoted in Berger et al. 1974, p. 172). On the other hand, the use of this root metaphor to justify maintaining the status quo, which also occurs, fails to recognize that an organism (a society) continually evolves. The other problem associated with the misuse of the root metaphor is the failure to recognize that in putting in focus certain likenesses that increase our ability to understand, it also puts dissimilarities out of focus.

Nyerere's recognition of being "rooted" in the past and of having central traditions that must be taken into account is quite different from the technicist liberalism of Skinner where a culture is viewed "like the experimental space used in the analysis of behavior." The root metaphor here represents society as a machine made up of interdependent parts; improvement in the control mechanism is simply a matter of experimenting with the variables (parts). For the other liberal educational theorists, society is viewed as an arena within which a collection of individuals grow in their capacity to escape from embeddedness in tradition. In terms of this root metaphor, which puts out of focus the cultural traditions that provide the sense of conceptual order and meaning necessary to human experience, new ideas and technologies can be introduced willy-nilly into society as long as they are viewed as progressive. It does not matter that the ideas and technologies may be derived from another culture or that the innovations represent a form of experimentation with the basic fabric of the culture. The emphasis on change as inherently progressive and on individual empowerment, both of which are extrapolated from the liberal metaphor of society, lessens concern for the culturally disruptive effects of that change.

Another point that separates the philosophical conservative from liberal thinkers is the conservative's ability to think in a dialectical manner that does not assume the progressive nature of history. Merleau-Ponty, in *Adventures of the Dialectic*, describes this form of dialectical thinking as involving a "junction of a subject, of being, and of other subjects: between *those* opposites, in *that* reciprocal action, in *that* constellation, in *that* becoming, which not only becomes, but becomes for itself, there is room, without contradiction and without magic, for relationships with double meanings, for reversals, for opposite and inseparable truths, for sublations, for a perpetual genesis, for a plurality of levels or orders" (1973, pp. 203–4). Aside from removing the part of the liberal conceptual formula that automatically associates certain terms (individualism, resistance, consciousness-raising, and so forth) with progress, this form of dialectically thinking more easily recognizes the complexity of society and human experience. It also involves an awareness that abstract theory, which often represents elements of idealism as well as the more invisible expression of power, must be evaluated against the mixed record of human achievement. But in requiring a "reality check," it does not preclude the need to strive continually for social improvements.

This dialectical form of thinking is especially prominent in the way the philosophical conservative refuses to take a doctrinaire stand. For anybody who has bothered to read the writings of philosophical conservatives, it quickly becomes evident that they do not fit the conventional stereotype of the conservative who is both against individualism and social progress and for protecting the advantages of the privileged, maintaining the status quo, and assuming an unquestioning attitude toward tradition. Nor, as a group, do they take an identifiable position in support of capitalism. In suggesting that philosophical conservatives cannot be identified with a specific political platform, I do not intend to imply that they do not have clearly formed ideas on the nature and prospects of the commonwealth. Their strength is reflected in their ability to examine critically the ideals, assumptions, and programs that most of us have been conditioned to accept at face value; it is also reflected in their ability to ask questions and to sound a cautionary warning in a manner that seems to contradict the most basic ground rules of liberal discourse. It is these intellectual qualities, as well as the power of their insights, that led Heilbroner to urge that socialist theory could be strengthened by taking seriously the more radical thinking (in the sense of going to the root issues and questions) of the philosophical conservative (1972, pp. 5–6).

Merleau-Ponty's view of dialectical thinking as involving "relationships with double meanings, reversals . . . [and] a plurality of levels or orders" applies directly to the style of thinking of philosophical conservatives. Like Burke, they share a basic distrust of abstract theory; but when forced to state and defend their ideas, they fully explore reversals, different levels, and double meanings—even when this involves ideals that others are willing to take for granted. The brief overview of their views on human nature, rationalism, progress, and individualism will indicate the error of identifying them with the economic conservatives, the group most liberal educational theorists have in mind when they use the term "conservative." Such an overview will also put in focus areas of kinship between philosophic conservatives and those of a more temperamental and cultural persuasion.

On the question of human nature—which is crucial to how we view both the nature of freedom and the prospects for individual self-determination—some philosophical conservatives urge that the mixed record of human achievement be given careful consideration. Others like Russell Kirk, whom Rossiter referred to as a "man born one hundred and fifty years too late and in the wrong country," see in human beings an unregenerate element (original sin) that will, despite the best educational efforts, continue to manifest itself in selfish, irrational, and destructive behavior. Yet those who look to human history rather than to the Old Testament for guidance on this question arrive at a somewhat less pessimistic view of human nature. As Rossiter put it, "man . . . is a fabulous composite of some good and much evil, a blend of several ennobling excellencies and several more degrading imperfections" (p. 21). For liberals who view this as a shockingly pessimistic prognosis, the philosophical conservative can point to the educated men and women who maintained the Nazi death camps, to the gulags in Russia, and, closer to home, to the senseless violence of the street and the calculated acts of will and selfishness that occur in the gray offices of our bureaucracies and the opulent boardrooms of our corporations. If William Golding's *Lord of the Flies* is unconvincing that the philosophical conservative's view of human nature is more correct than the "essential goodness" doctrine of the liberal, then the reader might be directed to read Foucault's documentation of the new technologies of power used in schools and work places and by the policing functions of the state. The exercise of power, while often invisible to both the user and the victim, expresses not only social and technological norms, but also the deeper psychological forces that the philosophical conservative wants to be included in any inventory of human nature.

Their view of human nature, which holds that the person is capable of both rational and irrational acts, of selflessness and selfishness, and of a will to power that frees and nourishes and, at the other extreme, controls and detracts, has important implications for liberals who want to organize society in ways that maximize human freedom and self-direction. Reflecting on the philosophically conservative view of human nature, Heilbroner noted an important policy implication that must be considered by reformers who take for granted the limitless perfectability of man:

> In a word, the conservative sees that man, at the very center of his being, is "free" in the sense of being unpredictable and untameable; and that this freedom is not an attribute that is necessarily congenial to social order. It is thus a view of man once more hopeful and more skeptical than that of the radical—more hopeful in its denial that men can be totally programmed, more skeptical in its denial that this unexpungeable individuality is an attribute that unfailingly redounds to the higher purposes of society. (p. 11)

Unlike the liberal-radical or socialist view of endless perfectability, Heilbroner sees in the philosophical conservative position a check on the seemingly limitless power of the state to use the technologies of power, including the use in schools of political technologies created by experts, against the individual. As he identifies a key assumption upon which reform policy is grounded, it is important to let him put the argument in its most elegant form:

> If the "conservative" conception is correct in emphasizing elements or layers of the personality that cannot be managed—or that can be invaded only at the cost of destroying the person—then socialism must reconsider its utopian image of what man can be. This involves the painful admission that perfectability is not a process that can proceed indefinitely. More than that, it requires the admission that perfectability is a process that socialism does not want to press indefinitely. In the end a socialist society must reconcile itself to an indeterminate space within which men can express their wishes and drives, *whether or not these conform to the ideals and goals* of socialism itself. (p. 12)

In contrast to Heilbroner's concern about the limits of social reconstruction and management of the person in the name of perfecting human nature, Alexander Solzhenitsyn sounds a different warning.

The liberal-bourgeois view of human nature, according to Solzhenitsyn, assumes that human nature reaches its moral apogee through unlimited self-expression and acquisitiveness. When this view is translated into social policy, it engenders endless conflict as individuals and social groups attempt to expand their domain of influence and economic advantage at the expense of the less powerful. In contrast to the notion of endless expansion, which he traces back to a false understanding of human freedom, Solzhenitsyn urges a shift away from a view of human nature that stresses outward development towards one that takes seriously the inward, more spiritual dimension of existence. This would be expressed in terms of living a life that is characterized by self-limitation. As Solzhenitsyn put it, "Freedom is *self-restriction*. Restriction of the self for the sake of others" (Solzhenitsyn et al. 1974, p. 136).

Like many philosophical conservatives, Solzhenitsyn recognizes that religion provides the basis of the moral authority he sees missing in modern consciousness, and he urges that moral regeneration begin with the rediscovery of repentance at both the individual and national level. This term, which appears as a moral and intellectual anachronism to liberals who view human nature as essentially good and thus in no need of being repentant about anything, involves a complex set of attitudes essential to spiritual awakening—and, as Solzhenitsyn tirelessly warns, to global survival itself. Repentance is an ethical impulse of the individual that involves the acknowledgment that one's actions have wronged others, the desire to forgive and be forgiven for injuries done (to others and to the environment), and the recognition of the moral limits within which one must live. As Solzhenitsyn put it, "Repentance is only a clearing of the ground, the establishment of a clean basis for further moral actions—what in the life of the individual is called 'reform'" (p. 135). It is, in his view, a sensitivity toward life that makes it possible to live according to the principle of self-limitation.

Terms like repentance, sanctity, and self-limitation are easily associated with a long history of religious fanaticism grounded in ignorance, cruelty, and indifference to human rights. The temptation of the liberal is thus to dismiss these terms as reactionarism, unless, of course, they happened to be uttered by a Zen master or taken from the sayings of somebody like Black Elk, the Oglala Sioux holy man. Then such terms would likely be associated with the raising of ecological consciousness, the awakened mind, and a less materialistic form of liberalism. Aside from the interesting phenomenon of the liberal's willingness to accept religious insights from non-Western sources while rejecting the insights of his own religious traditions, a more important issue here must be put in focus if we are to understand clearly the difference between the philosophical conservative and liberal views of human nature. The ideas of repentance and self-limitation (or the awareness of "sanctity," another word seldom seen in the liberal lexicon) recognize that the individual is not the center of the universe and thus is not the absolute source of authority and meaning.

The philosophical conservative views the individual's nature as too complex to be categorized as inherently good (and thus capable of complete self-direction) or as infinitely malleable (and thus a variable to be considered as part of a social engineering process). This combination of a non-anthropocentric view of the universe and a view of human nature that recognizes both positive and negative elements leads the philosophical conservative to recommend a prescriptive form of education (e.g., that found in Adler's *The Paideia Proposal*) and to urge a spiritual awakening within the individual. In commenting on the "cardinal sin" of the liberal view of the individual, Abraham Heschel in *Who Is Man?* observed that "deprived of the ability to praise" and to sense the mystery of being "modern man seeks to be entertained." In contrast to the mind that knows no uncertainty or deeper sense of meaning, Heschel echoes Solzhenitsyn when he writes: "*I am commanded— therefore I am.* There is a built-in *sense of indebtedness in the consciousness of man*, an awareness of *owing gratitude*, of being called upon at certain moments to reciprocate, to answer, to live in a way which is compatible with the grandeur and mystery of living" (1965, p. 111). This is indeed fundamentally different from the secularizing discourse of the liberal educational theorists we have looked at. Whether the more religiously open discourse of the philosophical conservative provides an acceptable alternative to the anomic tendencies inherent in the liberal notion of enlightened self-interest (which is supposed to serve as the self-limiting moral gyroscope) is an issue that we shall address in later chapters.

The philosophic conservative's view of a mixed human nature, which can be substantiated more effectively by the recent historical record than by theological arguments, influences their views on the role and nature of education, government, and even progress. For example, the educational views of Robert Hutchins, Mortimer Adler, and Hannah Arendt reflect the philosophic conservative position that children, when left to educate themselves, will not naturally strengthen our more civilizing institutions and traditions. As Adler said, "The ultimate goal of the educational process is to help human beings become educated persons" (1982, p. 10). For him, being an educated person means, among other things, developing a disciplined mind—informed by the best of the intellectual and cultural achievements of our past and capable of exercising critical judgment within the discourses of adult life. Phrases such as "disciplined conversation," "improving the mind," "raise their minds to a state of understanding [and] appreciating more," are common in Adler's writing, and reflect the philosophical conservative view that individual empowerment is most effectively achieved through a process that systematically transmits and renews cultural traditions. As Arendt put it, "Exactly for the sake of what is new and revolutionary in every child, education must be conservative; it must preserve this newness and introduce it as a new thing into an old world, which however revolutionary its actions may be, is always, from the standpoint of the next generation, superannuated and close to destruction" (1963, pp. 192-93).

Beyond the area of education, which is seen as too important to be left to the initiative of the child, the philosophical conservative view of man as a "composite of some good and much evil" leads to the argument for a form of government characterized by checks and balances and by separation of powers. Human nature being as indeterminate as it is, people in positions of power and public trust must operate within set restrictions to insure that they do not subvert democratic institutions. Just as education leads to internalizing checks and balances at the symbolic level, the liberty of the individual in public office is circumscribed by the Constitution, the tradition of the law, and a diffusion of power within separate branches of government. In effect, freedom must be restrained in order to insure that it does not turn into a form of authoritarianism that threatens the accumulated freedoms built into our institutions and patterns of daily life. As one observer noted (Clecak 1977, pp. 118-19), the philosophical conservative is thinking of the relationship between freedom and government in dialectical terms. Similarly, Samuel Huntington has argued that the recent surge of populist demands for an enlargement of governmental activity has served to undermine the legitimacy of government authority. In effect, too much democracy (the unleasing of individual demands on government) began to cripple the ability of democratic institutions to represent the interests of the people (1975, p. 15).

The remark by Peter Clecak that philosophic conservatives view democratic socialism as "too democratic in theory, and insufficiently democratic in practice" brings us to another characteristic that sets them apart from liberal thinkers. Although conservatives value the rational process, especially ideas that have endured over time, they are deeply suspicious of abstract ideas and theory. They are even more set against any form of social experimentation based on a blueprint of a more ideal society. As Rossiter put it, again reflecting a dialectical way of thinking that recognizes "plurality of levels" rather than linear progress, "reason is one of man's most precious gifts" and "a useful tool in the realm of instrumentality." However, reason "must be handled with prudence and skepticism. It must be applied within the limits of history, facts, human nature as we know all these to be; it must be squared with the inherited wisdom of the community and the sound instincts of the virtuous man" (pp. 50-51). Michael Oakeshott identified a second major reason for the philosophical conservative's penchant for distrusting abstract theory as a guide to social action. Experience, for the philosophical conservative, has always been recognized as a source of knowledge and even wisdom. But according to Oakeshott, the two forms of knowledge that are part of every human activity—knowledge of technique and knowledge of practice—have been artificially separated by thinkers who were unable to recognize experience as a source of tacit, more implicit forms of knowledge. By separating technical knowledge (which can be made explicit and communicated as theory to others on the assumption that its context is superfluous) from practical knowledge (which cannot be made explicit and communicated to others), the former has been given a dominant position in our culture (1962, pp. 7–8). The part of knowledge that is learned in context over a period of time cannot be directly taught or learned, although it can be acquired from someone who practices it; thus, it becomes devalued. The result is that abstract knowledge, because it appears systematic, measurable, and cost effective, is adopted by well-intentioned people who then ignore the technical-practical knowledge that underpins the ability to solve problems, practice skills, and express creative impulses. In effect, abstract ideas and theory represent what Oakeshott called "half-knowledge"; without concern for the complementary form of knowledge rooted in experience, this half-knowledge, externally imposed, becomes a source of defective practice.

Philosophic conservatism's suspicion of abstract thought as a potential source of unchecked power is matched by its basic skepticism toward the idea of progress. The possibility of genuine reversals, which was recognized in Merleau-Ponty's understanding of a dialectical process, is taken seriously by philosophical conservatives. Their ambivalent view of human nature and their distrust of abstract ideas as a guide to social action prevent them from embracing the myth of history moving progressively. Added to the intellectual grounds for questioning the assumption that change is inherently progressive is the depressing abundance of evidence of recent years: the increased danger of nuclear war precipitated by the technological and political elites; the ravaging of the ecosystems by technologies and social systems (again involving the active complicity of our most highly educated classes); the growing power of the state to disrupt the self-sustaining patterns of community life and to extend its control through ever more elaborate surveillance networks; and the growing crisis of what constitutes the basis of authority in both the public and private sectors—to cite just a few of the more obvious examples. It is not a matter of the philosophical conservative being against progress (recall Rossiter's remark that a "Society cannot be static. Change is the rule of life."); rather, it is a matter of wanting to insure that change, in the Burkean sense, preserves what is worthwhile in society while improving on what has become deficient and outmoded. In short, the philosophical conservative takes the position that change, guided by a prudent form of common sense and a sensitivity to the fact that a living tradition cannot be restored once it is lost, is possible but not inevitable.

For the philosophical conservative, progress exists in a continual state of tension with the traditions that serve as the guiding patterns for everyday life. But unlike the liberal committed to escaping from embeddedness in the past, the philosophical conservative tends to give greater attention to the fact, noted by Shils, that "traditions are not independently self-reproductive or self-elaborating" and that "only living, knowing, deserving human beings can enact them and re-enact them." The basic difference between the two orientations was clearly expressed by Heilbroner. "The radical," he noted, "views life as an epic, a quest to be consummated in the future. The conservative views it as a process of re-enactment, of renewal, to be justified in the present" (pp. 12–13). According to the liberal, emancipation should be viewed as progressive and thus beyond skepticism. To emphasize the contrasts, Heilbroner elaborates the more complex stance of the philosophical conservative: "Liberate man? By all means! But liberate him from what? From all that is personal as well as all that is selfish? From all that is ancient as well as all that is archaic? From all that is ritual as well as all that is rote? From everything nonrational as well as everything that is mistaken? From all faith as well as all fetish?" (p. 13). As Heilbroner's questions suggest, the philosophical conservative is unable to segment life into discrete parts and then emphasize one part (i.e., individualism or progress) by putting out of focus what Giddons called the "time-space" dimensions of human embeddedness. It is the complexity of this embeddedness, both at a social and symbolic level, that the philosophical conservative wants to take into account when thinking about progress and emancipation. The attitude of the philosophical conservative was succinctly expressed by Oakeshott when he wrote that "the conservative is not inclined to think that nothing is happening unless great changes are afoot."

The last characteristic of philosophic conservatism we want to take up relates to its view of the individual, whose needs and interests are *always* viewed in relation to the community. The idea of a self-directing and economically competitive individual represents the classical liberal tradition of thought. Burke viewed the nature of the individual as "intricate"; but in viewing the needs and traditions of society as involving the "greatest complexity," he came out for the primacy of the latter.

Again the dialectical quality of conservative thought appears. Rossiter clearly demonstrated the philosophical conservative's interest in finding the balance—which cannot be represented as an abstract political formula, because circumstances are continually changing. Writing before the awareness of gender discrimination, Rossiter observed that:

> In the world as it is, the world in which men live, it is often necessary to make a hard choice between individual and community. In such instances the Conservative says, the interests of the community come first. This does not mean that every instance of friction will be resolved in favor of society, nor does it mean disrespect for the dignity of the man's person or the inviolability of his soul. It does mean that society, the individual's fellow men considered as a collective entity, must get first consideration in all difficult cases. If the community is visibly decayed or arbitrary, the margin of doubt swings to the individual. . . . If a man has needs that force him to submit to the community, he also has rights that the community must honor. (1962, p. 39)

The needs of individuals include the social structure and symbolic order essential to social and economic well-being and to the development of thought and self-awareness, as well as the legal, Constitutional, and historical traditions essential to protecting their "natural" rights.

Because philosophical conservatives view the relationship of the private and public realms as intertwined, they again argue for a sense of balance. They oppose the liberal view of society as a collection of atomistic individuals pursuing self-interest by calling for an accepted theory of political obligation. At the same time they express concern about the intrusion of the state, with its tendencies toward centralization of power and its wide array of political technologies, into the private sector. To protect the latter some philosophical conservatives have called for strengthening the patterns of political organization that nourish local, voluntary, and decentralized forms of association. Robert Nisbet, in writing on the need to check the political power of the state by a rediscovery of the social, quotes Dewey (he could have also cited Ivan Illich) on the importance of voluntary groups and associations:

> Individuals who are not bound together in associations whether domestic, economic, religious, political, artistic, or educational, are monstrosities. It is absurd to suppose that the ties which hold them together are merely external and do not react into mentality and character, producing the framework of personal disposition. (1975, p. 269)

Concluding Remarks

In the first chapter it was suggested that unless we are aware of the influence of language, it can do much of our thinking for us. It is now time to return to that part of the argument in order to put in perspective how the present chapter expands the boundaries of liberal discourse beyond rigid liberal-conservative distinctions and provides a basis for the formulation of a post-liberal theory of education. Language involves both vocabulary and epistemological categories that enable us to impose a conceptual organization upon the world. The interplay between vocabulary and episteme establishes, in a sense, a regime of truth—the ideas and values that determine the categories and outer boundaries of legitimate thought. At the same time it creates areas of silence—ideas and values that are viewed as not legitimate for responsible people to consider. The special vocabulary of liberal educational theorists ("methods of intelligence," "authentic being," "emancipation," "freedom," and so forth) represents such a regime of truth. As this vocabulary is viewed by liberal theorists as placing them on the side of truth and progress, it is difficult to question its real explanatory power, its class and cultural origins, or its functions as part of a strategy of power. A more reflective attitude toward such terms as "emancipation" and "authentic being" becomes, in a sense, an act of intellectual and moral betrayal. At this point liberal educational theorists are locked into a regime of truth dictated by their language that then exerts an even more controlling influence on their thought.

The examination of the different forms of conservatism was not meant as an invitation to change ideological allegiance. Rather it was to show, along with the analysis of our embeddedness in a social, linguistic, and cultural world, how much is ignored by the language frameworks of liberal educational theorists. It was also intended as a basis for reconceptualizing a liberal approach to education. To suggest that the conceptual foundations of a liberal theory of education can be strengthened by taking seriously the social, linguistic, and cultural influences on individual thought and identity is one thing; to suggest that if liberalism is to be taken seriously today it must develop a sensitivity to the nature of the various forms of conservatism is likely to cause shock and deep dismay. The argument that the nature of embeddedness makes the notion of the self-directing individual untenable is difficult to refute; or, as with the ideas of conservatives, should it simply be rejected as reactionary. As the immediate response of many readers who view themselves as dedicated liberals is likely to be less than friendly to my proposal, I would like to put in clearer focus some implications of conservatism that should be considered by educational theorists.

As conservatism can be understood both as an ideology and as a term that describes inescapable aspects of human existence, it does not really make a lot of sense to declare categorically that one is for or against conservatism. The taken for granted patterns of thought and behavior, as well as the conceptual conventions embedded in our language systems, make us all conservatives in both the temperamental and cultural sense of the term. For liberal educational theorists, conditioned (culturally) to think of themselves as autonomous individuals exercising rational thought about the educational strategies necessary for the equally complete emancipation of others, the suggestion that we all live lives that unconsciously reproduce the cultural patterns of the past will undoubtedly sound heretical. Following Heilbroner's lead, it is important to recognize that both temperamental and cultural conservatism represent limits to the process of emancipation. These forms of conservatism, which are as varied and complex as the range of cultures themselves, also challenge us to recognize that emancipation is exceedingly complex and not always progressive—unless, of course, one "thinks" within a conceptual framework that is teleological.

Conservative ideologies—that is, the set of ideas and values pertaining to the ordering of society—represent a different set of problems for educational theorists. Whereas temperamental and cultural expressions of conservatism are reproduced unconsciously by liberal educational theorists, even when their discourse represents the individual as in a continual process of self-transcendence, the ideological expressions of conservatism force us to recognize how language sets the boundaries within which we think. At the ideological level, educational theorists must confront the challenge of conservatism at a more conscious level; and this will involve confronting the intellectual and moral dilemmas that arise as we begin to take seriously the arguments of conservative thinkers. At this more conscious level of intellectual confrontation, conservatism is both troubling and stimulating. Here we are speaking only of philosophical expressions of conservatism, as economic conservatism is really a progressive and modernizing ideology (i.e., classical liberalism).

The two lines of argument within conservative thought that are the most troubling are that social classes are both inevitable and culturally necessary and that, because human nature is flawed, a healthy society requires the imposition of a shared moral code. Both lines of thought open a Pandora's box of disturbing possibilities; yet in spite of the potential abuses these ideas can be used to justify, they nevertheless confront liberal assumptions about equality and individual self-direction (two key pillars of liberal educational thought) with a serious challenge. Essentially, this is the argument of Ortega y Gasset that egalitarianism oppresses the "noble" and creative individuals who achieve their fullest potential through extraordinary effort and an inborn sense of responsibility. In contrast stands the common or "mass-man" who "accepts the stock of common places, prejudices, fag-ends of ideas or simply empty words which chance has piled up within his mind, and with a boldness only explicable by his ingenuousness, is prepared to impose them everywhere" (1957, p. 70). T. S. Eliot expressed the same concern about the need to differentiate responsibility according to a natural ordering of social classes when he wrote, "A democracy in which everybody had an equal responsibility in everything would be oppressive for the conscientious and licentious for the rest" (1962, p. 48).

The observations of both Ortega and Eliot about the existential divisions that separate those who view their lives as a quest for a deeper sense of meaning and self-development from those who are content to live on the surface (and thus ignore the challenge of exploring the depth either of the received cultural traditions or their own experience) cannot be ignored. On the other hand, the problem of excellence and existential responsibility cannot be resolved by accepting the conservative argument for the natural ordering of social classes—which too often reflects economic and political interests. Although an adequate solution has not been even conceived, the problem of balancing the need to nourish more conscientious and creative individuals while preserving the rights and opportunities of all citizens will remain a continuing challenge to educational theorists. While the more appealing moral vision is found in the liberal concern with achieving a more egalitarian society, the long tradition of populist hostility toward genuine cultural achievement (in the aesthetic sense of the term) insures the continual relevance of the conservative's concern.

The concern of the philosophical conservative about the nihilistic effects of reducing the shared moral code to a matter of subjective judgment puts an important social problem in focus, but leaves unanswered the question of how to achieve a socially integrating moral code that does not involve new forms of cultural domination. The view of the philosophic conservative that the moral code, excluding minor variations, is handed down from one generation to the next is supported by Emile Durkheim's arguments on the social origins and functions of morality. It also reflects the philosophical conservative's metaphor of society as an organism that evolves, with the shared moral code arising out of the collective experience of a people. If one reads Christina Hoff Sommer's (1984) account of the moral confusion and absurdity that arises in classrooms where students are encouraged to discover their own moral values, one can easily see the Achilles' heel of the liberal practice of locating moral authority within the individual. Individuals often agree on processes and techniques but not on the nature of the moral values that are to become the basis of community life. Critical reflection and the need to defend the authority of subjective judgment are continual threats to any attempt to impose a new set of moral standards. This difference in the view of the origin of a moral code—the philosophical conservative arguing that it is part of the prereflective experience of the people passed on as a part of living traditions (a form of tacit knowledge), the liberal taking the position that morality ought to be a matter of the reflective judgment of the individual—represents positions not easily reconciled. Again, the liberal's faith in the power of the individual has great appeal, but the philosophical conservative's position more accurately reflects how a culture reproduces itself in the conceptual and moral orientations of its individual members. The latter may also have a deeper understanding that the moral codes that strengthen the bonds of community are part of the tacit knowledge shared in everyday conversation, including the process of story-telling.

The problem for liberal educational theorists is to rethink whether the idea of individualism, in terms of the rational process and moral judgment, can be upheld in the face of the arguments that the individual is really a social-cultural being (i.e., that language unconsciously influences the patterns of thought and that the individual is a carrier of tacit cultural knowledge that is experienced as part of the natural attitude). If the atomistic individual is a myth, the problem of identifying the cultural sources of a moral code, as well as its basis of legitimation, must be faced by liberal educational theorists. Another problem is the widespread acceptance of the liberal position that moral values should be discovered and then imposed on people in order to lift them up to a higher plane of moral existence. To put it another way, if liberal educational theorists cannot identify and transmit the moral standards that are part of lived cultural traditions, they are then faced with either arbitrating between special interest groups who want their own view of morality taught in schools or adopting the nihilistic position that morality is a matter of subjective judgment (with the teacher acting as an agent of "values clarification").

Philosophical conservatives are concerned with other issues that cannot be ignored by liberal educational theorists. As these issues will be central to the reconceptualization of liberal theories of education, it will suffice to identify them in the briefest manner. The first issue relates to problems of integrating within the field of progressive emancipatory action a sensitivity toward conserving worthwhile traditions and preserving the natural environment (adopting a sense of stewardship—to use a conservative metaphor—in the name of the unborn generations to come). The second issue relates to recognizing the limits of abstract thought, with a corresponding recognition of the legitimacy and power of the tacit forms of knowledge that underpin everyday experience. In effect, the philosophical conservative urges the restoration of a dialectical tension between abstract reflection (expressed in theory and technical forms of critical analyses) and the common-sense knowledge that grows out of experience. The third issue put in focus by the philosophical conservative relates to the relationship of the individual to the community. Finding the proper balance is not, as the philosophical conservative would be quick to point out, reducible to a simple formula. It involves fundamental questions pertaining to the community's basis of authority, as well as to the rights and responsibilities of the individual. Again, it involves thinking dialectically, which involves a more complex discourse than liberal educational theorists are accustomed to.

Our task now is to utilize a de-centered view of individualism, as well as the insights of the various forms of conservatism, as a basis for reconceptualizing the four liberal educational theories discussed in chapter two. Paramount concerns will be to strengthen those elements of liberal educational theory that seem legitimate and defensible in view of conservative caveats and then to reformulate those that contribute to the nihilistic tendencies in modern society.

5

Reconsidering Liberal Theories of Education

Now that we have examined the nature of individual embeddedness and identified the many faces of conservatism, it is time to attempt a reformulation of the archetypes of educational liberalism. Our purpose will be to determine those elements of liberal theory that must be abandoned entirely because of conceptual errors and those that can be strengthened by taking account of the issues and perspectives introduced in the two previous chapters. In effect, we will be attempting to expand the discourse to include issues that must be considered if liberal educational theories are to remain creditable. But the attempt to revitalize liberal elements in educational thought by eliminating the categorical distinctions used in the past to separate liberalism from conservatism will leave us with a synthesis of ideas and values that may exceed the connotative capacity of both political labels. At this point in their history the traditional political metaphors may simply be too unyielding and too encumbered with the traditional baggage of stereotypes and restricted conceptual boundaries to encompass a more complex way of understanding. Thus the synthesis, if it can be achieved, may force us to recognize that we are moving into a period of thought that no longer correlates with the limited explanatory power of the old political labels. This new period of thought, which really involves a transition that retains important continuities, can be understood as a post-liberal era, if one does not make the mistake of assuming that this phrase implies sharp disjunctures between new and traditional elements rather than a synthesis of them (a point of view that fits Shils' argument that innovations are always interconnected with the threads of tradition). The image of a post-liberal theory of education simply suggests that over the last fifty years we have been moving toward a fundamental reconceptualization of the ideas of individualism, rational process, progress, tradition, and so forth, that have served as the conceptual foundations for maintaining the distinctness of political labels. The idea of a post-liberal era of thought thus represents a stage of development that has not yet produced a satisfactory political label that could carry the full weight of the new way of understanding, yet it represents a level of understanding that would be severely circumscribed by the use of the label of liberalism.

Rogers and Skinner

The educational ideas of Rogers and Skinner represent the romantic and technicist streams in liberal thought; although the two positions have little in common, they will be examined together as examples of educational theories that cannot be reformulated. Both adopt extreme positions—Rogers locates authority entirely within the self-directing individual, while Skinner views the environment as the source of agency in selecting and shaping behavior—with the result that their theories cannot really evolve further without overturning the basic assumptions upon which these theories rest. Nevertheless, it is important to identify the conceptual weaknesses of both theorists' ideas, as well as to explore the implications of using their ideas as the basis of education.

Although the romantic and technicist positions appear irreconcilable, they are likely to remain related in a strangely causal way. In effect, the continuing emphasis on reducing human relationships, including education, to the calculus of social engineering will make the extremism of Rogers' position an attractive alternative for those who want to rebel against the reductionism of the technicist position. Rogers' emphasis on the authority of individual judgment is equally extreme and is likely to drive reform-minded individuals to find in Skinner, and others who share his ideological orientation toward an engineering approach to improving the human condition, the technology that the romantic position lacks. With the spread of rationalism into more areas of individual and social life, the romantic vision of free and autonomous individuals will continue into the future as an alternative vision. Because of its simplicity, attempts to translate the romantic vision into a set of social practices for the real world, as in recent attempts to establish alternative schools, will periodically direct attention away from the efforts of the technicists to extend their systems of rational control.

The attractiveness of Rogers' position is its uncomplicated faith in the worth and agency of the individual. It is, in effect, a reaffirmation of the Enlightenment doctrine that we are both free and equal. Although the originators of this view wanted to locate the source of individual agency in the rational process, Rogers' position avoids the potential distinctions in rational ability. Free choice and inner feelings become equally important in Rogers' view, and thus cancel the privileged position the Enlightened philosophers granted to the rational capacity. As Rogers put it, "The free person moves voluntarily, freely, responsibly, to play her significant part in a world whose determined events move through her and through her spontaneous choice and will" (1983, p. 276). By locating authority entirely within the individual, and by recognizing everything from "spontaneous choice," intuition, authentic feelings, freedom as an "inner thing," and rational thought as a source of authority, Rogers must also adopt the other liberal assumptions: the essential goodness of human nature, the progressive nature of change, and the view that moral and intellectual relativism is essential to a healthy and open society. Arguments that individual thought is culturally influenced and that individuals enact living traditions that are not recognized because they are experienced as part of the taken-for-granted world would threaten Rogers' conceptual starting point: that growth is toward the condition of absolute autonomy of the individual.

Similarly, the concerns of the philosophic conservative—a mixed view of human nature, a skepticism about the progressive nature of change, a concern that emancipation be balanced by the preservation of worthwhile traditions and that political institutions be organized according to the principle of checks and balances, and a concern with the crisis of legitimacy and disintegration of the authority of the autonomous individual—cannot be taken seriously without bringing into question the authority of the autonomous individual. The lack of complexity that characterizes Rogers' conceptual starting point restricts the scope of discourse to a reiteration of liberal assumptions about the individual and social progress. These assumptions, in turn, lead to a view of the teacher as a facilitator and to using student interest as the basis for determining curricular content.

Because Rogers' position provides a positive vision of human possibilities that contrasts sharply with the unresponsiveness of bureaucracies and the life-threatening technologies that are part of the legacy of our scientific-technicist traditions, it is likely to attract a number of adherents. It is therefore important to see the implications of embracing Rogers' approach to education uncritically. Although Rogers suggests that the role of the teacher is to make available learning resources that expand individual and group awareness, his real concern is with utilizing the freedom and authority of the individual learner as the basis of the educational process. As the argument that I want to develop is that

Rogers' approach to education contributes to an anomic form of individualism that, in turn, allows the state to expand what Foucault called its "pastoral" power, it is important to have Rogers restate his own position: "To free curiosity, to permit individuals to go charging off in new directions dictated by their own interests; to unleash the sense of inquiry; to open everything to questioning and exploration; to recognize that everything is in process of change—here is an experience I can never forget" (p. 120). Rogers' view of a completely relativistic world (everything changes except for the values of individual freedom and critical inquiry—both powerful contributors to relativizing all forms of authority) represents the particular form of individual that Foucault (1982) saw as essential to the expanding power of the pastoral state. Individuals may think of themselves as free and self-directing but be conceptually unable to resist subjugation to the political technologies the state uses to extend its control over social institutions and processes within which the individual must be integrated (p. 215). By making free choice and critical inquiry the basis of authority, which in turn is relativized by the freedom and critical judgment of other individuals, the individual ceases to be a source of authority that can challenge the state's ability to impose a purposive, administrative mode of thought as the basis of moral and intellectual authority. Foucault noted that pastoral power not only commands, but also looks after the well-being of the society and, in turn, the life of the individual. The pastoral function of the state is enhanced through the development of technologies that allow the state to monitor the activities and thoughts of individual members; this knowledge, in turn, is essential for guiding the individual. The pastoral function of the state is threatened by cohesive communities and cultural groups who have not succumbed to the nihilism of modernization (i.e., the relativization of norms and values). In knowing the basis of their authority—which may be tradition, communal norms, sacred books, and so forth—individuals are able to contest the state's claims to being the arbitrator of authority. Similarly, individuals who possess a knowledge of the traditions of their culture are more able to exercise communicative competence in holding others (including the state) accountable for the accurate representation of the past and in negotiating the basis of authority for introducing changes into the culture.

This brings us to the crux of the problem; namely, whether Rogers' approach to education would provide the conceptual foundations for recognizing authoritative norms shared by the community, as well as for making informed individual judgments. Rogers' view of the temporality of the individual puts in focus both the present and the future, which is also understood in terms of subjective interests. But the past seems to have no significance, either as a repository of a collective memory or as the basis for gaining an informed perspective on the present. By reinforcing the myth that individuals are free and self-directing, Rogers fails to recognize both the influence of language on thought and the social and traditional forms of embeddedness of the individual. In effect, his position promotes a rootless form of individuality, one that is continually in search of more fulfilling and unique experiences. This is a basic characteristic of anomie, as the emphasis on the relativism of all experiences, values, and ideas is also characteristic of nihilism. The irony of Rogers' position is that, in emphasizing the primacy of individual autonomy, the conceptual and cultural foundations that might serve as the basis of individual authority are undermined.

Skinner's translation of liberal principles into an educational theory is equally flawed, but for different reasons. Like Rogers, Skinner bases his theory on a simplistic view of the nature of the individual; the result is that his theory cannot be reconceptualized to take account of culture, language, tradition, or any of the issues raised by the philosophic conservatives without overturning the basis of his paradigm. This observation is not intended to negate Skinner's contribution to understanding that the individual must always be viewed as situated in an environment and that this environment involves positive and negative reinforcements that do, in fact, influence behavior. Skinner, however, takes the more extreme position that behavior is not just influenced but "shaped and maintained" by the environment (contingencies of reinforcement). Thus he reduces the individual to a genetic susceptibility to reinforcement, a view not unlike Thomas Hobbes' view of the individual as driven by the pleasure-pain nexus. By reducing values ("good things are positive reinforcers") and thought ("it is always the environment which builds behavior") to contingencies of reinforcement, Skinner leaves no room for rational thought and individual responsibility, much less the more complex view of the individual as a member of a language community and a sustainer of tradition.

Yet for all his denials of the efficacy of the rational process and his attempt to empty the individual of cultural influence, Skinner himself is heavily influenced by liberal assumptions: change is progressive; theory should be combined with the experimentalism of science and used to guide social change; techniques that provide efficient and rational control should supplant traditional forms of knowledge; authority for social planning should be located in an elite class of "cultural designers"; culture can be improved only through experimentation. Although his behaviorist orientation leads him to rework these liberal assumptions into an anti-democratic view of society, he succeeds in establishing himself as a leading spokesperson for the technicist stream of liberalism. Similarly, he replaces the liberal view of education as a form of individual empowerment with the view that education is the rational ordering of contingencies of reinforcement for the purpose of developing skills and predictable behaviors. Education thus becomes part of manpower planning for the technicist society: the result is that as behaviorism and systems thinking become unified into a theory of social action, decision-making must become increasingly centralized and abstracted from the life world of the individual.

In effect, Skinner reworks part of the liberal tradition into a technicist ideology where the individual is understood only in terms of an object of technological manipulation—justified, of course, in terms of humanistic and pastoral values. Aside from the irony of attempting to bring social and individual life under rational control in order to compensate for the individual's inability to exercise rational thought, Skinner leaves us with a view of education (and the human condition) that cannot be reconstructed by taking account of cultural and linguistic embeddedness or the issues raised by the philosophical conservative. His views reinforce technological nihilism and provide a rationale for centralizing power and authority within the state. What his theory succeeds in demonstrating, among other things, is that when certain liberal principles are carried to an extreme they can result in a non-liberal society, and that the more humane aspects of liberal society are nourished by a sensitivity to the concerns of philosophical conservatives. To put it another way, Skinner's theory demonstrates the dangers of a limited discourse, one that does not provide a conceptual basis for questioning the limits of progress, the rational experimentation for purposes of social engineering, the implications of not taking human nature into account in the development and use of powerful technologies, the need for checks and balances, and the implications of substituting reinforcement schedules for a shared moral code. More than anything, the sobering political implications of Skinner's theory strengthens the main argument of this book for a dialogue that takes account of liberal and conservative concerns.

Reconceptualizing Dewey's Educational Ideas

Dewey's *Liberalism and Social Action* represented an attempt to reformulate the conceptual foundations of liberalism and in many ways anticipated the theoretical developments that are pushing us into a post-liberal period of thought. Although many of Dewey's ideas were ahead of his time, he continued to incorporate into his theory liberal assumptions that have been called into question by recent social developments and by the deepening ecological crisis. Our task here is to identify the elements of his educational and social theory that can be used to conceptualize an approach to education that no longer takes for granted the idea of the autonomous individual, a belief in the socially ameliorative effects of competition and the pursuit of self-interest, and the assumption that the cultural crises that characterize the discovery of new scientific and technological knowledge can always be contained by our present level of political skill and understanding. In effect, our task is learning from Dewey how to think in the post-liberal era we are now entering; but as he himself did not fully grasp the transition we are undergoing, we can use other aspects of his thought to illuminate how our conceptual metaphors lead us to interpret the present in terms of past mythologies.

Dewey was breaking with the liberal discourse of atomistic individualism when he wrote in 1899 that the "end in view is the development of a spirit of social cooperation and community life" (1956, p. 16). In *Democracy and Education* (1916) he argued that personal independence is an "illusion." By 1935, when he wrote *Liberalism and Social Action*, Dewey was restating a familiar theme in his writings: that the old liberal "ideas of liberty, of individuality and of freed intelligence" have to be radically reconceptualized. "Liberalism," as he put it, "has to assume the responsibility for making it clear that intelligence is a social asset and is clothed with a function as public as is its origin, in the concrete, in social cooperation" (p. 67).

The basis for what Dewey saw as a radical break with the assumptions of classical liberalism was his understanding of the social nature of intelligence, which he wanted to base on the scientific method of problem-solving. The testing of ideas and values under conditions of experimental inquiry required the widest possible communication among members of society to insure the deepest understanding of the problematic situation, the goals to be attained, and the progressive refinement of the ideas to be acted upon. Dewey, in effect, anticipated the current understanding of the socially shaping and sustaining nature of communication. But unlike the sociology of knowledge of Berger and Luckmann, which centers communication as the medium that sustains the shared definitions of social reality, Dewey emphasized the efficacy of communication to the method of intelligence. This, in turn, led him to stress that "democracy is more than a form of government, it is primarily a mode of associated living, of conjoint communicated experience" (1916, p. 101).

By stressing the importance of communication to a more democratic form of problem solving, Dewey substituted the ideas of social cooperation and social intelligence for the more traditional liberal view of society being enhanced by the individual pursuit of self-interest. His position also challenged the liberal idea that the reflective individual is the ultimate source of rational and moral authority. Education was to provide a social setting for learning how to cooperate and share experiences that related to collective problem solving—in a word, to foster "interdependence." The discourse that Dewey used, and envisioned as the basis of a reconstructed liberalism, emphasized the social dimension of such terms as individualism, intelligence, growth, and democracy. By locating authority in experimental inquiry as a form of cooperative effort, Dewey overcame the old liberal dichotomy that separated the individual from the community. In Dewey's view, individuals realize their capacities more fully as they join with others in the renewal of community life.

Yet it was in his understanding of the nature of community renewal, both in terms of its scope and one best method, that we find Dewey being controlled by assumptions of the liberal discourse he attempted to escape. Although he clearly grasped the formative influence of the environment on the plasticity of the individual, Dewey proceeded to formulate a view of the rational process that provided, in his view, the only form of authority allowable in a world of changing relationships. For Dewey, "the test of ideas, of thinking generally, is found in the consequences of the acts to which the ideas lead, that is in the arrangements of things which are brought into existence" (1960, p. 136). Dewey argued tirelessly that thinking is a directed activity ("knowing marks the conversion of undirected change into changes directed toward an intended conclusion"), but his view of human agency failed to take into account the influence of culture on thought and behavior. As one aspect of culture, language provides the conceptual framework (the categories, assumptions, and epistemic filters that influence what will be attended to and ignored) within which thought occurs. As pointed out earlier, language can be understood as directing thought, even the experimental model of thinking that Dewey equated with progress and enlightenment. This inability to recognize the conceptual filters inherent in the epistemic traditions of a language community prevented Dewey from recognizing how he had incorporated into his own theory the cultural and ideological assumptions of his times: the progressive nature of change, the efficacy of rational thought to control and direct human affairs, the ameliorative effects of the scientific method, and the ability of society to incorporate an accelerating rate of change.

A second limitation with Dewey's thought relates to his failure to recognize that tacit forms of knowledge can be a positive form of authority in people's lives. Dewey's theory of habit can be viewed as an attempt on his part to take account of the unconscious learning that enables us to perform in culturally prescribed ways with effectiveness and predictability. Although Dewey recognized habits as an indispensable "form of executive skills, of efficiency in doing," he made an important distinction between types of habits in order to retain the primacy of explicit-experimental forms of knowledge. "Habit as habituation," as he put it, "is indeed something relatively passive" (1916, p. 57). Habits can also be understood as dispositions, including an intellectual disposition. In the end, Dewey uses the presence of rational thought as the basis for distinguishing between good and bad habits. Routine habits ("bad") are "unthinking habits," whereas in the other variety "the intellectual element in a habit fixes the relation of the habit to varied and elastic use, and hence to continued growth" (pp. 58-59). Although his understanding of habit has merit, he lacks an adequate grasp of the nature of tacit-implicit forms of cultural knowledge and their importance to the authority of cultural practices and beliefs in people's lives. By not recognizing how tacit-implicit knowledge is, to put it in Mary Douglas's words, "the necessary foundation of social intercourse," Dewey's position ends up making community contingent upon the outcome of a higher politicized process that combines democratic decision making with an experimental approach to establishing the relative authority of ideas and values.

As the distinction between Dewey's view of knowledge and the tacit-implicit forms that characterize how much of culture is learned is particularly pertinent to understanding the *limits* of basing the life of community entirely on explicit and politically negotiable understandings, it is important to quote Mary Douglas at length:

> By a less extreme process of relegation, some information is treated as self-evident. The logical steps by which other knowledge has to be justified are not required. This kind of information, never being made explicit, furnishes the stable background on which more coherent meanings are based. It is referred to obliquely as a set of known truths about the earth, the weight and powers of objects, the physiology of humans, and so on. This is a completely different pigeonhole of oblivion from the first. Whereas the former knowledge is destroyed by being labelled untrue, the latter is regarded as too true to warrant discussion. It provides the necessary unexamined assumptions upon which ordinary discourse takes place. Its stability is an illusion, for a large part of discourse is dedicated to creating, revising and obliquely affirming this

implicit background, without ever directing explicit attention upon it. When the background of assumptions upholds what is verbally explicit, meanings come across loud and clear. Through these implicit channels of meaning, human society itself is achieved, clarity and speed of clue-reading ensured. In the elusive exchange between explicit and implicit meanings a perceived-to-be-regular universe establishes itself precariously, shifts, topples and sets itself up again. (1975, pp. 3–4)

This interplay between explicit and implicit forms of understanding, which occurs in all areas of human activity—from the use of language in an argument to telling a joke or eating a meal—raises two issues in relation to Dewey's position.

The first has to do with Dewey's assumption (part of the "background of assumptions" necessary to the cogency of Dewey's theory) that knowledge must be viewed as instrumental and capable of rational reformulation in experimental situations. Partly because Dewey's theory does not take account of the "natural attitude" that characterizes how most of everyday life is experienced, he is faced with dividing experience into two categories: passive habituations, and the use of intelligence to reconstruct experience in order to organize human affairs rationally. Given his conceptual categories, including the cultural biases he unconsciously acquired as a Western philosopher, it is understandable why he is unable to abandon the idea that "experimental inquiry" should be applied to all areas of experience. Had Dewey understood the way in which the natural attitude "hides" the background knowledge that provides a stable frame of reference for reconceptualizing specific aspects of our thought and experience, he might have been able to acknowledge that intelligence, as a form of consciously directed activity, is always limited and never entirely free from the implicit assumptions of the culture. This, in turn, would have led to a more qualified, less ontological view of the role of experimental inquiry. Without recognizing the limits of the method of intelligence, Dewey's position creates a heavy burden of guilt for the conscientious who are never able to fully live up to the moral requirements of his philosophy; for others with a more common-sense understanding of how the natural attitude is embedded with implicit understandings, Dewey's ideas are likely to be rejected as unrealistic.

The second problem with Dewey's position relates to an issue raised earlier, namely, whether politicizing the authority of the rules and assumptions that bind individuals together into a moral community leads to the relativization of its foundations and eventually to its transformation into a society of individuals easily governed by the state

(Bowers 1986). This is an especially complex issue that is only now beginning to be recognized by thinkers concerned with the increasing power of the state to control the foundations of intellectual and moral authority. Consequently we shall only be able to touch on part of the problem by raising several questions about whether Dewey's view of the method of intelligence takes account of the effects of the politicizing process on the cohesiveness and authority of community life. Part of the appeal of Dewey's position is that he sees active participation in decision making as central to the existence of community. In effect, he recovers the idea of speech as a human characteristic that binds women and men together as a community and argues that the power of speech (and thought) provides for the possibility of a politics based on negotiation rather than violence and force. This model of politics, which is derived from the early Greek experience of the *polis*, is altered by certain aspects of Dewey's ideas and given a burden of responsibility that may exceed the capacity of the political process itself.

Briefly stated, the *polis* characteristic of the early Greek city-state involved a limited number of members drawn from a specific social class. Their freedom to participate in the political space of the *polis* was based on a distinction between the public realm and the household; it also involved a political economy that made possible leisure time for speech among peers on matters pertaining to a highly circumscribed public realm. In effect, the social-cultural system provided a stable background for a political process that operated within highly restricted boundaries. Dewey's idea of a community that contributes to the efficacy of the experimental method of problem solving through active communication has no limits on what can be viewed as problematic and thus as a political issue. All of the cultural foundations of the community are open to reconstruction according to the canons of experimental inquiry. This expectation, in effect, assumes that the observation of the consequences of directed action (even when the guiding method of intelligence has the broadest social basis) will lead to a new consensus on what constitutes the authority for action and belief. The issue here is whether the authority that serves as the basis of legitimation can be established directly through the political process, as Dewey assumed. This question is not intended to imply that the relativizing and redefining of "what is," which are essential aspects of the political process, do not at some future time lead to new forms of authority that are then experienced as part of the natural attitude toward everyday life. Rather, it pertains to the assumption about the creative and restorative powers of the political process itself, particularly in relation to the tacit characteristics of cultural knowledge that Douglas identified.

A second question about Dewey's view of the unlimited political community has to do with his assumption about the power of scientific evidence (the consequences that follow the testing of ideas and values) to establish a new consensus. As Alfonso Damico observed, Dewey's attempt to fuse experimental inquiry and a democratic form of politics is based on the assumption that objective evidence will lead intelligent people to change their beliefs (1978, p. 62). What Dewey never quite grasped is that there are profoundly divergent belief systems in the world—not all of which can be viewed as reactionary and inferior to the form of knowledge he associated with the scientific method. Dewey recognized the more obvious fact of political life, namely that not everybody would automatically participate in the collective reconstruction of experience: "The problem under discussion is precisely *how* conflicting claims are to be settled in the interest of the widest possible contribution to the interests of all—or at least the majority. The method of democracy," he continued, "—insofar as it is that or organized intelligence—is to bring these conflicts out into the open where their special claims can be seen and appraised, where they can be discussed and judged in light of more inclusive interests than are represented by either of them separately" (1963, p. 79). When communication and the power of objective evidence fail to produce the necessary consensus, particularly when the majority of society has "entered upon the path of social experimentation," Dewey is willing to accept, though with great reluctance, the possibility that "force may be *intelligently* employed to subdue and disarm the recalcitrant minority" (italics added) (p. 87). What is beyond challenge for Dewey is the authority of his mode of inquiry—even though that mode of inquiry is grounded in the authority of an ever-shifting consensus and the limited warrant of the inquiry process. This inability to recognize that his own ideological framework could legitimately be challenged by people who grounded their own belief systems in a less relativistic form of authority also led Dewey to ignore both the complexity of human nature and the possibility that the technologies made available through scientific advances might be used to "reconstruct" the ideas and values of those who dissent from the social consensus. Human nature is essentially good in Dewey's view, and he saw no need to build a system of checks and balances into a democratic society—particularly when they might circumscribe the unlimited political community he envisaged.

The last aspect of Dewey's liberalism that needs to be reconceptualized relates to his understanding of tradition, which he reduced to the question of how to use history instrumentally for the purpose of understanding present problems. Although he understood experience in terms of continuities and interactions, the emphasis Dewey placed on the method of intelligence led him to a sense of temporality in which the present and future become dominant. He believed that unless the past could meet the instrumental criterion of useful knowledge, there was a danger that it would become a competing source of authority in people's lives and thus become a substitute for the method of intelligence. If a knowledge of the past does not help to illuminate the problematic aspects of current social life, Dewey was prepared to close the door on what he saw as idle and unproductive curiosity: "The past is the past, and the dead may be safely left to bury its dead" (p. 150).

Tradition, as Shils describes it, is not the same as Dewey's understanding of history: "Tradition is whatever is persistent or recurrent through transmission, regardless of the substance and institutional setting" (1968, p. 150). Phenomenologically, tradition is experienced as a vital, taken-for-granted aspect of experience. It has authority in people's lives, in the sense of Arendt's distinction between an internalized form of authority and the external and coercive character of authoritarianism. In terms of Dewey's reductionist view of tradition, individuals are to make a critical judgment about relevance, use historical knowledge as part of the problem-solving process, and use the method of intelligence to give direction to social experience. In effect, the use of intelligence enables individuals to escape from their own historical embeddedness. This is where Dewey's own thinking reflects an embeddedness in traditional liberal assumptions. The basic problem, as pointed out earlier, is that Dewey failed to recognize forms of cultural knowledge that did not fit his scientific model of knowledge as explicit and instrumentally intentional. The oversight was partly due to his inability to take account of the natural attitude toward the tacit understandings of cultural traditions. It could also be argued that Dewey's totalizing view of the method of intelligence as the only legitimate source of authority led him to ignore other forms of cultural authority, such as the reenactment of traditions and so forth.

One of the consequences of Dewey's misunderstanding of the nature of tradition is an approach to education that gives students an erroneous understanding of their own temporality. Dewey's view of education as growth in the democratic use of experimental inquiry not only assumes a degree of rational autonomy from the conceptual controls of culture that is questionable, but it also reinforces the sense of "living forward." The present is important because it is the context that must be understood if ideas, as plans of action, are to be adequately formulated; but it is the future that has real significance. The importance of assessing consequences means that the ideas and values (relative as they are) upon which the reconstructed experiences are to be based give the future a special status, since it becomes the dimension of temporality within which success and growth are determined. This emphasis on growth (which involves the dialectic of inquiry and action) tends to deemphasize the continuity of cultural patterns—that is, the persistence of the past in the present. Dewey's stress on reconstructing experience causes students to misread their powers of rational self-direction, as well as the degree their lives represent the "end-state of a sequence of transmissions and modifications" that connects them to the cultural achievements of the past.

Two implications of Dewey's position have particular significance for education. The first relates to how Dewey's view of knowledge, which is always instrumentally oriented toward directing the process of growth, is likely to desensitize students from being able to recognize the problematic aspects of tradition toward which they have a natural attitude of taken-for-grantedness. Dewey makes the uncertainty surrounding the problematic situation the starting point of the inquiry process; thus, what is taken for granted, the assumptions "regarded as too true to warrant discussion" to quote Douglas, is not likely to receive attention in Dewey's approach to education until some future point in time—when the consequences may be simply too overwhelming to do anything about them. To put it another way, education that involves cultural literacy—the ability to read or decode the assumptions which underlie the patterns of thought, social practices, institutions, and so forth of the culture—will not occur until after some aspect of the taken-for-granted culture confronts us as problematic. The massive evidence that certain aspects of our belief system are ecologically damaging and morally corrupt should lead, it could be argued, to a careful examination of the basic beliefs we take for granted (the epistemic patterns) in order to understand the control they exert on our thought and social existence, their relation to problems we are aware of, and their historical origins. This approach recognizes the importance of the future, but puts greater emphasis on understanding how the present is unconsciously influenced by the past (Bowers 1974).

The second implication of Dewey's emphasis on education as growth in the reconstruction of experience raises the issue of whether there is a place in the political process (which Dewey saw as synonymous with education) for conserving worthwhile traditions. Dewey would be the first to admit that the reconstruction of social experience involves a synthesis of the new and the traditional, but his stress on the instrumental value of traditions and on the need to test ideas in experimental situations easily leads to a view of politics as negotiating only new arrangements. Since Dewey's time, we have come more under the influence of certain aspects of the ideas he was promoting—though not in the democratic configuration he intended. Driven by scientific discovery and technological achievement, change has itself become a new form of authority in our lives. In deauthorizing beliefs and values that serve as a source of resistance, politics has increasingly come under the influence of the instrumentalism of technology. The result has been an emphasis on the politics of change. By promoting the experimental mode of thinking in the classroom, the idea that everything is in a process of change, and the authority of objective evidence, a Deweyian approach to education is likely to reinforce a mind-set in students that can be more easily exploited by experts and others who use scientific evidence and technological mastery to advance special interests. Dewey's advocacy of teaching the skills necessary for a participatory form of democracy is not likely to become the dominant concern of education when the political process is manipulated by technical experts who can claim to be operating within the scientific tradition Dewey himself championed. Given the emphasis on using politics to engineer changes, the educational challenge is to provide students with a conceptual basis for understanding what aspects of culture and the natural environment must be conserved. Knowledge of the traditions that are a source of meaning, humane social relationships, and material and spiritual well-being, is not acquired through Dewey's problem-solving approach to education. Learning about the formative traditions of the culture should not be divorced from the student's phenomenological world; but it involves a more systematic approach. At times the student may not always be aware of the instrumental significance of what is being learned. Arendt clearly put in focus an aspect of learning essential to reflective participation in the political process when she made a distinction between teaching students what the world is like and instructing them in the art of living (including Dewey's art of how to think). "Since the world is old," she writes, "always older than the [students], learning inevitably turns toward the past, no matter how much living will spend itself in the present" (1961, p. 195). A knowledge of the past is thus essential if the political process is to involve renewing a shared world, as opposed to engineering the material and symbolic aspects of our cultural traditions to fit the requirements of technological innovations. Ironically, the traditional liberal form of education, as Mortimer Adler argued, is more likely to contribute to Dewey's vision of a democratic polity than the problem-solving approach that Dewey advocated.

Reconceptualizing the Ideas of Freire

Like Dewey, Freire's ideas are too complex to be uncritically accepted or arbitrarily dismissed. But unlike Dewey, whose work is sufficiently distant from us to allow a more measured appraisal, Freire utilizes a highly charged metaphorical language that gives his writings a charismatic quality. His distinction between liberation and domination, conscientization and a banking approach to education, clearly separates the forces of good from the forces of evil. In Third World countries where the fact of oppression and exploitation is not debatable, Freire's ideas represent unequivocal demands for liberation. Even in this country his ideas are viewed by reform-minded educators as working guidelines for revolutionary action. As one educational theorist put it, Freire "is not only a man of the present, but also a man of the future" (Freire 1985, p. xxv). Given the near cult status accorded to him by some of his followers, it is important to inform the reader that the following is not meant to diminish his genuine achievements in formulating the rationale and strategy for a powerful pedagogy. Our task is to identify those elements of his theory that seem compatible with the more dialectical view of the rational process and individualism that characterizes post-liberal thinking. Efforts will also be made to point out those aspects of his thought that are based on cultural assumptions that are both environmentally and socially problematic and indefensible in terms of what we now understand about the individual as a social-cultural being. A more critical understanding of Freire's ideas, it can be argued, will help to insure that his ideas are given serious attention beyond the time when his metaphors lose their power to unify and motivate.

Before sorting out the strengths and weaknesses in Freire's position, it is important to make a distinction between his pedagogy and his philosophical anthropology (i.e., the assumptions about the nature of man that he raises to the level of an ontology). This distinction is being suggested with the full awareness that the justification of his pedagogy is based on his assumptions about the interrelationship of consciousness, language, and freedom—key elements of a philosophical anthropology that are formulated in a highly problematic manner. Freire's pedagogy, which involves documenting the taken-for-granted aspects of the subject's life world (limit situations) for the purpose of reflecting critically on the possibilities of new forms of actions, is a powerful and appropriate educational strategy for raising the level of consciousness of people to the extent that they take responsibility for the social conditions of their existence. Such a pedagogy should be used with adult groups within this society and is appropriate within certain contexts of public education (Shor, 1980). It should also be used both as a basis for literacy programs and more generally as a strategy for politicizing oppressed groups in non-Western countries. But as I pointed out elsewhere (1983), Freire's pedagogy is based on Western assumptions about man, freedom, progress, and the authority of the rational process. As the use of his pedagogy contributes to a modernizing and Westernizing way of thinking, the question of cultural invasion needs to be considered, especially in non-Western cultures that still have substantive traditions. If one recognizes that, contrary to Freire's argument, there is more than one form of pedagogy that empowers, it then becomes a matter of determining which pedagogy is most appropriate to the context. Thus the question of Freire's pedagogy cannot be decided in the abstract.

What does need to be discussed here, however, is the adequacy of Freire's philosophical anthropology—an existential view of man he represents as culturally invariant. In sorting out the elements of Freire's thought that should be retained as part of a post-liberal theory of education from those that should either be reformulated or abandoned entirely, we must keep in mind the time-space relationships of the discussion. In effect, this assessment of Freire's ideas must be understood within the context of a modern Western society that threatens to destroy the ecological system upon which it depends and is faced with an equally disturbing crisis in its moral and conceptual foundations. Freire's philosophical anthropology might be assessed quite differently within the context of Chinese, Indian, or Islamic culture.

Freire's basic assumptions about the human situation have much in common with Dewey's position; consequently, an analysis of Freire's ideas will touch on similar themes. Yet there are important differences between them. For now we shall focus on those aspects of Freire's position that seem essentially sound and consistent with the revival of social responsibility. Like Dewey, Freire views human life as submerged in an historical process, with nothing fixed except for the capacity of critical reflection. The danger, as both thinkers viewed it, was to accept passively the received conditions of social existence. As unthinking acceptance represents a state of alienation from essential human capacities, it must be overcome by raising consciousness to critical awareness of the individual's power to reflect and thus change the conditions of his own existence as well as the social conditions that are the source of his dehumanization. For Dewey the scientific method served as the basis of human authority; in terms of Freire's theory, critical reflection becomes the legitimate basis of human action. Although it will be necessary to return later to a more careful analysis of Freire's understanding of the role critical reflection is to play in creating history, for now it is sufficient to emphasize the importance of his idea of empowerment. This idea is, of course, not original with Freire. But in this increasingly technicist and dehumanizing era, it is important to have a powerful reaffirmation that people can have commitments, take responsibility for the world they live in, and use critical reflection to change restrictive social conditions. It is also important to recognize that the idea of empowerment might be interpreted more in terms of the social group than it ordinarily would be in the West. In any case, Freire provides an eloquent defense of the view that critical awareness is a "transforming act."

Another aspect of Freire's thinking that seems especially pertinent to countering the excessive pursuit of individual self-interest that characterizes modern society is the connection he makes between dialogue and community. His view of dialogue reflects his understanding of the world as a process of transformation. Individuals stand in an open relationship to this world where speech and thought involve reciprocity with others who are equally open to participating in the transformative process. As Freire put it, "If it is in speaking their word that men, by naming the world, transform it, dialogue imposes itself as the way by which men achieve significance as men. Dialogue is thus an existential necessity" (1971, p. 77). The qualities that must be present when dialogue occurs—mutuality, confirmation of the other, openness, trust, critical thinking—provide a vital sense of community free of coercion. The participants are indeed bonded together in a transforming experience that retains a sense of wholeness and deep trust.

Empowerment of the individual and dialogue are highly desirable values upon which to base an educational theory; unfortunately, Freire tends to enshrine them within a theoretical framework that has the effect of putting them beyond critical assessment. They become, in effect, synonymous with truth, progress, and the just society. Although empowerment and dialogue are important values, they must be qualified if we are to take them seriously. In Freire's thinking, critical reflection is both the source of empowerment (authority) and the expression of one's essential human nature. To quote Freire, "One of the important points in conscientization is to provoke recognition of the world, not as a 'given' world, but as a world dynamically 'in the making.' . . . It is precisely this creation of a new reality, prefigured in the revolutionary criticism of the old one, that cannot exhaust the conscientization process, a process as permanent as any real revolution" (1985, pp. 106-7). As this culturally specific view of change corresponds to the rational attitude of his followers who are under similar linguistic controls, it is imperative to make explicit the implications of his position. Freire's view of the transformative dynamic of existence is nearly identical to Dewey's position; thus, many of the criticisms of the latter also apply directly to Freire. In spite of the danger of repetition, it is necessary to specify why Freire's position tends to reinforce the values and assumption that characterize the remissive form of modernization we are experiencing in the West. The charisma now surrounding Freire may lead his followers to acknowledge readily the criticism directed at Dewey's ideas but prevent them from recognizing that Freire's position manifests nearly the same inadequacies.

The problem with Freire's position is not that he advocates critical reflection but that he makes it the only legitimate source of knowledge and authority. To not guide action by critical reflection is to be submerged in an "'unclear' vision" as he put it. This position, which rests on Freire's assumption that "making history" is always progressive in nature, is problematic for a number of reasons that cannot be explored within the context of Freire's own discourse. In spite of his advocacy of critical reflection, he seems unable to adopt a reflexive stand toward the categories, epistemic orientation, and mythologies embedded in the language within which he thinks. By adopting a more ideologically open language that enables us to articulate the problematic nature of modern liberalism, it is possible to put a number of issues in focus.

Although Freire stresses the importance of dialogue as an essential aspect of critical reflection, this mode of thought shifts the locus of authority from that of community and tradition to the individual who unifies thought and action in a new praxis. Critical reflection may reach deeper levels of problematizing through dialogue with others, but it nevertheless remains an activity that occurs within the individual. The process of liberation, as formulated by Freire, thus strengthens the individual as the center of moral and intellectual authority. In the case of a conflict between the majority consensus of a community and the reflective individual, which often happens in Western societies, Freire's emphasis on the primacy of the critical reflective act suggests the logic of his position would lead to supporting the latter. Yet he also argues *against* a privatized form of individualism and *for* the solidarity of the social group. The potential conflict between the authority of critical reflection and the authority of the community, which may not entirely be grounded in the reflective process Freire envisages, cannot be resolved by Freire because of his failure to recognize other forms of authority, i.e., the authority of community norms and the authority of substantive traditions.

A possible reason Freire does not address how to resolve the conflict between the individual, who is to unite critical reflection with action, and the expectations of community is that he has an essentially positive view of human nature. Unlike the philosophic conservatives who take seriously the historical evidence of the betrayal of reason and ideals by individuals who were not always able to hold in check their desire for power and material advantage, Freire assumes that the person with a raised state of consciousness will be essentially selfless in the pursuit of the common good. In effect, the critically rational powers of the mind are seen as on the side of truth, progress, and community; the oppressors, "who oppress, exploit and rape by virtue of their power," lack the ability to reflect critically and thus must be liberated by the oppressed. Freire warns against the oppressed simply reversing roles with the oppressors and urges that the qualities associated with dialogue—love, humility, trust, faith in man's ability to recreate the world continually— must be part of the revolutionary process that illuminates the structural and psychological sources of oppression and transforms them into the conditions of liberated existence. Aside from this warning, Freire ignores the possibility that critical reflection may unite with self-interest to produce a more powerful and socially disruptive individual. Unlike the philosophical conservatives who argue that a system of checks and balances within the structure of society itself is a necessary supplement to the assumption that rationality should serve as an adequate guide to social action, Freire places complete trust in the emancipatory powers of education to free individuals from undesirable character traits. Freire also places a great deal of trust in the progressive nature of change that is initiated and guided by critical reflection.

Freire's use of dichotomous categories creates a discourse that is largely incapable of examining the dark side of his own vision of revolutionary consciousness. The oppressive and the dehumanizing, by the logic of his categories, are associated with exploitive economic systems, an uncritical acceptance of traditional culture, and a passive, alienated state of individual existence. That the process of conscientization might lead to new forms of oppression and dehumanization is a conceptual impossibility within his theoretical framework. Yet a case can be made that Freire's ideas, in spite of his good intentions, are inherently nihilistic and that their use as the basis for conducting the affairs of society could lead to new forms of oppression and dehumanization.

Freire's radical ontology (man must continually "*name* the world, to change it") and his view of conscientization as "constant clarification of what remains hidden" suggests that the continual transformation of social beliefs, norms, and institutions is the ultimate goal. On the surface, the image of people confronting reality in order to invest it with their own sense of meaning has high appeal, but there is another dimension that is generally ignored by Freire and his followers. The continual problematizing of the natural attitude in order to transcend "limit situations" means that the authority of all ideas, values, norms, and institutions would be continually relativized. That is, they would cease to have authority within the context of people's lives (in Arendt's sense of the term), with the result that the basis of social relations would not be predictable. As the dialectic of reflective thought and action is carried out by all members of society, the most basic of cultural norms, as well as the supporting symbolic order, would need to be continually renegotiated. Aside from the crucial issue of whether this negotiation process would always involve dialogue and democratic participation, there is the even more perplexing problem of cultural nihilism which we have discussed before. By locating authority in the process of critical reflection, Freire has put in focus the demystifying potential of human intelligence, but he has not addressed the problem of how to restore a shared sense of authority. What his position leaves us with is a world in which all forms of authority are relativized—that is, there would be no shared moral, intellectual, or social claims for the individual that would inspire commitment. Individuals, exercising their ontological right to name the world in terms of the dictates of their own critical judgment, continually would have to establish the conceptual and moral basis of authority for social life. As the newly established basis of authority would be continually relativized by the ongoing process of critical reflection, everything would become meaningless. Like Dewey's theory, Freire's representation of reality as process demonstrates a lack of understanding of the cultural embeddedness of the individual and of how the relativizing of all beliefs leads to a loss of meaning and commitment.

A discourse that organizes reality into neat dichotomous categories dominates Freire's thought to such an extent that he is unable to acknowledge the network of tacit understandings that provides the degree of certainty (the "stable background," to use Douglas' phrase) necessary for rendering outworn traditions and oppressive social arrangements problematic. The dialectical process between tacit and explicit forms of meaning escapes Freire's attention; in this process, the achievements of explicit forms of understanding, including critical reflection, lead over time to changes in the belief system and social practice that, in turn, become part of the tacit understanding that endures until viewed as problematic. The dialectic is thus one of renewal within the relationship of implicit-explicit understanding.

This inability to recognize embeddedness in the tacit dimensions of culture (which include the shaping influence of language) may result from Freire's attitude toward history as a source of alienation and constraint. Although he urges colonized people "to preserve their native language" (1985, p. 186)—presumably because it provides the basis of a collective memory essential for resistance, Freire represents the act of critical reflection as the means of transcending the hold of the past. "History makes us while we make it," he wrote. "Again my suggestion is that we attempt to emerge from this alienating daily routine that repeats itself. . . . We need to be subjects of history, even if we cannot totally stop being objects of history. . . . As active participants and real subjects, we can make history only when we are continually critical of our very lives" (p. 199). If Freire were dealing with oppressive conditions in a particular society, one could readily agree that, within context, a radical transformation of the society would be justified—which would include a rejection of the oppressive traditions of that society. But Freire is not addressing the problems of a specific group of people; he is, in fact, addressing a problem of the human condition that presumably applies universally without regard for the traditions of different cultural groups. Aside from the uniquely Western patterns of thought embedded in Freire's statement, as can be seen in his bias toward literacy over orality, there is another problem that is particularly acute in societies such as ours that make a virtue of a form of individualism that is self-directing and thus free of the past.

This problem is related to the recent rise of the state as the most powerful source of political power. Foucault's analysis of the nature of power includes an observation that the particular form of the state, and the political technologies it uses to exercise power, require a linkage with a particular form of individualism (1982, p. 216). Ironically, the acceptance of Freire's philosophical anthropology (i.e., that people must create their own history by continually renaming the world), contributes to the rootless form of individualism that serves the interests of the modern state. Freire's bias against tradition as a specter ("these cultural remnants" as he referred to it) is almost a logical requirement of the epistemic categories that underlie his pattern of thinking. His uncritical acceptance of the metaphorical images of the individual and critical reflection as sources of rational autonomy and moral self-direction, as well as of the idea that change can be given rational direction, prevented him from recognizing that the emergence of the state, with its need for rational planning as the basis of administrative control, threatens the foundations of his own more populist vision. Freire warns in several places that the state must represent the democratic will of the people, but in his letters to co-workers in Guinea-Bissau he acknowledges the importance of an overall "plan of the government and of the Party." He even suggests that the literacy program is essential to creating "information of inestimable value to the government" (1978, p. 119). The point is not that Freire is supportive of the authoritarian state (he definitely is not!), but rather that he lacks an understanding of how his bias against tradition may contribute to a rootless and anomic form of individualism easily manipulated by the state.

In order to question the power relations rooted in the system of social networks established and maintained by the state, it is essential for the individual to be able to put issues, policies, and even language itself into a broader perspective. This ability to understand the implications of how power is being exercised, both in terms of individual and communal well-being, requires the exercise of memory. As Shils points out, "Memory is the vessel which retains in the present the record of the experiences undergone in the past and of knowledge gained through the recorded and remembered experiences of others, living and dead" (p. 50). Shils further notes that the image of self, in part, reaches backward and incorporates the recollections and memories of a complex social past. The self also involves imagination and the intentionality of critical intelligence (as both Dewey and Freire emphasize). Yet without memory of meaningful traditions (i.e., the ability to recall a collective history), the individual would lack an important conceptual element necessary to judging the exercise of power by the state. In her essay, "What Is Authority?" Hannah Arendt made an observation that is particularly germane to understanding the importance of memory to political empowerment: "We are in danger of forgetting, and such an oblivion—quite apart from the contents themselves that could be lost—would mean that, humanly speaking, we would deprive ourselves of one dimension of depth in human experience. For memory and depth are the same, or rather, depth cannot be reached by man except through remembrance" (1961, p. 94). It is this depth of understanding and meaning (a critical sense of temporality) that can also serve as the source of authority for resisting manipulation by the state. Unfortunately, the theoretical orientation of Freire's discourse prevents him from recognizing that traditions are more than specters and "cultural remnants."

Two of the most important aspects of Freire's thinking, that individuals have the power to invest language with meaning that expresses an awareness of their existential conditions and that the renaming of the world occurs through dialogue, also must be reconceptualized. Because of the great moral appeal of Freire's vision of the critical transformation of the world through dialogue, it is necessary to reiterate essential agreement with his understanding of the ability of individuals to use language to create an ever-new social reality, as well as his view of dialogue as the only basis of authentic human interaction.

Perhaps the clearest statement on the power of individuals to speak a "true word" is the following: "Human existence cannot be silent, nor can it be nourished by false words, but only by true words, with which men transform the world. To exist, humanly, is to *name* the world, to change it. Once named, the word in its turn reappears to the namers as a problem and requires of them a new *naming*. Men are not built in silence, but in word, in work, in action-reflection" (1974, p. 76). There is no question that Freire is partly correct: through reflection language becomes the vessel into which new meanings are put and the lens for a new way of seeing. But language is far more complex than Freire's statement would lead us to understand. The idea of a true word, of naming the world as though it involved an authentic act of creation, does not make a great deal of sense in terms of our present understanding of language as a carrier of the epistemological categories of a culture. We learn to think within these conceptual categories as we acquire our native language. The important point overlooked by Freire is that even though we may take advantage of a certain degree of the symbolic openness of our language to express a "new" sense of meaning, to illuminate "new" relationships, and to reconceptualize elements of our natural attitude and the epistemological orientation reflected in the basic cultural paradigm, language continues to exert a powerful and largely unconscious influence on thought.

Whereas Freire organizes the world into the dichotomous categories of speaking true and false words (the latter denoting a passive and alienated form of existence), language imprints the act of critical reflection itself with the conceptual categories and assumptions that characterize the cognitive orientation of the culture. Words like authentic, reflection, and true must be viewed as iconic metaphors that reflect the epistemic orientations of the root metaphor or world view of the culture in which they are used. There is an important difference between blind acceptance of the world named by others and the act of critical reflection, but even the most rigorous attempts to be authentic and to think critically cannot escape entirely from the control of language.

Freire's own use of language provides the best evidence of how critically reflective thought, while advancing our understanding in significant ways, reproduces a culturally specific conceptual orientation. While he uses language to change our understanding, the language continues to organize his thoughts into culturally recognizable patterns. His metaphorical way of thinking about individualism, revolutionary change, authentic being, tradition, and so forth reflect the deep epistemic patterns of the Western world view. If there is doubt about the culturally specific categories that Freire uses to formulate his philosophic anthropology and his pedagogy of liberation, a comparison can easily be made with linguistic categories and cognitive orientation of non-Western cultural groups. For example we could compare Freire's view of the person with that of the Northern Ojibwa, whose linguistic conventions include both the animate and the inanimate within their concept of the person. Within their conceptual categories, the process of emancipation would take on an entirely different meaning than it has within the conceptual categories that are part of Freire's natural attitude. It might also be useful to compare his ethno-metaphysics with that of a language community in India or China. The point is that, regardless of the purity of revolutionary intent, individuals may significantly change certain aspects of their social-conceptual world, but they can never be completely autonomous from the controls of their own language community. This in turn raises another issue, namely that the problem of emancipation (which Freire uses as a context-free metaphor) cannot be conceptualized entirely outside the conceptual categories of a language community; perhaps the recognition of this will lead to recognizing that emancipation may take different cultural forms.

The second and last aspect of Freire's thinking that needs reformulation relates to his understanding of dialogue as the only authentic and mutually emancipatory form of communication. The connection between Freire's philosophic anthropology, dialogue, and his habit of thinking in dichotomous categories can be seen in the following statement:

> But while to say the true word—which is work, which is praxis—is to transform the world, saying that word is not the privilege of some few men, but the right of every man. Consequently, no one can say a true word alone—nor can he say it *for* another, in a prescriptive act which robs others of their words. Dialogue is the encounter between men, mediated by the world, in order to name the world. (1971, p. 76)

When stated in this way, dialogue appears as the only form of communicative relationship that avoids domination. But the social world is more complex than Freire's vision of the ever-renewed dialogical praxis; it also involves myriad traditions (in Shils' sense of the term) that form the basis of organizing and sustaining social life: beliefs, practices, institutions, technologies, and so forth. The introduction of youth into the ways of society (even revolutionary societies), as well as the interaction of already socialized members, cannot always take the form of dialogue. Not everything in society can be renegotiated at the same time; certain expectations must be communicated without the open-ended and transforming expectation associated with dialogue.

Martin Buber, the philosopher who had the deepest understanding of dialogue, clearly recognized that most of our communication would not have the characteristics that he identified with genuine dialogue. Nor did Buber assume that everybody, at all time of their lives, would be psychologically capable of entering into this special relationship with others and the world. Although he views dialogue as having the elements that Freire associates with it—trust, mutuality, love, humility, presentness, and so forth—Buber understood it in almost Nietzschean terms. People who are able to meet life in terms of its novelty, who are able to make the other present, and who are free from doubt about their self-identity and from other anxieties that could cause them to control the dynamics of the relationship, are capable of entering into dialogue. Children and the psychologically mature experience dialogue, which means that dialogue is a fairly rare experience—particularly since it requires encountering others who are similarly prepared to say "Thou." Buber recognized that the nature of society—its norms, patterns of thinking, values, economy, technology, and so forth—influence the degree to which people are capable of entering into a dialogical relationship. He too urged radical changes in society for the purpose of achieving community, but he did not envision dialogue as the commonplace that Freire makes it.

6

Education and
the Restoration of Community

IN *Habits of the Heart*, Robert Bellah and his coauthors observe that as a society "we have never been, and are not, a collection of private individuals who, except for a conscious contract to create a minimal government, have nothing in common" (Bellah et al. 1985, p. 282). Yet the authors note that the "language of individualism" limits our ability to understand our embeddedness in what they have termed a "social ecology" and also threatens to erode the moral and republican traditions that have given depth to individual membership in community life. The "language of individualism" is not the only threat to the social ecology; the ability to maintain the commitments and moral understandings essential to a viable community is also threatened by excessive concentrations of wealth in the hands of a privileged few, by distortions in the work place, and by the progressive corruption of the democratic process. A common denominator among these threats to shared moral understandings, social practices, and institutional supports of community is the pursuit of short-sighted interests—economic, technological, and personal. Although schools cannot be expected to carry the full weight of correcting these problems, educators can nevertheless address themselves to aspects of the problem that are essentially educational in nature. The part of the analysis that is particularly germane to educators is the idea that we are not "a collection of private individuals." This myth, while strengthened by forces within modern society, confronts educators with a special challenge—to understand how the "social ecology" forms and nourishes the individual.

This brings us back to one of the main themes explored in the previous chapters, namely, developing a conceptual basis for a discourse that allows us to consider the full interrelatedness of individual and community. For Bellah and his coauthors, the word community is not used in a casual manner. To them it refers to a group of people living interdependent lives shaped by collective participation in the decision-making processes and sharing a common past. Because their understanding of community so clearly differs from the sense of temporality built into the liberal theories of education we have examined, it is important to quote them more fully:

> Communities, in the sense in which we are using the term, have a history—in an important sense they are constituted by their past—and for this reason we can speak of a real community as a "community of memory," one that does not forget its past. In order not to forget that past, a community is involved in retelling its story, its constitutive narrative, and in so doing, it offers examples of the men and women who have embodied and exemplified the meaning of the community. These stories of collective history and exemplary individuals are an important part of the tradition that is so central to a community of memory.
>
> The stories that make up a tradition contain conceptions of character, of what a good person is like, and of the virtues that define such character. But the stories are not all exemplary, not all about successes and achievements. A genuine community of memory will also tell painful stories of shared suffering that sometimes create deeper identities than success. . . . And if the community is completely honest, it will remember stories not only of suffering but of suffering inflicted—dangerous memories, for they call the community to alter ancient evils. The communities of memory that tie us to the past also turn us toward the future as communities of hope. They carry a context of meaning that can allow us to connect our aspirations for ourselves and those closest to us with the aspirations of a larger whole and see our own efforts as being, in part, contributions to a common good. (p. 153)

The educational theories of Dewey and Freire possess many enduring strengths that must be incorporated into our understanding of the potential of public education, but their theories also contain serious omissions and distortions that reflect both their particular vantage point for viewing the problems of society and the conceptual bias toward "living forward" that has long been part of the discourse of educational liberalism. As suggested earlier, Dewey's emphasis on the social, participatory nature of problem solving strengthens the bonds of community; Freire's stress on dialogue, while more difficult to sustain, is also important to the restoration of community. Yet in making the "method of intelligence" and critical reflection the *only* legitimate form of authority, both theorists undermine the authority and educative effects of the "community of memory" that Bellah and his colleagues write so eloquently about. The retelling of its story, which is an integral part of socialization into the life of a community, involves the presentation of models (exemplary lives and examples of social pathologies) that are important to being educated as a person and as a member of a community. However, the moral authority of these models is easily relativized by an *overemphasis* on critical reflection, whether by the group or the individual. This emphasis on reflective thought—the hallmark of both theorists—ultimately makes individual judgment the source of moral and intellectual authority. The evidence, if not always reducible to a matter of subjective judgment, must be placed within a larger context of meaning (social, political, and moral) that, in turn, becomes a matter of individual interpretation. Faced with a view of the past as a source of constraint, which characterizes the position of both Dewey and Freire, the individual is likely to believe the liberal myth that self-determination requires escaping from the community of memory and its constitutive narratives.

In spite of their excessively limited view that learning occurs only in social problem solving, Dewey and Freire make a contribution that is particularly vital to overcoming the fragmentation and anomie that characterize modernization. An essential element in their respective pedagogies, overshadowed by their concern with critical reflection, is the idea that speech is central to the political life of the community. The differences between Dewey's participatory approach to scientific problem solving and Freire's "thematic investigation circles" are, in fact, quite minor when compared to the political role they both assign to the power of individual speech—guided, of course, by reflective thought. Open communication involving all members of the community becomes, in terms of their theories, the primary way of expressing civic responsibility. What separates their view of speech and action, as civic virtues, from the current trend of liberal thought is a profound (some would say "unrealistic") belief that the purpose of political (educational) action is to serve the common good. As Theodore Lowi (1979) pointed out, current liberalism views society as an aggregate of individuals who unite as members of an interest group for the purpose of bargaining for as much of a share of public resources and power as they can obtain. Their gain represents a loss for the rest of the public, but collectively the different claims made by competing interest groups are interpreted as an accurate weathervane of what public policy should be. Dewey and Freire do not define the public in terms of competing interest groups, but they do stress the importance of common interest and participatory involvement—civic virtues essential to the idea of community advanced by Bellah and his colleagues.

Aside from the decidedly more contemporary assumptions Dewey and Freire base their theories upon, their ideas on the importance of the civic commons represent a return to the ancient Greek idea of politics. For the Greeks, "to be political, to live in a *polis*, meant that everything was decided through words and persuasion and not through force and violence" (Arendt 1958, p. 27). For Dewey, speech performs an essential political function but is to be guided by the consequences that follow from the testing of ideas; Freire, on the other hand, would make speech within a communal setting contingent upon the critical reflection that undercovers the deep codes underlying the limiting patterns of daily life. Yet they both make communication within a political community the medium that connects thought and action. This aspect of their thought provides an important sense of direction for thinking about the role education can play in strengthening the foundations of community. However, as pointed out previously, their theories also contain assumptions that contribute to the modern forms of nihilism highly detrimental to community. Our task will, therefore, be to formulate the outlines of a theory of education that addresses the problem of enabling people to exercise communicative competence (a more contemporary way of thinking about the role of speech in the *polis*) while avoiding the liberal assumptions that strengthen the myth of individual autonomy.

Such a theory must address R. Freeman Butts' (1980) concern with strengthening civic learning in the schools; but it must encompass other elements essential to achieving a healthier balance between nurturing individual talents and integration into "the web of moral understandings and commitments that tie people together in a community," as Bellah and his coauthors put it. Butts urges schools to more directly engage students in the study of the values associated with democratic institutions and the history of political institutions and political issues. He also argues that education for civic participation must involve teaching the skills necessary for utilizing and improving democratic institutions. But education appropriate to renewing the foundations of community must include other elements, especially those that bond people together in a manner that prevents the increased political efficacy of individual members from destroying the delicate balance within the social ecology and between the social and natural ecology. Although Butts is urging the revival of civic humanism, his emphasis on political understanding, when interpreted within the liberal framework of individual self-determination, could degenerate into utilizing democratic institutions for the purpose of achieving the interests of special groups. Elements needed to guard against this development include: (1) a shared stock of tacit knowledge, including models of what a good person is like; (2) a knowledge of traditions that will enable students to participate more fully as members in the "community of memory"; (3) an understanding of self as a social being (i.e., understanding the social forces that influence identity and consciousness and the implications of being part of a social-natural ecology); and (4) the conceptual foundations necessary for the exercise of communicative competence.

This list of educational objectives may appear overwhelming to teachers already burdened with socializing functions normally carried out by other social institutions. But an argument can be made that the fragmentation of activity and responsibility caused by the values of modern society—which in turn adds to the burden placed on public schools—will simply be increased if teachers, as well as others, do not address the educational aspects of restoring a sense of community. Interest groups pressure schools to take on an increasing number of curricular and supervisory responsibilities, and as long as teachers reinforce in the consciousness of students the beliefs associated with the ideology of modernization (the individual as a self-directing being, the progressive nature of change, the relative nature of all values, the authority of purposive rational thought, and so forth), they will face a continued series of demands from members of society no longer capable of distinguishing between the private and the public good.

Further reflection on what is being proposed as part of a post-liberal theory of education leads to a different way of understanding the nature of the public education and its relationship to the process of cultural transmission. This new understanding, in turn, leads to a different approach to what occurs in the classroom as the old paradigm, with its increasingly technicist interpretation of liberal assumptions, shapes the current natural attitude of teachers. To put it another way, an approach to education that contributes to the restoration of community will involve looking at the nature of teaching and the curriculum through a different set of conceptual lenses. This different way of "seeing" leads naturally to using the traditional curricula in ways that strengthen the bonding and participatory processes necessary for membership in a healthy social-natural ecology. It will also lead to recognizing how to incorporate into the curriculum the relevant culture of the community.

The suggestion that public education be understood within a different paradigm or conceptual framework has special implications for institutions concerned with the education and professional development of teachers. Although many critics would claim that these institutions are conservative in orientation, a more defensible claim is that their programs are based on liberal assumptions about the autonomous nature of the individual, the progressive nature of change (witness the largely uncritical embrace of computers as the long-awaited educational panacea), the authority of measurement, and the need to prepare for living in the future by not learning anything about the past, since the past might become a source of encumbrance. The elaboration of a post-liberal theory of education, particularly in terms of how such a theory would lead to a different classroom practice, will remain largely an empty exercise if the people who control the direction of teacher education do not take seriously the need to rethink the liberal paradigm that is proving to be increasingly problematic in both a social and ecological sense.

Instead of basing education in the classroom on a concept of the individual as a self-contained being and a view of learning as a process that achieves various degrees of correspondence between the thought processes occurring within the individual's mind and the external reality, it would make more sense to use the image of the individual as a social-cultural being as the starting point for rethinking formal education. The prevailing orthodoxy about the nature of the individual and the processes of thought, both of which represent surviving remnants of the classical liberal paradigm, is too easily interpreted in behavioral terms where measurable results become the dominant concern. The problem with this approach is that it puts out of focus the individual as a member of a language community that provides both the patterns and conceptual boundaries of thought and the basis of self-identity. In effect, it ignores the most fundamental aspect of how we exist in the world, which was effectively summarized in Hanna Pitkin's statement—which I shall repeat:

> One insight that the model of language membership suggests, then, is that the customary distinctions between individual and society, between self and some larger whole to which it belongs, are not fixed, mutually exclusive categories. Rather they concern different aspects of, different perspectives on, a single reality. Society is not just "outside" the individual, confronting him, but inside him as well, part of who he is. (1972, p. 195)

This statement recognizes language as the constituting ground of individual being; ideology—which represents our attempts to reflect on the meaning of this ground—must recognize this as the basic starting point for a theory of education.

By viewing education as a central aspect of the dynamics of language membership, we immediately establish a basic point relevant to the concerns of Bellah and his coauthors about the restoration of a sense of the public order. The myth is that we are autonomous, self-directing individuals; the fact is that we begin life as members of a language community and grow in the capacity to individualize the expression of the communal inheritance we receive. Community is not something that has to be reinvented; but it can become attenuated and take on distorting and pathological characteristics. The restoration of community has to do with its moral foundations, its vision of good and evil, and its ability to adjust the daily routines, institutions, and structural characteristics to the requirements of its moral aspirations. Education of the individual begins as a communal activity, and it remains one—even when it is carried on within an ideological framework that emphasizes the pursuit of self-interest, competition, and the irrelevance of traditions as a source of sustenance and authority. This "egocentric orientation," as Jonas Soltis termed it (1981, p. 97), reflects the epistemic and moral orientation of the community, but it is an orientation that ironically, and tragically, puts out of focus the legitimate claims of the community on the individual.

Pitkin's view of the primacy of language membership also makes it easier to recognize the relation between the forms of education carried on in public schools and in the larger culture. Culture, as Clifford Geertz tells us, can be understood, in part, as "an historically transmitted pattern of meanings embodied in symbols, a system of inherited conceptions expressed in symbolic forms by means of which men communicate, perpetuate, and develop their knowledge about and attitudes toward life" (1973, p. 89). Although this explanation of the nature of culture emphasizes symbolic, at the expense of the physical, manifestations, it adds an important dimension to understanding membership in a language community. The "patterns of meaning embodied in symbols" are embedded in the language, and as individuals learn the language of their cultural group, they are acquiring the "guide to 'social reality,'" as Edward Sapir put it (1970, p. 69). More recently Ward Goodenough summarized how cultural learning occurs through language acquisition: "To learn the language—that is, to learn to use its vocabulary acceptably—is indispensable for learning the cultural forms its vocabulary encodes" (1981, p. 66). As education involves communication (language), it also involves, in addition to explicit and prescriptive instruction in how to think and act in a social setting, learning at the tacit level the symbolic codes essential to organizing everyday life into mutually recognizable patterns.

Viewing education as a language process that involves the transmission, and some negotiation, of culture is helpful for keeping in focus the dangers of reducing it to a question of the relationship between strategy and measurable outcomes; but it does not go quite far enough in helping to clarify what is unique about education (cultural transmission) in the classroom. In the everyday world where traditional patterns are re-enacted, adjusted, and transmitted to the culturally uninitiated, education is largely tacit, in that conversation and performance (the pragmatic aspect of cultural learning) are often experienced as part of the natural attitude toward dealing with the task at hand, e.g., the mother explaining to the child how to play with another child, the new teacher learning the areas of decision-making that are the province of the administrator, the adolescent learning the rules and expectations connected with driving a car. Learning in social settings involves the ability to perform in terms of shared expectations; it also involves learning the cultural codes (symbolic patterns) that underlie the cultural patterns. It does not, as a rule, involve learning and using a language code that is more complex than required for sharing knowledge that is taken for granted. To put it another way, education outside of school—in the work place, the market place, and the home (which includes the enculturating power of television)—usually involves a certain parsimony of language. Agents of enculturation—parents, peers, people who must teach the patterns and norms relevant to their activities—usually do not provide the more elaborated vocabulary necessary for putting cultural norms or activities into a complex theoretical framework or for developing a sense of conceptual distance necessary for critical thought. Successful performance in accordance with cultural norms, rather than in expanding the individual's ability to think about the cultural process or event, is the primary emphasis in education outside of schools.

Cultural transmission in schools, while involving learning at the tacit level many of the cultural norms and routines appropriate to existence within schools, also involves learning how to *think* about the institutions, practices, and norms that make up the culture. This form of learning is generally separated from context (in contrast to most learning outside of schools), is highly abstracted in that it relies on words and concepts instead of direct experience to represent cultural reality, and often cannot be tested against the real world of experience. The curriculum—which includes primarily talk and reading about work, technology, history, literature, and a myriad of other facets of the culture—is intended to provide students with the conceptual foundations (vocabulary, concepts, and theory) necessary for thinking and talking about their culture. The student's later performance in a social context may be aided by this symbolic knowledge, but in many instances the explicit symbolic knowledge acquired in schools will prove unrelated to the requirements of the real world. For example, the difference between the explanation of the work process in most schools and what is encountered in the work setting illustrates the uniqueness of cultural transmission within schools. The symbolic knowledge—the words and concepts necessary for thinking about the nature and purpose of work—often oversimplifies the complexities of the work process and obscures the political issues requiring negotiation.

The emphasis within schools on explicit forms of knowledge—learning what and how to think—gives the teacher extraordinary power to manipulate the language game of socialization that initiates youth into the patterns of thought shared by members of the language community. One way to understand the power of the teacher is to view the classroom as an interacting set of language systems, involving verbal and non-verbal communication (use of space, time, body language, and so forth). The teacher consciously and unconsciously orchestrates the dynamics of this language environment to influence the student's thought and behavior. Often, as the teacher is making available to the student the vocabulary and concepts for learning about an aspect of the culture, the language processes exert control over the teacher—with the control being experienced as part of the teacher's natural attitude. Standing in front of the class; using cultural prescribed body language to communicate messages related to frustration, concern, and encouragement; organizing thought in terms of dichotomous categories; and using the conventional rules of grammar—these are just a few of the expressions of how the teacher remains under control of the cultural codes embedded in the language. The culture that is part of the teacher's natural attitude is thus transmitted to the students who are likely, under certain conditions, to accept it at the same taken-for-granted level. Understanding how to use the dynamics of these language processes, as well as being aware of how language manipulates thought and behavior, are essential to being an effective teacher. They are also essential to understanding the ideological orientation being transmitted to students, along with all the facts and concepts that are part of the teacher's explicit teaching. Lastly, awareness of the language processes that sustain cultural transmission in the classroom is vital to understanding the connection between making socialization (cultural transmission) explicit and the student's growth in communicative competence.

This brings us back to the concern about the relationship between education and community, particularly the form of community membership that involves political participation directed toward common goals. The challenge facing public teachers is to understand how they exercise control over the dynamics of the socialization process, how changing the dynamics of the language processes contributes to the student's communicative competence, and how the content of the learning process relates to different ideological orientations—i.e., either the liberalism of individual self-interest and progressive change or a post-liberal understanding of mutual enrichment between individualism and community. As many teachers are likely to say that these issues are too abstract and unrelated to what they do in the classroom, it is necessary to emphasize that the teacher and students, like fish in water, are immersed, sustained, and controlled by the language processes that constitute the milieu of the classroom; that teachers transmit directly a particular image of individualism as well as other conceptual categories that collectively constitute a particular view of society; and lastly, that the teacher's control over language acquisition during the phase of primary socialization is related to the student's ability to use language as a way of making explicit those areas of cultural experience that are problematic and thus in need of negotiation. Teachers may choose not to make the effort to understand how they are implicated, but they cannot escape being implicated.

As I have already written about the connection between the student's growth in communicative competence and the teacher's control over primary socialization in the classroom (1984), I would like to summarize how primary socialization in the classroom can be used to provide students with the basis for various understandings: of themselves as social beings, of the reciprocal relationship between self and community, of the continuities between the present and the past, and of the political nature of the extended *polis* within which they now live—and thus of the need for being able to exercise communicative competence if this ongoing cultural experiment is to retain democratic characteristics. In effect, I would like to explain how viewing education in the classroom as a "language game" helps to put in focus the ideological orientation, and thus the form of society, that is being strengthened by the teacher's choices within the context of the socialization process. This view of education, which draws heavily from the sociology of knowledge of Alfred Schutz, Peter Berger, and Thomas Luckmann, shares similarities with the ideas of Dewey and Freire, but it also involves fundamental differences. As we proceed, attempts will be made to clarify how their ideas can be integrated into the post-liberal theory of education that is being developed here.

Briefly stated, education within the classroom involves students, as they encounter areas of the curriculum (culture) that they have not learned to think about before, in the process of primary socialization. They may already have developed a functional-implicit knowledge of cultural patterns, like how to fit one's activities into the cultural patterns for organizing time, but they undergo primary socialization as they listen to the teacher's explanation of how to "tell time" (i.e., think about time). Similarly, students will have learned at the functional-implicit level the cultural episteme for organizing thought and integrating a "taste" for the nutritional habits reinforced within the culture. Primary socialization in the classroom will provide them the vocabulary and conceptual framework for making explicit this part of their cultural knowledge (knowledge they can demonstrate in context but not necessarily reproduce at a conceptual level). Primary socialization—that is, exposure to how to talk and think about aspects of the collective experience of the cultural group—may leave the students with the vocabulary and conceptual framework that reinforces and thus stabilizes the sense of taken-for-grantedness; or it can provide the linguistic tools essential for illuminating aspects of experience—the assumptions about time, work, nutrition, and so forth—by providing a conceptual framework necessary for reflection, for comparing perspectives, and for testing conceptual understanding against the complexities of the life world. In effect, primary socialization can lead to the ability to participate in the public discourse by providing the conceptual-linguistic foundations of speech, or it can limit the student both conceptually and linguistically to the point where the natural attitude dictates what can be expressed to others. When the latter occurs, discourse becomes one-dimensional in that what is taken for granted circumscribes the boundaries of reflection and imagination.

Primary socialization occurs whenever students are dependent upon a significant other (a teacher, peer, media personality, etc.) to explain and model an aspect of cultural experience they have not encountered before. Thus the curriculum, insofar as it introduces students to new areas of the cultural territory, always involves socialization at the primary level; it also involves reinforcement of conceptual patterns and taken-for-granted knowledge learned previously. By looking at primary socialization as a language game, it is possible to identify key moves that bear on the issues of individualism, communicative competence, and community. The essential "moves" in the language game of primary socialization involve: (1) the significant other (the teacher) presenting the curriculum by defining "What Is," which involves making available the initial vocabulary and conceptual framework for thinking and talking (the initial explanation or readings); (2) communicating, along with the explicit message of what is being named and thought about, a natural attitude that may vary from taken-for-grantedness to "let's not accept anything without questioning it"; (3) the content of communication often being represented as any objective statement of fact; and (4) the reinforcement of the deep conceptual patterns (the paradigm) that make it possible for the initial explanation—the language and concepts used to establish "what is"—to take on a sense of coherence with the totality of a world view.

Because there are many variables that come into play as the teacher selects and interprets the culture to the students (differences within conceptual frameworks, natural attitudes, identities, moods, and so forth), primary socialization is never as efficient or as entirely under the control of the teacher as we think—or as some of us would like. But when certain variables are present (i.e., the teacher is seen as a significant other, students and teachers are members of the same language (epistemic) community, a certain degree of symmetry exists in what is taken for granted, and so forth), the teacher's control over the dynamics of primary socialization can have a powerful effect on the student.

Teachers who do not really know the material they are teaching or share the same taken-for-granted beliefs embedded in the curriculum materials will be likely to manipulate the language game so that the student is left with a limited vocabulary and conceptual framework (language will be limited to constituting what the significant others take for granted), with a model of the natural attitude that should be adopted toward what is being learned, with a sense that the explanations are factual and objective, and with the deep organizing and sustaining assumptions that make up the world view. For many students, whose initial thoughts about new areas of cultural experience will be both facilitated and constrained by the language made available to them, socialization involving these particular "moves" will limit their capacity for communicative competence. Quite simply they will lack the conceptual basis necessary to reflect on their newly acquired beliefs, since those beliefs will be taken for granted.

On the other hand, teachers who have a good understanding of what they are teaching or who know how to use the lived culture of the community to supplement the curriculum, provide students with a more complex vocabulary and conceptual framework (the initial phase of the language game). The more the "What Is" phase of socialization involves extended discussion and comparison of explanations with the experiences of people who have diverse backgrounds, the more complex the student's conceptual map will be. At the same time the teacher will be communicating (modeling) a different natural attitude, one that takes for granted the importance of assessing the explanatory power of "What Is" statements in terms of the complexities of the life world. The emphasis on perspective and complexity leads naturally to changing the third move in the language game from the false sense of objectivity to an awareness that everything has a past and that an understanding of historical development is essential to making a judgment about the contemporary merit of beliefs, social practices, and institutions. Examination of the underlying assumptions of the cultural paradigm is also possible. Often the teacher who knows the subject well and who retains the degree of intellectual curiosity necessary to avoid the reduction of knowledge into neatly packaged formulas will naturally alter the moves in the language game in a manner that provides the conceptual foundations necessary for communicative competence. Although this "common sense" approach of the teacher has implications for viewing the teacher as a liberally educated person rather than a classroom manager, there is also a case to be made for teachers possessing a more explicit understanding of the dynamic relationship between culture, language, and the structures of consciousness within the classroom setting. A knowledge of how language influences thought, as well as of the language processes going on in the classroom, would provide a more clinical understanding of the process of cultural transmission.

It is now time to consider more specifically how an understanding of primary socialization can lead to addressing the larger social issues that were previously raised. Sensitivity within the classroom to how we use language and how language uses us, as well as to an historical perspective, helps to constitute a different image of individualism. As the teacher talks about time, for example, in terms of the language used to think about it (What is the dominant metaphorical image of time? Where did we get the notion that time is measurable? How did advances in technology change our metaphor image of time? How does our understanding of time influence other areas of thought?), it will become quite obvious that students share similar images and that the language they use in everyday conversation provides the conceptual patterns that makes possible mutual understanding. For the student this is, in effect, the opening to a different metaphorical image of self as an individual. Instead of the liberal image of the autonomous, self-directing individual (this metaphorical image being derived from early liberal psychological and social contract theory), students are confronted with an image of individuality that takes account of the constituting function of language; that is, they can recognize themselves as social-cultural beings because of a shared language. It must be emphasized, however, that as students are continually being reinforced to think of themselves as independent agents, responsible for their own thoughts and actions, it will be necessary for teachers to make explicit how a shared language and embeddedness in cultural patterns and traditions leads to a view of individualized expression of the shared cultural patterns—what Geertz referred to as the "extra-personal mechanisms for perception, understanding, judgment and manipulation of the world."

By including in primary socialization an historical perspective on the "What Is" statements ("Work can be understood in terms of the categories of mental and manual labor," "Objectives are specific, concrete, and observable," and so forth), students are provided a basis for considering how conceptual categories, as well as the metaphorical nature of language, influence not only their way of thinking but, more generally, the formulation of social policy itself. The historical perspective (When did we begin to separate work into mental and manual categories? When did we get the idea that objectives are free of value judgments and political interests?) helps introduce students into the community of memory, and to viewing themselves as agents in the reenactment of traditions. Primary socialization can involve accepting a tradition of thought at the taken-for-granted level. On the other hand, an awareness of historical development involves a substantially different form of involvement in the reenactment of cultural traditions. The "retelling of the stories" essential to participation in the community of memory provides a critical perspective that enables students to understand the historical legacy both as an achievement of the past and, at the same time, as problematic in the present. As students think about the immediate problems, they reenact traditional thought patterns; they are also involved with tradition as agents of renewal as they come to grips with current social issues. As Bellah and his coauthors point out, the community of memory not only enables students to put the present in perspective in a manner that challenges the idea of the autonomous, self-directing individual, it also turns them "toward the future as communities of hope." The rethinking of traditions—of what has been handed down from the past—provides, in effect, a special opportunity to introduce a critical perspective into the dynamics of reenactment that continues to occur—even when the student has been socialized to adopt a taken-for-granted attitude toward the traditions that constitute the life world.

Political participation in community, as Butts and others have pointed out, requires a balancing of values. On the one hand, public education must involve teaching values and forms of understanding that promote cohesion within a democratic society; on the other, it must also provide a conceptual and moral basis for cultural pluralism and individual development. This involves introducing into the constituting process of primary socialization a sense of balance between freedom and social responsibility; it also involves a sense of balance between critical reflection and the conceptual and moral culture that will be transmitted at the implicit level of understanding. The latter is essential to the bonding process that enables members of a community to share a common stock of taken-for-granted knowledge that governs much of their social life, e.g., the spacing patterns that operate in different social settings, the rituals of body language, the protocols of speech acts, and so forth. As the balance between social cohesion and individualism is a delicate one, it is important to stress that primary socialization can lead to the development of a conceptual map that views all forms of tacit knowledge as backward, unemancipated, and reactionary. This is likely to occur when the student encounters "What Is" statements that over-generalize the power and authority of critical reflection. Statements that universalize critical reflection as the only form of authority ("Question everything") and suggest that freedom can be totalized may result in the development of a conceptual framework that blinds individuals to their cultural embeddedness and fosters the myth that they are responsible only to the dictates of their individual judgment. Primary socialization to abstractions that are universalized (no matter how ideal the abstract idea or value is) introduces into the culture a form of individualism that acts like a loose canon—smashing into cultural practices without any sense of direction or awareness of what is being destroyed.

The distinction between telling students they are free (autonomous), rational (or emotive), self-directing beings and providing them with the conceptual basis for understanding the social world they live in is crucial to the question of what constitutes the basis of communicative competence. In recent years, liberal and radical educational theorists have emphasized the importance of understanding the free, autonomous nature of one's being. Carl Rogers represents the more emotive end of the ideological spectrum, while Giroux and Freire equate freedom with the power of critical reflection. Being told that one is a free and morally and rationally self-directing agent can be a heady message, particularly if it is learned at the stage of primary socialization when the initial conceptual map that establishes the nature of self and its relationship to the world is being first constituted. Few students have the maturity or conceptual basis for questioning a cultural myth that, at the same time, enhances the sense of self. Aside from creating confusion about how to reconcile the authority of individual reflection with other forms of authority and from being incorrect in terms of what we now understand about the inescapable influence of language and culture, learning that one is free and self-directing does not necessarily lead to communicative competence. Although the metaphorical representation may appear on the surface to support democratic forms of participation in community life, it can easily be misinterpreted—i.e., taken in the literal sense that one is wholly free, even of those responsibilities that involve accommodating self-interest to the needs of the larger community.

Effective participation in the *polis* as we know it involves an ability to speak, that is, to participate in the discourse that shapes the course of social events. As traditional forms of authority—institutions, values, social practices—are deauthorized by the forces of modernization, it is necessary to reestablish the basis of belief and social practice. This involves negotiating how problems are to be defined and what constitutes acceptable solutions. For example, the feminist movement deauthorized traditional beliefs and practices, which in turn led to negotiating (involving a complex discourse that cut across gender and ethnic lines) a new basis of understanding. Changes in technology (robots, medical technology, computers, nuclear power, etc.) are politicizing practices formerly taken for granted and opening up new areas of public discourse. The ability to participate in these discourses is not automatically assured by learning that critical reflection leads to individual self-direction. As a constituting part of consciousness, this metaphorical image of self can just as easily be translated into pursuing of self-interest—and to locating other individuals who will form themselves into a special interest group. This would take us back politically to the liberal idea of the competitive society, where the success of the dominant interest groups is interpreted as advancing the common good.

Communicative competence is often acquired as part of the socialization (and resocialization) process that occurs outside of schools. People dealing with changes in the work place, with the threat of nuclear power, and so forth, have acquired the knowledge of relevant issues necessary to participate in the ongoing discourse. Yet the conceptual basis of communicative competence can be affected in a positive manner by the kind of primary socialization that occurs in schools.

The ability to enter into a discussion of politically significant issues requires that one be able to communicate the results of one's reflections through words, to organize words into coherent statements, and to listen intelligently to the arguments and views of others. This is not a startlingly new description of the role of language in the political process. But it helps put in focus a fundamental issue that is pertinent to considering the relationship between primary socialization in schools and the exercise of communicative competence in the political world of adults. Without getting bogged down in a theoretical discussion of whether the constituent elements of an "ideal speech situation" have been met, it is possible to identify language as foundational to the development of the more cognitive aspects of communicative competence. Put in the most basic terms, if primary socialization leaves individuals with a limited vocabulary and conceptual understanding, an attitude that takes for granted the social phenomena they are learning about, and a false sense of objectivity about the new information, the students will simply not have the language necessary for doing anything more than communicating their taken-for-granted beliefs. The language given to them by the significant other (the teacher) will not only help to constitute the natural attitude but will also structure thought in accordance with the epistemic patterns of language. If students learn about work, technology, language, the authority of expert knowledge, and so forth at this level, they will lack the language necessary for illuminating these aspects of experience obscured by the natural attitude toward taken-for-granted beliefs. Without the language necessary for formulating thoughts, it will be impossible to participate in the discourse that determines the outcome of political issues.

How the "moves" in the language game of primary socialization—naming "What Is," communicating a natural attitude, representing the knowledge as objective, and reproducing the assumptions of the conceptual (cultural) paradigm—are played out in the student's encounter with the curriculum and interpretative framework of the teacher influences whether a linguistic-conceptual basis is being laid for the future exercise of communicative competence. Recognizing that how the culture is divided up and transmitted as a part of the school curriculum takes us to a more basic stage of education for civic participation. Students may be exposed to "the value claims of political democracy," "scholarly political knowledge," and the "participation skills" necessary for a democratic political system, as Butts urges (p. 116); but they must also possess a more explicit knowledge of the culture—particularly those elements politicized by the forces of modernization—if they are to bring a greater depth of understanding to their involvement in the political process. Put another way, education for civic involvement can lead to a form of democratic decision-making where the cultural assumptions, embedded in the natural attitudes of the participants, continue to direct the course of the decision-making process. But engaging the deeper structural and epistemic aspects of the political issues to be decided—the cultural dimension of the problem—requires a knowledge of what is taken for granted, an historical awareness that serves to deobjectify what might otherwise be taken as fact or as objectively real, and an understanding of the cultural assumptions that underlie the practices and beliefs that are being renegotiated as part of the political process. Participants who possess this knowledge will help deepen the level of the discourses they participate in.

This brings us back to the question of what is unique about primary socialization (cultural transmission) in schools. The range of cultural experiences that will be talked and read about in schools, as well as the tendency toward a rationalized (and sometimes critical) form of presentation, make the school quite unique in the form of socialization it sanctions. Outside of the school there are often genuine penalties connected with asking to make assumptions explicit, inquiring about the origins of ideas and social practices, and examining whether the definitions used as the basis of thought and social action represent the complexity of human experience. Generally, primary socialization in the work place, public meetings, and other social settings involves transmission in a language that tends to normalize perceptions and understanding in accordance with what the significant other takes for granted. There are important variables in these encounters, but rarely are alternative moves in the language game of socialization reinforced. Schools provide a unique site for a more complex and empowering form of socialization. Here more complex explanations can be presented and evaluated against the real world; the teacher can provide the sense of trust and support necessary as students suspend the natural attitude in order to enter the liminal space where definitions and ways of perceptions can be negotiated; and there are both opportunities and resources for developing an historical perspective of the issues at hand. There is also the opportunity to examine how individualism and community are to be reconciled within the wider context of public debate on policy issues. A more empowering form of socialization is dependent, however, on the teacher's understanding of and sensitivity to the power of the natural attitude—among all participants in the socialization process—to conceal the very areas of shared culture that need to be named (illuminated) and examined. This is the variable that makes problematic a form of socialization that contributes to communicative competence.

That teachers exercise a significant form of control over the language process (over how initial conceptual maps are constituted and thus will influence subsequent thought and political behavior) and that they have a responsibility for contributing to the conceptual foundations of communicative competence bring back into focus the importance of certain aspects of the theories of Dewey and Freire. The responsibility that Dewey assigned to the teacher for thinking about curriculum in terms of enhancing the student's ability to participate in the political life of the community must be more widely recognized. The connection between language and thought makes the language acquisition process inherently political; regardless of whether teachers are providing students a limited or more complex language code, they are participating in an ecology of language, culture, and thought that involves the exercise of power and thus a form of political control. Teachers cannot escape being political agents; consequently, the question is whether or not they will use the curriculum (both received and consciously selected) as an opportunity to think more deeply about the cultural patterns, traditions, and forces that seem increasingly problematic. The conservative argument that schools should reflect and renew the traditions of the larger society strengthens the idea that teachers have a responsibility to provide students a curriculum and form of learning that enhances their ability to participate in our long-standing tradition of democratic decision-making. This is another point where Dewey's ideas, particularly the connection he saw between social intelligence and the democratic process, provide support for a post-liberal understanding of education.

Dewey's emphasis on preparing to live in a world of social change is also important. As Shils recognized, traditions of thought, technologies, institutions, and so forth, are never entirely adequate responses to the current situations we find ourselves in. Furthermore, we have developed certain traditions (modes of inquiry, views of individualism, segmenting patterns of thought, and technologies) that make a virtue of accelerating the rate of cultural change. Dewey's perception that we must become a nation of problem solvers is thus partly correct; he is also compelling in his arguments that problem solving should involve a social form of intelligence—of participatory decision-making within the horizon of the common good rather than individual self-interest.

Yet other aspects of Dewey's liberalism can now be seen as more clearly aligned with the patterns of thought that underlie the social and ecological crisis we now face. Among these, his emphasis on the scientific method of thought as the only foundation of authority, his view of change as natural and progressive, and his understanding of technology all seem increasingly problematic—especially when judged against the insights of current rethinking of how community and tradition are sources of empowerment. By taking into account how the individual is embedded culturally and linguistically and by recognizing the empowering nature of traditions that have been reappropriated within the context of the present, it is possible to avoid these more nihilistic elements in Dewey's thought.

Although Freire bases his pedagogy on a number of assumptions that reflect the conceptual blind spots he shares with Dewey (the progressive nature of change, critical reflection as the only legitimate source of authority, the ability of individuals to escape their cultural embeddedness, the culture-free nature of the human condition), his theory of education nevertheless contains elements essential to a post-liberal theory of education. The form of socialization, for example, that contributes to the conceptual foundations of communicative competence involves making taken-for-granted beliefs and practices explicit—a major concern of Freire. Although the classroom does not involve the same political and economic risks as the life world, students still must deal with certain psychological uncertainties as they enter the liminality of the inquiry process. Problematizing the conceptual foundations of the natural attitude involves a period of uncertainty as a new basis of thought is sought. During both the problematizing and renegotiation phase, it is absolutely essential that the teacher and student share a sense of trust; it is also desirable that communication take on the form of dialogue as Freire understands it. But the dynamics of socialization cannot, and do not always have to, reach the level of communion that Freire envisages as the minimum condition for non-repressive education to occur. As Martin Buber points out, "however intense the mutuality of giving and taking" with which the teacher is bound to the students, "inclusion cannot be entirely mutual"; the teacher "experiences the pupils being educated, but the pupil cannot experience the educating of the educator" (1959, p. 100). That is, the students are limited by their past socialization (their natural attitude, the linguistic zones of competence, and so forth) from always understanding why the teacher changes the "moves" in the language game of socialization—asking the question that forces the students to check whether the explanation takes account of the complexity of the life world, suggesting that students put issues in an historical perspective, introducing a cross-cultural perspective or including information that brings into question certain aspects of the student's taken-for-granted beliefs. Students must have confidence in their teachers in order to participate in this conceptually broadening experience, but they cannot attain the degree of equality in the educational process that Freire suggests. As stated earlier, being a significant other means a lack of symmetry in symbolic worlds; the teacher also has the added responsibility, as Dewey and Arendt understood, of introducing into the curriculum those aspects of the social world that need to be renewed. This cannot always be negotiated with students.

Freire's insights into the political nature of language must also be integrated into a post-liberal view of education. Indeed, language involves a controlling form of power, and thus it must be viewed as inherently political. Although we can take seriously Freire's concern with an empowering form of linguistic competence (i.e., that students be able to invest language with meaning that reflects their existential situation), it is impossible to ignore the complex interaction of cultural episteme and language. As argued earlier, individuals cannot "*name the* world," in quite the way Freire suggests. Individuals are born into a language environment which includes the conceptual categories and metaphorical images that reproduce the world view of the culture. They may introduce new metaphorical images, make explicit some of the conceptual categories, and refurbish other aspects of their linguistic household, but on the whole, the conceptual conventions of their language will endure, even as they are modified. In spite of his unfounded optimism in the individual's ability to become emancipated from the control of language, Freire introduces into educational theory an awareness of the political nature of language that was not there before, and for this we are indebted to him.

Although both Dewey and Freire make an important contribution to understanding how education can be used to strengthen participation in community life, we cannot address other issues basic to a reciprocal individual-community relationship without taking seriously the question of what should be conserved. The discourse of the liberal educational theorists, including that of Dewey and Freire, provides an overly restrictive understanding of this basic issue. Change, the desideratum of Dewey and Freire, is becoming increasingly the dominant cultural orientation. Within this context individuals who exercise communicative competence must be as sensitive to preserving meaningful traditions as they are to the more technical aspects of affecting social change. This involves, in part, a process of self-definition in terms of the traditions enacted in the context of daily life. An understanding of embeddedness, of continuities, and of cultural and community membership seems essential to the formal educational process carried on in the classroom, but this understanding needs to be balanced by an ability to make explicit (and thus politicize) aspects of taken-for-granted beliefs and practices that are injurious in both an individual and communal sense. Finding the balance between continuity and renewal, bonding and critical reflection, will be the real test of our ability to articulate the nature of communicative competence. The discourse necessary to this task must involve an openness to the insights and concerns of both liberal and conservative thinkers.

Implications of Bioregionalism
for a Radical Theory of Education

OVER the last decade we have witnessed a variety of radical models for thinking about education; but in the diversity that ranged from the free classroom of the neoromantics to the engineered classroom of the behaviorists (not to mention the more purely ideological proposals of the neo-Marxists that were never tested in the classroom), there was a common thread of understanding that betrayed what has been traditionally meant by the term "radical." The original meaning of the word *radicalis* involved going back to the most basic and fundamental source. When used in this way, radical thought means going beyond the view of reality framed by an ideological position. Thus, in a very real sense it means going beyond the ideological formulations of the various streams of liberalism and conservatism in order to get at the root issues. It does not mean, as interpreted by recent educational theorists, developing a complicated rationale for addressing the problem of individual freedom and empowerment. This view of radicalism simply involved working out the programmatic implications of the modern mind-set that was already taken for granted. A radical thinker, by way of contrast, pushes the starting point back to the most basic issues; and in today's world the maximizing of individual freedom is not the most basic issue we face.

Just as it can be argued, to paraphrase Gary Snyder, that photosynthesis rather than labor is the true origin of wealth, there are a deeper set of issues that make problematic the very foundations of the bourgeois consciousness that characterizes current radical educational theory. These issues have to do with the destruction of our habitat and with the hubris of modern consciousness that rejects the possibility that we might learn from the wisdom of preliterate societies. Thus, the genuinely radical thinker is more likely to be considering the implications of Eric Havelock's *Preface to Plato* and Herbert Schneidau's *Sacred Dis-*

content than a revisionist interpretation of Marxism. The problems of inequality and restricted individual empowerment are not nearly as important as the cultural roots of our alienation from nature. Regardless of how our agenda for social reform is framed, the bottom line has to do with reversing the global ecological deterioration we are now witnessing.

The ecology movement of the sixties and early seventies helped to awaken many from the cultural myth that held out the promise of unending growth, but it lacked the conceptual sophistication necessary for a radical rethinking of the cultural roots of the problem. Pollution controls, recycling of materials, and campaigns to save endangered species were a few of the genuine achievements. Conservation seemed to be the key metaphor that designated the thrust of this political movement. Recently, a more radical movement made up of loosely affiliated groups in Europe, Great Britain, and North America has emerged. Known as die Grünen in the Federal Republic of Germany, the Ecology Party in Great Britain, the bioregionalists in North America, these groups are concerned with alleviating the danger of nuclear war, the ravaging effects of an industrial social order on the environment, and exploitive relationships between First and Third World countries. For our purposes, however, what is most important about this emergent movement are the conceptual foundations it is helping to lay for a genuinely radical critique of our culture and thus of our approach to education. The bioregionalists in North America seem to be the least controlled by the assumptions of modernization and thus are able to ask the most probing questions about the belief systems that underlie our social practices. To accord them the serious attention they deserve, readers must be able to free themselves from the control of the mental habits reinforced by the language of the liberal paradigm.

The following resolution passed unanimously at a cattleman's meeting in Texas (1898) epitomizes the modern mind-set that the bioregionalists view as a form of cultural neurosis:

> *Resolved,* that none of us know, or care to know, anything about grasses, native or otherwise, outside the fact that for the present there are lots of them, the best on record, and we are after getting the most out of them while they last. (cited in Shepard 1982, p. 2)

This mind-set represents in its worst form the attitude of the invader who exploits the resources and moves on; when expressed in its most constructive form, it represents the attitude of the experimenter-explorer who turns inquiry into technology and moves on to the next intellectual quest without being concerned with the ensuing disruptions in either the cultural or physical environment. Both the invader and experimenter-explorer are driven by an inner quest: the one for profits and the other for truth and power. In both cases, the interdependencies that characterize the biotic community are put out of focus.

Echoing the warnings of earlier environmentalists about depleting resources faster than they can be replaced locally and then drawing down the resource base of distant habitats, the bioregionalists have directed their attention to the development of a culture that is rooted in the natural world. As Kirkpatrick Sale put it, a sustainable culture is "in harmony with natural systems and rhythms, constrained by natural limits and capacities and developed according to the natural configurations of the earth and its inherent life forms" (Sale 1985, p. 24). The model for a culture that involves participation of responsible ecological citizens rather than mastery over nature through rational control is not, according to the bioregionalists, to be found in futuristic thinking that seeks power through science and technology. The genuine radicalness of their thinking is clearly reflected in Sale's observation that, if we are to become dwellers within rather than masters over the biotic community, "we must try to regain the spirit of the ancient Greeks, who considered the earth as a living creature, which they worshiped with the name Gaea. We must try to learn that she is, in every real sense, *sacred*, and that there is therefore a holy way to confront her and her works, a way of awe and admiration and respect and veneration that simply will not permit despoliation or abuse" (Sale, p. 24). The suggestion that preliterate ancient societies possessed a form of wisdom that we must recover as part of our living traditions and that we must include the non-human in our sense of community, as well as develop a "sacramental food-chain mutual sharing consciousnesss"—to quote Gary Snyder, presents a real challenge to the assumptions upon which modern consciousness is based. Yet there is more to the bioregional position that we will touch on briefly before turning to educational implications.

The bioregionalists also take a strong stand against the current organization of society into nation states. Existing political boundaries that influence economic and social practices, as well as the manner in which citizens think about themselves, reflect the historical outcome of political struggles for power and administrative control. The bioregional view is that politics should be attuned to the requirements of a life-territory, which must take account of the life-sustaining characteristics of a habitat—the watershed, soils, and renewable and non-renewable resources that make up the biotic community. The word "place" is often used by bioregionalists as a way of designating a form of politics attuned to nature rather than the dictates of ideology. Thus they reject the current view of the nation state and suggest that a new basis for political units might be found in the way North American Indian tribes occupied distinct bioregions.

In place of the major activities that occupy a modern society—internationalization of economic activity (both in terms of production and mass markets), advancement of scientific forms of knowledge, and a continual quest for more efficient and rationally controlled technologies—the bioregionalists offer an alternative vision that is likely to have little appeal to anomic individuals who are habituated to the fast and flashy pace of modern consumerism. In place of hi-tech and the impersonality of the market place, they urge a rediscovery of how to use our hands and bodies in dealing with the fundamentals of life-cultivating activities, such as growing and preparing food, and in sharing the common tasks of the community as it adjusts to the cycles of the seasons. Their view involves a more communal life style, the use of intermediate, less energy-intensive technologies, and the recovery of the symbolic richness of oral traditions. This is not a vision that will have immediate appeal to many people; in fact, it is likely to be viewed as a backward step from the conveniences associated with modern society.

Judgments about a life style that involve a completely different set of criteria for determining the meaning of human fulfillment will in part be distorted by the ideological conditioning of the existing culture. Yet at a deeper level, the question of whether the views of the bioregionalists should be taken seriously will *not* turn on whether a society organized according to the principles of self-sufficiency and ecological balance will provide as much personal pleasure, leisure, and freedom as some of us now enjoy. We will have to take them seriously, I suspect, because their arguments about what happens when a dominant species within an ecosystem depletes the life-sustaining resources have been thoroughly documented. In the terminology of the bioregionalists, the draw-down of the resource base is followed by an overshoot stage in which severe disruptions and conflicts over increasingly limited resources occur, followed by a crash where the population is reduced to a level where the resources can recover. It occurs in all species, and the historical record indicates that human cultures are not exempt from the fate of exceeding environmental equilibrium. In *Always Coming Home*, which Ursula Le Guin referred to as an "archeology of the future," a group of people, the Kesh, choose to remain behind in a devastated environment from which everyone else has escaped in a galactic spaceship that is no longer dependent upon minerals, plants, and soil (a common escape scenario for technicists who believe meaningful life can be sustained in a totally artificial environment). Instead, the Kesh, the people of the future Le Guin projects as inhabiting a valley in Northern California, live in small clans as hunters and gatherers. Their technology, form of education, ceremonies, and customs do not represent a progression beyond what we have today; they are instead remarkably similar to premodern cultures that were attuned to the rhythms of the environment. Equally missing from their mythology is our own belief that purposive rationality is an ultimate source of power, allowing us to escape the laws that require other species to live within ecological balance. I suspect that Le Guin, raised in a family that was sensitive to the wisdom of subsistence cultures toward their habitats, represents the more prophetic bioregionalist voice.

Regardless of the questions we may have about the implications of the bioregionalists' argument (Do we have to abandon our credit cards and cities? Do we really have to give up our fossil fuel addiction?), we cannot ignore the evidence that we are now nearing "overshoot" where the demands of an increasingly world-wide consumer culture will exhaust essential resources. The main issue facing educators now is to decide whether to wait for more definitive evidence that we have exceeded ecological limits or to take the threat seriously by beginning to rethink those aspects of our belief system that do not take into account our ecological interdependence. The first approach would involve thinking about the relationship between education and society within the current conceptual framework that associates empowerment with continued progress in the areas of individualism and rationality. In effect, the current cultural trajectory would be supported by a form of education based on any one of the four archetypal models of educational liberalism discussed in the earlier sections of this book—neoromantic free classrooms, the engineered classroom in the Skinner-Taylor mold, the Deweyian classroom that teaches the method of scientific problemsolving, and the emancipatory, consciousness-raising pedagogy of Freire.

A second approach for educational theorists is to give serious attention to some of the basic concepts of bioregional thinking, partly because the concepts are fundamentally sound in their own right and partly because they take into account the forms of understanding we must possess as ecological limits force us to modify our cultural beliefs and practices. This is where educational theorists must be able to free themselves from a restrictive discourse where the vocabulary and conceptual categories force thought into predetermined directions. The basic concepts essential to the bioregionalist position, as stated earlier, represent a radical turning away from the assumptions that underlie the ideological positions that evolved out of the Enlightenment, including Marxism (Bookchin 1971).

Alienation, a key concept in the thinking of bioregionalists, is one of those powerful images that can be given a substantially different meaning by changing the root metaphor. Existentialist literature, for example, often started with assumptions that the individual is basically alone and that through an act of will individual life could be given authentic meaning and a sense of purpose. Those who could not find the authority for giving their own life a sense of direction escaped by living an inauthentic life dictated by group norms. Thus, for the existentialists, social conformity led to self-alienation. From a more Durkheimian perspective, alienation results from a breakdown in a shared normative framework, with the result being an anomic individual who experiences a loss of meaning. By contrast, the bioregionalist's understanding of alienation does not start with either the image of the authentic, self-sufficient individual or a concern with the social defenses against individual malaise. The root metaphor of the bioregionalists is the interdependency of all life forms. Consequently, for them, alienation is expressed in the illusion of being free to choose one's place, to be self-accountable for one's actions, and to be orientated toward fulfilling personal wants and goals (values highly regarded within some streams of liberalism). This is really to be rootless and to confuse real power with a cultural myth that equates happiness with freedom.

For the bioregionalists, overcoming alienation is knowing and being responsible for your place—which involves coming to terms with the most fundamental aspects of the spatial and temporal aspects of existence. In the words of Wendell Berry:

> From the perspective of the environmental crisis of our time I think we have to add . . . a further realization: if the land is made fit for human habitation by memory and "old association," it is also true that by memory and association men are made fit to inhabit the land. At present our society is almost entirely nomadic, without the comfort or discipline of such memories, and it is moving about on the face of the continent with a mindless destructiveness, of substance and of meaning and of value, that makes Sherman's march to the sea look like a prank. Without a complex knowledge of one's place, and without the faithfulness to one's place on which such knowledge depends, it is inevitable that the place will be used carelessly, and eventually destroyed. (1972, pp. 68–69)

Gary Snyder put it more succinctly: "You know whether or not a person knows where he is by whether or not he knows the plants. By whether or not he knows what the soils and waters do" (1980, p. 69). Stated somewhat differently, modern interpretations of alienation involve foregrounding the individual by putting out of focus the background (place or context). For the bioregionalist both are integral to each other.

Yet there is more to the bioregionalist position that has direct implications for thinking about the purpose of education, as well as for rethinking certain prejudices that have long held a privileged position in educational circles. A knowledge of place and a concern with rootedness is not the expression of a nostalgic desire to return to the simplicity of a more primitive past. The bioregionalists are really concerned with the problem of empowerment—and their way of understanding the process of empowerment leads them to deviate significantly from how it is conceptualized by the different interpreters of educational liberalism.

In contrast to the anthropocentrism that characterizes the four archetypal interpretations of educational liberalism, the bioregionalist views empowerment in terms of living in harmony with the rhythms of the environment. In more concrete terms, this means learning "how to give full rein to those cooperative and communal and participatory selves, those symbiotic and responsible and multi-dimensional selves that have been blunted and confined" by the binary pattern of thinking that has contributed to the cultural forms of alienation associated with modern consciousness (Sale 1985, p. 33). A brief overview of what has been lost through the long march to achieve the current individualistic and rationalistic mode of consciousness can be seen in how binary thinking progressed by declaring the absolute supremacy of one aspect of experience and denying its supposed opposite qualities. What was lost through this binary process of selection and rejection represents essential elements that must be recovered if we are to overcome the alienation that separates us from our environment.

The following overview of these areas of human experience that have become a casualty of binary thinking is really intended to identify issues that must become part of the discussion of educational reform; if you will, it will help to recover part of the language that will enable us to think about aspects of the educational process that the more restrictive discourses of educational liberalism put out of focus. The overview touches on exceedingly complicated cultural developments, many of which are still being argued, and it is in no way intended as a list of prescriptions for reforming public education. But it does suggest a sense of direction that deserves serious consideration.

The sense of estrangement from the environment that characterizes the modern attitude toward exploitation of resources and ownership is fundamentally different from the way in which many traditional cultures view the earth as alive and sacred. In a fascinating study of how monotheistic religions of the West introduced a binary separation in how the sacred was experienced, Herbert Schneidau (1976) makes the point that belief in a God that could not be located within the environment represented a radical and, in terms of its recent introduction, novel departure from the "animal-man-god interpenetration" that is essential to mythological consciousness. By investing the abstract Yahweh with absolute power, the cosmic continuum was disrupted; ancient religion, as a form of geography that "organized space into sacred configurations," to quote Schneidau (p. 71), was now viewed as paganism. The binary logic that made the sacred a transaction between man and God, rather than seeing all forms of giving and taking of life as bound up together, thus separated (alienated) humans from a religious sense of the interdependence of all life forms. Without this sense of interdependence, based on awe, reverence, and respect rather than self-interest and cost effectiveness, there are no limits on how far we can go in exploiting the animal, plant, and mineral resources.

The bioregionalists are very much aware that a culture living in harmony with the environment must recover this part of ancient memory that was so attuned to the sacred, as opposed to taking the modern approach of legislating limits and using expert-technicist studies as the basis of authority. In contrast to the natural attitude of those of us who operate within one or more of the conceptual configurations of educational liberalism (some of us are given to syncretistic tendencies where we borrow willy-nilly from all four streams), Native Americans such as the Navajos experience the sacred as a basic part of their sense of empowerment; and basic to their understanding of the alienation of the dominant Western culture. Part of the declaration signed by 64 elders of the Independent Dine' (Navajo) Nation at Big Mountain clearly puts in focus how different views of empowerment relate not only to spiritual but ecological survival: "Our sacred shrines have been destroyed. . . . Our Mother Earth is raped by the exploitation of coal, uranium, oil, natural gas, and helium. . . . We speak for the winged beings, the four-legged beings, and those gone before us and the coming generation. We seek no changes in our livelihood because this Natural life is our only known survival and it's our sacred law" (Mandler 1981, p. 1).

The binary thinking that separates rationalism and mythological consciousness, which many will see as the contending paradigms represented in this quotation, can also be seen in the way modern consciousness has privileged literacy over oral traditions. For the last one hundred and fifty years, literacy has been so closely intertwined with the idea of empowerment that it has become almost the chief criteria for determining whether people are to be considered as progressive and civilized or backward and primitive. The deeper connections between literacy and the rise of the public school are important both in terms of the social stratification that resulted from the stratification of knowledge and in terms of how schooled literacy contributed to the loss of localized cultural identities (Cook-Gumperz 1986, p. 36). Although the contribution of schooled literacy to the creation of a mass, rootless society is important to the bioregionalist's analysis of the ecological instability of modern society, our main concern is to clarify how the form of empowerment that we automatically associate with literacy contributes to alienation in the bioregional sense of the term. This part of the argument, in turn, puts in focus additional issues that need to be addressed as we move into a post-liberal era of thinking about how education, culture, and the environment interrelate. In looking at the dark side of literacy, it is important to remember the dangers of continuing to be caught up in the categories dictated by a binary form of thinking; thus our brief analysis of literacy is not meant to be interpreted as a total rejection of literacy in favor of an uncritical acceptance of orality as the chief means of sharing knowledge with others.

The work of Walter Ong, Eric Havelock, and others has largely overturned the long-held view that the introduction of the alphabet that made modern writing possible was primarily a technological advance in enabling us to be more rational and objective in our thinking and in contributing to the upward spiral of knowledge (civilization) through a more effective means of sharing knowledge with other rational individuals. Their contribution was in clarifying how literacy differs from oral communication, particularly in how the two modes of communication influence consciousness as well as patterns of social interaction. In contrast to the ideology that now privileges literacy as culturally superior to orality, they found that the transmission process of reading and writing amplifies certain human attributes and patterns and reduces others. Literacy, in brief, amplifies the sense of individualism (writing and reading are highly privatized experiences); an abstract form of thought that allows for a careful editorial refinement of text; a text that is divorced from the living person who produced it and thus fixed in time—allowing for analysis and comparison with other fixed texts; and impersonal communication where the writer has to imagine the reading public (Ong 1982). In addition to empowering the analytical mind, literacy contributes to the reification of the word and thus to the decontextualization of knowledge. Contrary to popular thinking, empowerment is not the binary opposite of alienation; in the case of literacy, it contributes to a form of consciousness that is alienated by virtue of what is reduced or eliminated in communicating knowledge to others.

Ong points out that in contrast to the printed word the spoken word is always a social event, an ongoing action, that allows intuition, context, non-verbal communication, memory, intonations, character of participants, and all the senses to be fully involved (1977, pp. 12-49). As a living event, oral communication involves adjusting the messages to the nuance of the social context and thus serves to renew the shared definitions of reality that underpin communal life. It is, in effect, more dialectical in that both the memory and perspective of the participants remodel what has become irrelevant in the collective experience, rather than, as with abstract thought, creating a disjuncture. As Havelock put it: "New information and new experience are continually grafted on to inherited models" (1963, p. 122). As the text, so to speak, is always updated in the oral tradition, education does not involve absorbing abstract and thus possibly irrelevant or destructive forms of knowledge. But this form of empowerment—in terms of communicating about what is lived—reduces those mental qualities associated with analysis, independent perspective, and the abstract accumulation of knowledge that can be later drawn upon.

Clearly both oral and literate cultures provide for their members different forms of empowerment and alienation. Yet this is not recognized by an ideology that represents literacy as the primary form of empowerment and the key for becoming a modern individual. For instance, Freire's arguments for literacy represent a belief that is so strong and unqualified that he fails to recognize that his educational reforms would contribute to structuring consciousness in a manner that supports the very form of society he wants to overthrow. Our real purpose here, however, is not to engage the blind spots in the thinking of liberal theorists of education; it is to understand how the alienating characteristics of literacy contribute to a form of culture that is out of harmony with its habitat.

Ron and Suzanne Scollon, two linguists who have thought a great deal about how orality and literacy relate to the problem of alienation in the modern world, go to the heart of the matter by reminding us that language is primarily about relationships and only secondarily about ideas (1985, p. 15). We have tended to emphasize the latter, which is really the signifying function of language or what could be called, in terms of the sociology of knowledge, the constituting function of language. But naming "What Is" also involves establishing how the relationships among the different entities named are to be understood, as well as the relationship between the speaker (writer) and that part of the world that is being symbolically represented. It is this latter function of language that the Scollons draw our attention to, particularly how orality and literacy constitute fundamentally different relationships.

The relationships that are reinforced through literacy are in part a function of what is amplified and reduced through the use of print technology; they also reflect our deepest metaphysical assumptions about the world and our place in it. In terms of print technology, the symbolic representation of ideas is amplified, but the relationship between the ideas and their phenomenological origins is reduced. Our cultural orientation of emphasizing writing in the third person and of representing our knowledge as objective (actually an orientation dictated by a class set of epistemological assumptions) fosters a relationship of separation between the word and the person. This separation, where the word takes on an independent, reified existence, creates a reversal in which abstract and fixed symbolic representations are taken to be real, while the life world of the writer (and reader) are put out of focus. The Scollons observed that as a language form, literacy alters our sense of relationship in the most fundamental way by shifting our "focus from what is primary to what is secondary." The primary is actually our embeddedness as sensory and cognitive beings in an interdependent biocommunity; the secondary is what we are able to represent in symbolic form about our existence. The reversal makes the abstract more real than what is experienced, which exceeds in richness, complexity, and depth what can be communicated through the technology of language—especially the printed word. For the Scollons the primacy given to literacy strengthens the kinds of relationships that are alienating, with abstractions being substituted for living relationships between people and between people and the biotic community. They also point out that literacy involves an asymmetry of power, in which the writer and reader relate to each other as sender and receiver (p. 19).

The consequences of the domination of literacy over orality can be seen in how we view knowledge and where it is to be located. As literacy de-emphasizes context as part of the message system, it has led to the distorted view that only the explicit forms of understanding capable of being represented in symbolic form can be viewed as valid knowledge. Tacit understanding of the cultural codes that regulate most aspects of social life thus tend to be ignored or downgraded in importance. The emphasis on literacy also privileges the analytical mind over the body, with the consequence that we fail to recognize the importance of embodied forms of knowledge to our sense of empowerment. David M. Levin makes the point that

> the body is, or is at, the source of all our knowledge. . . . As an ancestral body, an "ancient" body of genetically encoded reproduction, for example, it is the biophysical element which binds our existence to that of our mortal ancestors, even the earliest; as a cultural body, it transcends the

chains of nature, participates in the shaping of history, and serves, whether we will it or not—though our willingness makes a difference— as an impressionable medium for the transmission and sedimentation of cultural norms, values, and meanings. (1985, p. 171)

In addition to the attunements, dispositions and preestablished under- standings of the body, knowledge can be understood as embodied in our technologies. Becoming sensitive to these embodied forms of knowledge as the foundations of our empowerment also requires that we recognize the environment as a sustaining and shaping force.

In order to overcome the alienation that separates "the word from the body, the society from the earth, and our reason from our spiritual- ity," the Scollons suggest an approach to education that addresses the problems of relationships and empowerment—which they view as in- tertwined with each other (p. 32). Their educational proposals are grounded in the Confucian idea that the problems of the world, includ- ing the fate of the environment, cannot be separated from self-under- standing. But most importantly, self-understanding involves getting in touch with the basic organic categories of existence—past, place, rela- tionships, and future possibilities. These are the most fundamental of human relations that are put out of focus by the rationalistic, anthropo- centric view of the universe that comes down from the Enlightenment and is currently reinforced in the four interpretations of educational liberalism that continue to serve as our primary models for thinking about education. Their educational proposal addresses the connection between the problem of empowerment and the need for a culture that is in ecological balance—two issues that should be a central concern to educational theorists.

A curriculum guided by a concern with helping students get in touch with the organic categories of their existence must begin with learning about the past. For the Scollons this should include, in addition to the past preserved as part of the Western literate tradition, the legacy of the oral traditions: e.g., the *Iliad* and the *Odyssey* of Homer, the Bible, the Koran, as well as the wisdom given us by the great thinkers of India and China. Learning the oral traditions of the past, as well as the present, provides insight into the archetypal models of how people have con- fronted and resolved the deepest existential questions. It also involves acquiring the conceptual basis necessary for recognizing the past in the present, including those aspects of earlier forms of consciousness that were more attuned to the cycles of life. By viewing the self (as a carrier of language) as part of a symbolic continuum that stretches back to the earliest formation of our conceptual maps, learning the past is really a way of learning about the self. Yet just as there needs to be a balance between the oral and literate traditions of the past, there also needs to be a balance between being immersed in the oral patterns of retelling important stories and the individualizing analytical form of thought that is associated with literacy. Learning the past through the spoken word helps to attune the student to relationships with others that are grounded in a shared context. The power of this form of learning can be seen in how individuals, in learning their native language, acquire efficacy while at the same time being bonded to the patterns of community life.

That all forms of life can only be understood as they are situated in their place or context suggests the importance of the second organic category. In contrast to the various expressions of educational liberalism that foreground the virtue of self-directing individuals by putting the background (place) out of focus, the Scollons echo the bioregional concern with understanding the life-sustaining processes and resources of one's place. In the past the more explicit part of the school socialization process took the students' relationship to place for granted, with the result that, later as adults, they were caught up in culturally prescribed routines that were largely carried out without adequate awareness of their disruptive effects on other forms of life that shared the same place. A curriculum that takes the life-place seriously as one of the organic categories of existence would focus on the relationship between the cultural life style of students and the resource base of the region: soil, mineral, water, plant, and animal life. Yet learning about the relationship between self and place would not properly clarify the nature of the interdependencies if current cultural lenses were used. Studying the nature of soils (and which cultural practices deplete them) and the characteristics of animal and plant life as though they were being inventoried for future exploitation would simply exacerbate the problem. Learning about place really involves, as Berry, Snyder, and the Scollons remind us, developing a spiritual understanding of the earth as a reference point for understanding self.

This may sound strange to the ear attuned to a language that represents our relationship to the earth in terms of I–It rather than I–Thou. Nevertheless, the capacity to have an I–Thou relationship that is confirming, open, and transforming provides a way of recognizing that we do not have to live entirely by cultural models that involve exploitive and calculating relationships. In terms of curriculum, understanding place does not involve bringing religion, in the usual sense of the term, into the classroom. But it does provide a point of departure for examining the environmental consequences of cultural beliefs and patterns of action. This would involve examining the cultural beliefs that influence the sense of commitment (or lack of it) to place, as well as recognizing what human actions toward the environment are proscribed (and why). In terms of the Scollon's curricular recommendations, this would involve examining how bioregions are intersected by political-cultural lines, and how the bioregion has fared on both sides of the dividing line (p. 33). Comparisons between modern and transitional cultures (e.g., Hopi and Navajo) in terms of their respective impact on the environment would yield useful insights into how the spiritual aspects of culture influence our relationship to place.

The study of place should also involve examining the political and economic implications of how resources are utilized. This part of the curriculum would help students understand the problems connected with living within the resource base of a bioregion, the forms of dependencies that result from misuse of resources, the application of destructive technologies, and the political and economic relationships that do not represent the interests of the people living in a bioregion.

The two other organic categories, cultivating relationships and enlarging the future, have curricular implications that relate directly to learning past and place. Cultivating relationships, in curricular terms, requires an understanding of the models of good and evil that are exhibited in the world's great literature and oral traditions. Understanding what is right and wrong in others and how context may blur these categories is essential to being able to correct within oneself those personal characteristics that undermine mutually empowering relationships with others. The Scollons put in sharper focus the relationship between a curriculum that provides insight into the human character and the student's self-understanding and ability to cultivate relationships by using a quotation from Confucius: "If you hate something in your superiors, do not practice it on those below you; if you hate a thing in those below you, do not do it when working for those over you" (p. 35). Cultivating good relationships with others thus involves understanding self, and this is aided by studying the cultural models and values that both serve as reference points and have been internalized as part of self.

Enlarging the future, according to the Scollons, follows from the study of the past and place. One of the purposes of the latter is to help prepare for the future. The Scollons want to distinguish between planning for the future, which involves the purposive rational mind that often takes a Maginot Line approach to dealing with a changing environment, and preparing for the future. In curricular terms, enlarging (or preparing) for the future involves learning how to be open to new relationships and how to develop the capacities for negotiation and cooperation. It also involves developing as part of one's self, and encouraging in others, a vision of a shared future. Awareness of a future that is organized around an image of self-fulfillment or what one will do as an isolated individual is not as enlarging as a sense of future that includes relationships with others. This should also involve, as the Scollons remind us, a sense of the future that takes account of the characteristics of the bioregion. Thus, enlarging the individual's sense of future becomes tied to preserving the life sustaining characteristics of the larger biocommunity.

These general guidelines for organizing curricula allow for the specific content to be adjusted to the uniqueness of cultural groups and characteristics of the bioregion. The guiding questions—What soil series are you standing on? What species of animals and plants are on the verge of extinction in your area? and so forth—can be asked of each region, but the answers and thus curriculum content will reflect the diversity of regional characteristics and the teacher's imagination and resourcefulness. The important consideration here does not have so much to do with the fact that a bioregional approach to thinking about education leaves us without a fully fleshed out curriculum or set of pedagogical practices; rather it has to do with identifying a set of priorities that challenge in the most fundamental way the conceptual underpinnings of the liberal paradigm. The argument that literacy is the key to enlightened thinking, that locating authority in the rational judgment or emotive response of the individual, and that because of the progressive nature of change we should emancipate people from the authority of traditional beliefs and practices are all characteristic of the discourse of educational liberalism. The bioregional concern with understanding empowerment in terms of a culture that enables its members to live in harmony with the rhythms and resources of the natural environment introduces a new metaphorical language that makes sense only if we substantially revise the paradigm that has turned such words as progress, emancipation, individualism, critical rationality, and literacy into educational ideals that support an ecologically destructive ideology. By introducing into the discourse of educational and social reform the metaphorical language of cultural practices attuned to long-term survival, both in a spiritual and ecological sense, the bioregionalists are challenging us to reshape the language that will guide how we perceive the world. The task for educational theorists will be to reconcile Black Elk with John Dewey, Confucius with Skinner. This will involve a far more radical discourse than the one now driven by the variant forms of educational emancipation.

References

Aarsleff, Hans. 1982. *From Locke to Saussure: Essays in the Study of Language and Intellectual History*. Minneapolis: University of Minnesota Press.

Adler, Mortimer. 1982. *The Paideia Proposal*. New York: Macmillan Co.

Arendt, Hannah. 1958. *The Human Condition*. Chicago: University of Chicago Press.

———. 1961. *Between Past and Future*. Cleveland, Ohio: Meridian Books.

Aronowitz, Stanley, and Giroux, Henry. 1985. *Education Under Seige: The Conservative, Liberal and Radical Debate Over Schooling*. South Hadley, Mass.: Bergin & Garvey Publishers.

Bachelard, Baston. 1969. *The Poetics of Space*. Boston: Beacon Press.

Bell, Daniel. 1976. *The Cultural Contradictions of Capitalism*. New York: Basic Books.

Bellah, Robert N.; Madsen, Richard; Sullivan, William M.; Swidler, Ann; Tipton, Steven M. 1985. *Habits of the Heart: Individualism and Commitment in American Life*. Berkeley: University of California Press.

Berger, John. 1979. *Pig Earth*. New York: Pantheon Books.

Berger, Peter; Berger, Brigitte; Kellner, Hanstried. 1974. *The Homeless Mind: Modernization and Consciousness*. New York: Vintage Books.

Berger, Peter L., and Luckmann, Thomas. 1967. *The Social Construction of Reality: A Treatise in the Sociology of Knowledge*. Garden City, N.Y.: Anchor Books.

Bernstein, Basil. 1975. *Class, Codes and Control*. New York: Schocken Books.

Berry, Wendell. 1983. "Standing By Words." In *Standing By Words*. San Francisco: North Point Press.

———. 1972. *A Continuous Harmony: Essays Cultural and Agricultural*. New York: Harcourt Brace Jovanovich, Harvest Books.

Bookchin, Murray. 1971. *Post-Scarcity Anarchism*. Berkeley, Calif.: Ramparts Press.

Bourdieu, Pierre. 1971. "Systems of Education and Systems of Thought." In *Knowledge and Control: New Directions for the Sociology of Education*, edited by Michael F. D. Young. London: Collier-Macmillan Publishers.

Bowers, C. A. 1974. *Cultural Literacy for Freedom*. Eugene, Oreg.: Elan Publishers.

———. 1980a. "Curriculum as Cultural Reproduction: An Examination of

Metaphor as a Carrier of Ideology." *Teachers College Record* 82(Winter): 267–91.

———. 1980b. "Ideological Continuities in Technicism, Liberalism, and Education." *Teachers College Record* 81(Spring): 293–321.

———. 1983. "Linguistic Roots of Cultural Invasion in Paulo Freire's Pedagogy." *Teachers College Record* 84(Summer): 935–55.

———. 1984a. *The Promise of Theory: Education and the Politics of Cultural Change.* New York: Teachers College Press.

———. 1984b. "The Problem of Individualism and Community in Neo-Marxist Educational Thought." *Teachers College Record* 85(Spring): 365–91.

———. 1986. "The Dialectic of Nihilism and the State." *Educational Theory* 36(Summer): 225–32.

Buber, Martin. 1959. *Between Man and Man.* Boston: Beacon Press.

Butts, R. Freeman. 1980. *The Revival of Civic Learning.* Bloomington, Ind.: Phi Delta Kappan Educational Foundation.

Carroll, John. 1977. *Puritan, Paranoid, Remissive: A Sociology of Modern Culture.* London: Routledge & Kegan Paul.

Clecak, Peter. 1977. *Crooked Paths: Reflections on Socialism, Conservatism, and the Welfare State.* New York: Harper & Row, Colophon Books.

Cook-Gumperz, Jenny. 1986. *The Social Construction of Literacy.* Cambridge: Cambridge University Press.

Damico, Alfonso J. 1978. *Individuality and Community: The Social and Political Thought of John Dewey.* Gainsville: University of Florida Press.

Dewey, John. 1916. *Democracy and Education.* New York: Macmillan Co.

———. 1956. *The School and Society.* Chicago: University of Chicago Press.

———. 1957. *Reconstruction in Philosophy.* Boston: Beacon Press.

———. 1958. *Art as Experience.* New York: Capricorn Books.

———. 1960. *Quest for Certainty.* New York: Capricorn Books.

———. 1962. *Individualism Old and New.* New York: Capricorn Books.

———. 1963. *Liberalism and Social Action.* New York: Capricorn Books.

Douglas, Mary. 1975. *Implicit Meanings.* London: Routledge & Kegan Paul.

Dreyfus, Hubert L. 1981. "Knowledge and Human Values: A Geneology of Nihilism." *Teachers College Record* 80(Spring): 507–20.

Dunn, John. 1979. *Western Political Theory in the Face of the Future.* Cambridge: Cambridge University Press.

Eliot, T. S. 1962. *Notes Toward the Definition of Culture.* London: Faber & Faber.

English, Raymond. 1952. "Conservatism: The Forbidden Faith." *The American Scholar* 21(Autumn).

Foucault, Michel. 1977. *Language, Counter-Memory, Practice: Selected Essays and Interviews.* Ithaca, N.Y.: Cornell University Press.

———. 1979. *Discipline and Punish: The Birth of the Prison.* New York: Vintage Books.

———. 1982. "The Subject and Power." In *Michel Foucault: Beyond Structural-*

ism and Hermeneutics, edited by Hubert L. Dreyfus and Paul Rabinow. Chicago: University of Chicago Press.

Freire, Paulo. 1971. *Pedagogy of the Oppressed*. New York: Herder & Herder.

———. 1973. *Education for Critical Consciousness*. New York: Seabury Press.

———. 1978. *Pedagogy in Process: The Letters to Guinea-Bissau*. New York: Seabury Press.

———. 1985. *The Politics of Education: Culture, Power and Liberation*. South Hadley, Mass.: Bergin & Garvey Publishers.

Geertz, Clifford. 1973. *The Interpretation of Cultures*. New York: Basic Books.

Giddens, Anthony. 1981. *A Contemporary Critique of Historical Materialism*. Berkeley: University of California Press.

Goffman, Erving. 1971. *Relations in Public*. New York: Harper & Row, Colophon Books.

Goodenough, Ward H. 1981. *Culture, Language and Society*. Menlo Park, Calif.: The Benjamin/Cummings Publication Co.

Gouldner, Alvin. 1979. *The Future of Intellectuals and the Rise of a New Class*. New York: Seabury Press.

Habermas, Jürgen. 1973. *Legitimation Crisis*. Boston: Beacon Press.

Hall, Edward. 1977. *Beyond Culture*. Garden City, N.Y.: Anchor Books.

Harrington, Michael. 1983. *The Politics at God's Funeral*. New York: Penguin Books.

Havelock, Eric. 1963. *Preface to Plato*. Cambridge: Harvard University Press.

———. 1982. *The Literate Revolution in Greece and Its Cultural Consequences*. Princeton: Princeton University Press.

Heidegger, Martin. 1975. *Poetry, Language, Thought*. New York: Harper & Row, Colophon Books.

Heilbroner, Robert L. 1972. "A Radical View of Socialism." *Social Research* 39(Spring): 1-15.

Heschel, Abraham. 1965. *Who Is Man?* Stanford: Stanford University Press.

Hobsbawn, Eric, and Ranger, Terrance, eds. 1983. *The Invention of Tradition*. Cambridge: Cambridge University Press.

Hollis, Martin, and Lukes, Steven, eds. 1982. *Rationality and Relativism*. Cambridge: MIT Press.

Huntington, Samuel P. 1975. "The Democratic Distemper." *The Public Interest* 39(Fall): 9-38.

Johnston, Ken. 1981. "The Production of Conservative Educational Ideologies." *Discourse* 2(no. 1).

Kluckhohn, Clyde. 1972. "The Gift of Tongues." In *Intercultural Communication*, edited by Larry Samover and Richard Porter. Belmont, Calif.: Wadsworth Publishing.

Le Guin, Ursula K. 1985. *Always Coming Home*. New York: Harper & Row.

Levin, David Michael. 1985. *The Body's Recollection of Being*. London: Routledge & Kegan Paul.

Lilge, Frederic. 1977. "Lenin and the Politics of Education." In *Power and Ideology in Education*, edited by Jerome Karabel and A. H. Halsey. New York: Oxford University Press.

Lowi, Theodore J. 1979. *The End of Liberalism*. New York: W. W. Norton.

MacIntyre, Alasdair. 1984. *After Virtue*. Notre Dame, Ind.: University of Notre Dame Press.

MacPherson, C. B. 1962. *The Political Theory of Possessive Individualism*. Oxford: Clarendon Press.

Mandler, Jerry. 1981. "Kit Carson in a Three Piece Suit." *The CoEvolution Quarterly* (Winter).

Merleau-Ponty, Maurice. 1964. *The Primacy of Perception*. Evanston, Ill.: Northwestern University Press.

———. 1973. *Adventures of the Dialectic*. Evanston, Ill.: Northwestern University Press.

Mueller, Claus. 1973. *The Politics of Communication*. Oxford: Oxford University Press.

Nietzsche, Friedrich. 1968. *Will to Power*. New York: Vintage Books.

Nisbet, Robert. 1975. *Twilight of Authority*. New York: Oxford University Press.

Norberg-Schulz, Christian. 1980. *Genius Loci: Towards a Phenomenology of Architecture*. New York: Rizzoli International Publications.

Oakeshott, Michael. 1962. *Rationalism in Politics*. New York: Basic Books.

———. 1982. "On Being Conservative." In *The Portable Conservative Reader*, edited by Russell Kirk. New York: Penguin Books.

Ong, Walter. 1977. *Interfaces of the Word*. Ithaca, N.Y.: Cornell University Press.

———. 1982. *Orality and Literacy: The Technologizing of the Word*. London: Methuen.

Ortega y Gasset, Jose. 1957. *The Revolt of the Masses*. New York: W. W. Norton.

Pelikan, Jarvslar. 1984. *The Vindication of Tradition*. New Haven: Yale University Press.

Pitkin, Hanna F. 1972. *Wittgenstein and Justice*. Berkeley: University of California Press.

Rogers, Carl. 1983. *The Freedom to Learn for the 80's*. Columbus, Ohio: Charles E. Merrill Publishing Co.

Rosen, Stanley. 1969. *Nihilism: A Philosophic Essay*. New Haven: Yale University Press.

Rossiter, Clinton. 1962. *Conservatism in America*. New York: Vintage Books.

Sahlins, Marshall. 1972. *Stone Age Economics*. Chicago: Aldine-Atherton.

Sale, Kirkpatrick. 1985. *Dwellers in the Land: The Bioregional Vision*. San Francisco: Sierra Club Books.

Sapir, Edward. 1949. *Culture, Language and Personality*. Berkeley: University of California Press.

Sartori, Giovanni. 1978. "The Relevance of Liberalism in Retrospect." In *The*

Relevance of Liberalism, edited by the Staff of the Research Institute on International Change. Boulder, Colo.: Westview Press.

Schachtel, Ernest G. 1959. *Metamorphosis*. New York: Basic Books.

Schilpp, Paul Arthur, ed. 1951. *The Philosophy of John Dewey*. New York: Tudor Publishing Co.

Schneidau, Herbert N. 1976. *Sacred Discontent: The Bible and Western Tradition*. Baton Rouge: Louisiana State University Press.

Schumacher, E. F. 1979. *A Guide for the Perplexed*. New York: Harper & Row.

Scollon, Ron, and Scollon, Suzanne. 1985. "The Problem of Power" (monograph). Haines, Ala.: The Gutenberg Dump.

Shapiro, Jeremy J. 1976. "The Slime of History: Embeddedness in Nature and Critical Theory." In *On Critical Theory,* edited by John O'Neill. New York: Seabury Press.

Shapiro, Michael. 1981. *Language and Political Understanding: The Politics of Discursive Practices*. New Haven: Yale University Press.

Shepard, Paul. 1982. *Nature and Madness*. San Francisco: Sierra Club Books.

Shils, Edward. 1981. *Tradition*. Chicago: University of Chicago Press.

Shor, Ira. 1980. *Critical Teaching and Everyday Life*. Boston: South End Press.

Skinner, B. F. 1972. *Beyond Freedom and Dignity*. New York: Bantam/Vintage Books.

Snyder, Gary. 1980. *The Real Work: Interviews and Talks, 1964-1979*. New York: New Directions.

Soltis, Jonas F. 1981. "Education and the Concept of Knowledge." In *Philosophy and Education*, edited by J. F. Soltis. Chicago: National Society for the Study of Education.

Solzhenitsyn, Alexander; Agursky, A. B.; Barabanov, Evgeny; Korkakov, F.; Borisov, Vadim; Shafarevich, Igor. 1974. *From Under the Rubble*. Boston: Little Brown and Co.

Sommers, Christina Hoff. 1984. *Vice and Virtue in Everyday Life*. New York: Harcourt Brace Jovanovich.

Spring, Joel. 1975. *A Primer of Libertarian Education*. New York: Free Life Editions.

Strauss, Anslem. 1964. *George Herbert Mead on Social Psychology*. Chicago: University of Chicago Press.

Sullivan, William M. 1982. *Reconstructing Public History*. Berkeley: University of California Press.

Thompson, E. P. 1978. *The Poverty of Theory and Other Essays*. New York: Monthly Review Press.

Vygotsky, Lev Semenovich. 1962. *Thought and Language*. Cambridge: Mass.: MIT Press.

Wagner, Helmut, ed. 1973. *Alfred Schutz on Phenemolology and Social Relations*. Chicago: University of Chicago Press.

Wolin, Sheldon S. 1960. *Politics and Vision*. Boston: Little Brown and Co.

Zijderveld, Anton C. 1979. *On Clichés: The Supersedure of Meaning of Function in Modernity*. London: Routledge & Kegan Paul.

Index

About the Author

C. A. Bowers teaches Education and Social Thought in the College of Education at the University of Oregon. His previous publications include *The Progressive Educator and the Depression: The Radical Years* (1969), *Cultural Literacy for Freedom* (1974), and *The Promise of Theory: Education and the Politics of Cultural Change* (1984).